The

NORFOLK
Village Book

Compiled by the Norfolk Federation of
Women's Institutes from notes and illustrations sent
by Institutes in the County

Published jointly by
Countryside Books, Newbury
and the Norfolk Federation
of Women's Institutes, Norwich

❧ FOREWORD

Welcome to this new edition of *The Norfolk Village Book*. We hope you will enjoy dipping into its pages.

Compiled from contributions by WI members, it first appeared in 1990. The publishers having decided that a revision was due, again enlisted our help, so the entries have been updated and more villages added.

Norfolk is an exceptional county having a wonderfully varied landscape. With miles of coastline forming its northern and eastern boundaries, it encompasses broadland, breckland, marshland and fens. This has led to a diversity of occupation and building across a predominantly agricultural area, thus adding to its many attractions.

Here is ample evidence of Norfolk's history, its development and adaptation to the changing features of modern life, making it an ideal companion for those exploring Norfolk.

Members, justifiably proud of their heritage, were delighted to participate in the production of this book and it is they who have endowed it with its unique Norfolk flavour.

Yvonne Sizeland
Federation Chairman

COUNTY OF

o Hunstanton

o Fakenham

King's
Lynn O

East Dereham o

Swaffham o

o Thetford

NORFOLK

Cromer ○

○ Aylsham

Wroxham
○

NORWICH
◎

Great Yarmouth ○

○ Wymondham

E. Combe

❉ ACKNOWLEDGEMENTS

The production of this book was only made possible by the enthusiastic research of the contributors and the untiring efforts of Mrs Richmal Ashbee who co-ordinated the project, ably assisted by Mrs Eileen Gomme. To all these and to others who helped in any way the Norfolk Federation of Women's Institutes offer their grateful thanks.

Our thanks are also due to: Mr G. Amos (South Walsham); Mr E. C. Apling (Hingham and Woodrising); Mrs I. Birt (Toft Monks); Mrs P. Everson (Seething); Mrs M. A Garry (Castle Acre); Mr E. R. Grainger (Blofield); Mrs F. Gubb (Brampton); Mrs D. Havart (Thwaite); Mrs W. Hill (Blickling); Mr C. Kellehar (Ranworth); Mr M. Oldridge (Garvestone); Mr G. Pooley (Warham, Holkham and North & South Creake); Mr R. Richley (Kenninghall); Mr J. Thurston (South Wootton); Mr D. Tuck (Kettlestone); Mr D. Turner (Narborough); and Mrs C. Twinch (Bawburgh)

In addition to the above, the following people have helped with information for this updated edition: Mrs R. Ashbee (Roughton); Mrs J. Brasnett (East Winch); Mr Ron Brewer (Old Buckenham); Mr M. Eggleston (Three Holes); Mrs S. Florance (Framingham Earl and Framingham Pigot); Mrs E. Kidner (Earsham); Mr B. Makepeace (Swainsthorpe); Mrs Mountain (Great Massingham); Dr Pearce (Little Barningham); Mrs D. Reeve (Ketteringham); Mr G. Stocking (Walsingham); and Mrs B. Youngs (Trowse).

ACLE

Acle took on a new lease of life on 14th March 1989 when its long-awaited and long-overdue bypass was finally opened. After 62 years of collective battling the residents of Acle took to the streets to celebrate the end of a constant stream of juggernauts and the summer-long traffic jams that dominated the village centre en route to the east coast. Sanity had been restored to the streets of Acle.

With a growing population and the need for new housing, Acle now has several small developments on sites around the village. Both the old school and the thriving market that brought people to the village on Thursdays since the 13th century, have now been replaced with both housing and a new supermarket. A small market is still held every Thursday, but gone are the days of the traditional livestock auctions of the past.

To provide recreation for the local residents and the surrounding district Acle has many clubs and organisations from tennis, to bowls (which can be played all year round on the indoor rinks) and football and cricket clubs. The younger members have Cubs, Scouts, Guides, a youth club and a thriving playgroup. All year round, members from the flower club, ELCA, a ladies club, the Wl, the British Legion, and Acle and District 49 plus meet regularly.

A significant landmark in the village is the parish church of St Edmund King and Martyr, which in 1990 celebrated its 900th anniversary with great pageantry and pomp. The Methodist chapel is also home to Acle Voluntary Aid, which provides support and care for the sick, elderly and house-bound.

Members of the village take care and pride in the village as a whole and the dedication of their work resulted in the 1998 Best Kept Village Award. A walk through the village from the Acle War Memorial Hall will take you past the old Bridewell and through the street along to the Damgate Woodland walk, out on to Weavers Way and back to the newly planted Roman Wood.

With a library and a business centre providing the latest hands-on technology, Acle is certainly moving with the times into the next millennium, yet at the same time retaining part of the tradition of rural Norfolk. It is a living, working, dynamic community with all the facilities and qualities that make village life precious.

Acle is a gateway to the Broads and the starting point of thousands of memorable holidays. The village is surrounded by some of the most beautiful and most important wetland countryside in Britain.

❦ ALBY WITH THWAITE

The civil parishes of Alby and Thwaite, with about 70 houses between them, have been united since 1884. Alby is a small village of scattered houses and farms, about five miles north-east of Aylsham, and is dissected by the A140 Norwich/Cromer road. Travellers can find refreshment at the Horseshoes Inn or, for the greater part of the year, at the Buttery in Alby Crafts. The craft workshops and showrooms are housed in restored brick and flint farm buildings and have become a major tourist attraction in the area. The village lacks shops but one enterprising resident has opened a specialist children's bookshop in her home.

On a side road, signposted Aldborough, is Alby church dedicated in honour of St Ethelbert, King of East Anglia in the 8th century. It is a neat building of cut flint and freestone in the Early English style of architecture and the Old Rectory alongside, now a private residence, probably incorporates part of the medieval priest's house. The list of rectors goes back to Robert de Felbrigg in 1312. Over the years regular services were held, but for the time being St Ethelbert's is disused and under the care of the rector who lives in Erpingham, one of the seven parishes of the group benefice.

Over the parish boundary is Thwaite, called Tuit in the Domesday Book, and it would seem that there was a church there at least by 1035. All Saints' stands on rising ground, commanding extensive views over fields and common, and is a small building of Early English and Perpendicular styles with a round tower at the west end. A Sunday school room was added in 1835 by Mrs Lydia Baret who, in the same year, erected a public elementary school to hold 60 pupils with teacher's residence, at a cost of £800. This school, now a private house, was built in the village near the duck pond on Thwaite Common, and the area has retained its attractive rural setting. The young children from Alby and surrounding villages attend Aldborough school which, oddly enough, is sited within Alby!

🍁 ALDBOROUGH

Aldborough lies three miles west of the A140 between Aylsham and Cromer. The village and its church and mill are listed in the Domesday Book. The mill was working not so long ago, but has now been converted into three large homes, the outside still presenting a bargeboard first floor and a pleasant introduction to the village.

Like many Norfolk churches, St Mary's is some way from the village. There are still Saxon stones visible, though most of the church is 14th to 15th century. The church is now part of a five parish group. There is also a Methodist chapel. The present building opened in 1906, replacing one which is now Fern Cottage on the green. Prince Andrew's Chapel is Independent, and the present building opened in 1980, replacing the 70 year old Gospel Hall.

Aldborough has always had some importance as a trading centre. King John granted a charter for a fair to be held on or near 21st or 22nd June each year. This was originally for the sale of horses, livestock, poultry and household goods as well as a hiring fair for servants and labourers. In the late 19th century it gradually became more of a pleasure fair; and today the dodgems, shooting booths, roundabouts and all the fun of the fairground come to the green on the traditional dates.

The green is the main feature of the village and a natural centre. The shops and most of the older houses (one thatched) are grouped round it, the pub is at one corner, the community centre at another. There is a children's playground at one end, and the main part is a football pitch in winter and a cricket ground in summer. On a fine summer's day it presents an idyllic scene. The green has also enabled the village in recent years, in September, to mount a 'Trade & Leisure Fair' which draws in thousands of visitors, and raises thousands of pounds for a different charity each year.

Aldborough must have been self-sufficient in its trade and industries until the mid 20th century. (There was also some illicit trading: Watch Oak on Hall Road is reputed to have been a look-out point for a signal from Cromer that the brandy was ashore!) Glove making is mentioned in 14th century records and continued until the 19th century. There were two tanneries, two harness makers and saddlers, a whip maker and a basket maker, two bakeries, two butchers, a tailor and a dressmaker, two carpenters' workshops, a smithy and a watch maker, as well as four general stores, a post office, a boot and shoe shop, a

11

stationer's, two pubs and a garage: all these were still in existence when members of the WI wrote a village history and survey in 1937.

Today there are still shops around the green: one general grocery store, a post office combined with a shop selling shoes, stationery, clothing etc, an antiques shop, a butcher's, a public house and a restaurant. Off the green there are two cottage industries – a pottery and a printer's. Several mobile services come into the village, including a library and two fish and chip vans. There is still a doctors' surgery, now with two doctors and a community nurse, serving a much wider area than the village.

Although we know that the village and church have existed for so long, there is no authenticated evidence of domestic buildings from the medieval period. The Black Death affected this area and its population in the 14th century, and it is assumed that houses near the church were abandoned or destroyed and new houses built round the green. Part of a field is named 'Poison Green' in old maps and is reputed to be a plague pit. The oldest houses round the green are known to be late 17th and early 18th century: the Black Boys pub is probably one of the earliest, and is a listed building, as are some of the houses nearby. The main part of the Old Rectory was reconstructed in the reign of William IV, but the north wing is much earlier. It has been used as a private house for over 50 years, since the then rector married the owner of Aldborough Hall and went to live there. It is now the home and headquarters of the owners of 'Aldborough Apples', a thriving fruit business – the orchards lie between the church and the main part of the village.

Aldborough Hall is about a mile from the village in the direction of Holt. The oldest section is 16th century, with additions and alterations in 1636, 1750 and 1816. It was occupied by the Gay family from 1613 until the last member to bear the name married Rev Christopher Lilly: she is commemorated in the naming of Margaret Lilly Way. The Lilly family are still landowners and farmers though they no longer live at the Hall. The other chief landowner and farmer lives at Manor Farm, the house built on the site of the manor which had been burned down.

🍁 ALDEBY

The origins of Aldeby are deeply rooted in history. Originally a Viking settlement, this is commemorated in the attractive village sign. The area was at that time surrounded on three sides by water, so affording the Viking ships access.

The sea brought with it another 'invader' in the form of large gravel deposits. These deposits have provided Aldeby with one of its chief industries and the villagers have lived mostly in harmony with the gravel pit since the 1920s.

In addition to the Viking ship, the village sign features a sheaf of corn and a bunch of fruit to represent Aldeby's numerous farms and orchards. The orchards, together with Waveney Apple Growers (or, as it is known locally, the 'apple factory'), a collection, storage and packaging point for the fruit, have provided employment, albeit mostly seasonal, for many years. The workers were once primarily women and it is, perhaps, a sign of the times that nowadays more men are seeking casual employment.

There have been other changes over the years, notably in methods of farming and, in common with most villages, Aldeby has seen the departure of some local families and an influx of newcomers. The houses with their rich variation of period and style have, in many cases, been renovated, some from a state of near dereliction. Two former pubs, the Tuns and the Dun Cow, have become dwelling houses and the inhabitants of Aldeby need to go further afield to satisfy their thirsts and their social inclinations.

Impervious, or seemingly so, to all change, the parish church of St Mary stands beside the site of the old Benedictine priory. The latter, founded about 1100, was a cell to the priory in Norwich and the earliest section of the church was built to accommodate, separately, both monks and villagers. The present nave is, as a consequence, disproportionately long. Despite its air of timelessness the church has evolved over several centuries and the wall dividing the north chapel from the main body has been added within living memory.

Notwithstanding altering trends and attitudes there is a feeling of continuity in Aldeby. A walk in the churchyard (even at the risk of a sprained ankle) to see the recurring family names on the gravestones reinforces this feeling.

The loss of school and pubs, both prime meeting places, has inevitably detracted from the heart of Aldeby but she is still alive and most definitely kicking.

🍁 Anmer

Anmer lies off the beaten track, on the edge of the Royal estate of Sandringham. It is a small village of about 30 houses, mostly of flint and brick, and set in very pretty surroundings on the edge of Anmer Park.

Previously most of the houses were occupied by people who worked at Anmer Hall or in other parts of the Royal estate, and even today there are several people living in the village who work for the estate or who are retired, having spent most of their lives here. This gives a pleasant atmosphere of continuity, and a feeling that life goes on here much the same as it has always done.

The Hall itself is a very attractive Georgian house, surrounded by parkland with many fine trees; the country home until recently of the Duke and Duchess of Kent and their family. On one occasion the Royal Norfolk Show was held in the park. Near the Hall is the 14th century church of St Mary, which has an altar cloth given by Queen Mary.

The village has a special interest in the Royal Family, who are often seen when they are staying at Sandringham, and when shoots take place round the village. A special event during the summer is the Sandringham Show, when members of the estate staff compete for prizes for the best fruit, flowers, vegetables and gardens. Anmer residents have a tradition of doing well in these events, and the best garden is often one in the village.

Anmer has a long history going back before our present Royal Family bought Sandringham House in 1862. The name Anmer is thought to derive from the Old English meaning 'duck pond'. Tradition has it that another English queen, Boudicca, fought a battle against the Romans close by at Anmer Minque. Roman remains have been found here, and there are several ancient barrows or burial places dating from even earlier times. One of the long-distance green roads, Peddars Way, running from the north coast to Thetford and beyond, passes close to the village.

The village sign links the years. It shows a Roman soldier on one side and a Boy Scout on the other. It was given by the Norfolk Scouts to the Queen in appreciation of the privilege of holding their jamboree here in 1957.

14

❧ ASHILL

The name Ashill means 'ashy leas' or 'hill of ashes'. This is a very ancient settlement and evidence of a Roman encampment has been found. In 1874 a gold torque was discovered and a quantity of pottery in the area known as Quidney.

The two principal manors were Uphall and Panworth and prosperous farms of these names still exist. The Bedingfield family were lords of the manor from 1554 to 1682.

The church, which is over 700 years old and of flint construction, is dedicated to St Nicholas and is mostly in the Perpendicular style. There is a magnificent tower with an ogee headed doorway on the west front. On the second buttress on the south side near the chancel door is a scratch dial used to tell the time before Ashill had clocks. On the north side may be seen memorial tablets to Rev Bartholomew Edwards (1789–1889) and his wife. He lived to be 100, all but nine days, and was rector of Ashill for 76 years. This long ministry is recorded in the *Guinness Book of Records*. His photograph may be seen in the church.

The goose green and village pond are in the charge of the Village Trustees, who also administer charitable funds. Householders in the village have the right to run a goose and gander and followers on the green. Near the green is the village 'Call In' where coffee is served and lunches provided for the elderly and various classes and activities take place. This is run by Ashill Village Aid, which provides many services in the village such as car transport for those unable to visit doctors, hospitals etc by public transport. The old flint building, beautifully restored, housed the village fire engine in the past.

Ashill is now a thriving village community located between Watton and Swaffham, with a population of 1,450 people. The village has grown to its present size from a population of 500 in the mid 1960s. The newcomers live on a number of estates, which consist largely of bungalows. At the end of 1988 Ashill had a new school built to replace the over 100 year old buildings. Ashill Community Centre was opened in 1981.

Most of the employed people work outside the village; Watton, Swaffham, Thetford, East Dereham and Norwich being the usual places of employment. Inside the village the three larger farms employ a few men each and the engineering shop has five employees.

Ashill being a typical Norfolk village is basically self sufficient, with its varied retail outlets including a post office, farm shop (selling milk), market garden and an electrical shop. A fresh fish van, fish and chip van, milk float, baker's van and mobile library visit the village regularly.

🍁 ASHWELLTHORPE

Ashwellthorpe is a small village with a population of about 760, to the south of Wymondham. As well as a post office and general store, there is a garage and a hairdresser. The village hall is the home of various activities and there is also a well used recreation ground.

The church tower was built in the late 13th century and the chancel some years later in the early 14th century. There is an interesting alabaster monument between the north chapel and the chancel, possibly of Sir Edmund Thorpe, who died in 1417. The carved octagonal font is dated 1660, the year that Charles II was restored to the throne after Cromwell's Commonwealth had failed. On the green in front of the church is the village sign.

Ashwellthorpe Hall Hotel was originally the manor house of Sir Thomas Knyvett, 1596 to 1658. Today it is owned by the Disabled Drivers Association, who give holidays to the disabled. It is also open to non-residents.

The trotting track holds several race meetings a year and is on the boundary of Ashwellthorpe, though it is known as the Wreningham trot racing track. The White Horse public house is in the centre of the village, next to the village hall.

🍁 ASLACTON

Aslacton is a small village on the river Tas some 13 miles south of Norwich. It was founded by Oslac, a follower of Cuthrum the Dane who settled in East Anglia after a formal treaty with Alfred the Great. The village was sufficiently busy in the Middle Ages to be granted a weekly market in 1263.

The church of St Michael is a very early foundation and has one of the 120 round towers in Norfolk. It houses the oldest ring of five bells in the county. This replaced an earlier, heavier ring of three. It is unique in being the oldest complete ring by a single bellfounder in the county and the bells are dated 1604, 1607, 1607, 1607 and 1614.

There has been a primary school here since 1850. In the 1950s the children of the neighbouring village of Great Moulton were added to the roll and in 1986 those of the village of Tibenham. It became a National Board school in 1976. A new primary school building which continues to cater for the children of these three villages was completed in 1989.

Social activities, Women's Institute and playgroup are all shared with the adjoining village of Great Moulton.

🍁 ATTLEBOROUGH

Attleborough is a small market town midway between Norwich and Thetford. The heavy traffic using the A11 now uses the bypass opened in 1985, allowing Attleborough to regain some of its traditional market town flavour. It has grown considerably over recent years, with much residential and industrial development. However, with the older, traditional industries of brush making and turkey rearing still in evidence the town has incorporated the old and the new to the benefit and enjoyment of all. The community spirit can be fully appreciated each June during Carnival Week, when every organisation joins in a host of activities culminating in a splendid parade of floats and a highly festive afternoon on the recreation ground. At Christmastime there is a splendid display of festive lighting which improves every year due to community support and enthusiasm.

There are shops in the town to cater for every need, soon to be joined by a large supermarket. The excellent services, recreational and leisure facilities include a sports hall, health centre, doctors' surgeries, dentists, opticians, banks, building societies and all manner of retail outlets. Besides the recreation ground, Attleborough has 19 acres of land presented on the closure of Wm Gaymers Cider Company – the old apple orchards. This land is in full use for sporting activities and is also the site of the famous bi-annual Breckland Tattoo.

Educational provision is excellent, catering for all ages from pre-school to adult. There is also a school for handicapped children and an adult training centre for handicapped adults. The latter raised funds to build its own swimming pool from the proceeds of the Tattoo. Local social groups may hire the pool, which is in constant use.

A weekly market is held on Thursdays, continuing the 13th century Charter granted to the town by Edward I. The town is of Saxon origin and was already well established when in AD 856 St Edmund spent a year in the town in preparation for becoming King of the East Angles. St Edmund's Gate, St Edmund's Close and St Edmund's old people's home all bear his name.

The parish church of St Mary is of early Norman origin. It retains its Norman tower, a splendid 15th century rood screen, and well-preserved medieval wall paintings. Some residents of the town sailed with the Pilgrim Fathers to America where they founded Attleboro', Massachusetts, now a large city. A link, founded by one of the town's WI members, has been maintained for many years. Attleborough is now twinned with the French town of Neuil les Aubiers in the Dept Deux Sèvres. Very successful visits have taken place between townspeople and pupils from the High School of both 'twins'. Young people have also been welcomed on both sides for work experience and language enhancement.

🍁 AYLSHAM

Aylsham is a busy market community of over 5,000 people, set in rich farmlands on the river Bure. Its prosperity owed much to its position at the navigable head of the river. Wherries, the traditional black-sailed craft of Norfolk, traded up-river to Aylsham, making regular visits to the river basin above the mill. When the great flood of 1912 destroyed much of the locks, wherries could no longer be used for transport. A water mill is recorded on this site in the Domesday Book. It was rebuilt in its present form in 1798, and was used as a provender mill until 1960.

Its principal manor was owned by John of Gaunt. This manor later passed to the Hobart family, in nearby Blickling Hall, which is now owned by the National Trust; certain rights have passed regarding Aylsham Market Place and the Buttlands. The Buttlands is an old archery range, established in the reign of Edward III for longbow practice.

The height of Aylsham's own industry was between 1350–1800. The linen and canvas industry flourished in the 14th century and, later, the weaving of woollen and worstead cloths. Flemish weavers came over in the early 18th century, and their architectural influence can be seen in many houses of that period.

The beautiful flint-faced church of St Michael dominates the town, standing close to the Market Place. Its great 14th century tower houses a ring of ten bells, forming one of the finest rings in the county. The famous landscape gardener Humphry Repton lies buried here; his grave is carefully tended.

The Aylsham Market in Palmers Lane established a county reputation for the sale of live and dead stock. More recently, Mr G. Key developed sale-rooms on the same site, for the sale of antiques. Aylsham Market Place still has trading stalls on most days. They give a colourful picture of the life of the town.

Growth of the town has continued steadily in the last 30 years, and new housing estates have developed. The industrial estate on the north side of the town continues to expand, providing more jobs for local people. Local shops cover every requirement.

Aylsham Show is held annually in Blickling Park, on August Bank Holiday Monday, for local charities. It is one of the largest one-day shows in the country.

🍁 BACTON-ON-SEA

When the village of Bacton-on-Sea is mentioned probably the first thing that springs to mind is North Sea gas. We can however lay claim to more ancient fame.

The Baptist church at Bacton (founded in 1821) has a unique feature, a stained glass window. This was given in memory of George Pilgrim who was pastor here for 56 years. For 50 of those years he received no remuneration!

The present parish church, standing on a rise about a quarter of a mile from the sea, is about 500 years old, although heading the list of vicars which hangs in the church there is mentioned one Ralph in 1257. The church is dedicated to St Andrew and was granted to the prior of Bromholm by William de Glanville the founder.

An even older foundation was Bromholm Priory, or Bacton Abbey as it is commonly known. The priory, which was at one time several miles from the sea, was founded in 1113 as a cell to Castle Acre Priory. Only ruins remain of the former Cluniac monastery, which it is said was of vast proportions. Henry III came to Bacton in 1233 and the priory church was then stated to be 200 ft long.

19

The priory was mentioned by Chaucer in his *Canterbury Tales*, by the Miller's Wife crying 'Helpe Holy Cross of Bromholm'. The priory had in its possession a relic in the shape of 'a little cross' stated to have been made by St Helena (mother to Constantine the Great) out of those parts of the Saviour's Cross to which his hands and feet were nailed, particularly the part where it was most sprinkled with His blood. St Helena, having conveyed the cross to Constantinople, gave it to her son. In turn it came into the hands of Emperor Baldwin who employed a chaplain to say a daily mass before it. Later the office of chaplain passed to Hugh, a priest from Norfolk. After the death of Baldwin, Hugh stole it and gave it to the monastery of Bromholm, where in gratitude for the gift he and his two sons were maintained for their lifetimes. This cross brought great wealth to the monastery through the successive pilgrimages that were made to it. Many miracles were attributed to it including those of restoring the sight of 19 blind persons.

Sir John Paston was buried here in 1466 and it is recorded that before his funeral one man was employed for three days flaying beasts to be consumed; also many geese, capons and chickens were used together with 1,300 eggs, 20 gallons of milk and eight of cream. Provision was made of 13 barrels of beer, 27 of ale and many gallons of red wine. A barber was occupied for five days smartening the monks for the ceremony. At the funeral we are told, two panes of glass had to be removed by the priory glazier from the windows to prevent the smoke from the torches suffocating the mourners.

🍁 BARTON TURF

The village, or part of it, has in the past also been known as Barton Bury. The name Barton means an enclosure for barley and Turf refers to the peat dug out in medieval times for fuel, thus forming the second largest Broad in the county. The mud is being pumped from this Broad to bring back deeper water for sailing and, hopefully, wildlife. There are plans also to recreate the washed-away Pleasure Hill Island in the centre of this water to bring back some of its lost character. The acres of water and marsh on the eastern side of the village have for hundreds of years meant a living of hard work for wherrymen and marshmen who cut the peat, reed and sedge for thatching. Marsh litter (hay) for fodder and bedding, and bolders (rushes) for making baskets and horse collars were also cut.

The river Ant was used as a highway upstream and down to Yarmouth, Norwich and Lowestoft. Barton Broad is now a base for the Norfolk Punt Club, formed in 1926. The Coalhouse, built on the Parish Staithe and extended in the late 1800s, was used for the storage of waterborne goods.

The old cottages appear to have been built on the edges of commons in Pennygate. Staithe Road and the clay holes are now mistakenly called the Common; the large area of common land in the north-east was lost in the Enclosure Act of 1809.

The church of St Michael and All Angels stands well away from the present village. The lofty embattled tower has recently been rehung with six bells, and it is also well known for its rood screen. The small Methodist chapel was built in 1845 and restored in 1914. The excellent cricket ground has been home for the Norwich Wanderers for many years.

There are the remains of a lime kiln in the village, but all traces of the post mill have disappeared, as have some farm premises and all the 'little-doers' with two or three acres. Farm workers live in the village today.

One shop remains out of five and the school closed in 1965. There were once two blacksmiths, a carpenter, a coal merchant, several wherry owners, a basket-maker and two boatyards, one of which was the oldest family boatyard on the Broads until recently and still trades under that name.

🍁 BAWBURGH

The village of Bawburgh is only six miles from Norwich, and there can be few places where the compromise between town and country is more clearly seen. On hot sunny days in summer the city visitors make the village green resemble the French Riviera, while year-round patrons of the pub and restaurants are able to glimpse a unique part of rural Norfolk.

For most of the year Bawburgh is still a place where, in sight of the old multi-roofed mill, small boys can throw off their shoes and discover the delights in a jam jar of river water. The mill, mentioned in the Domesday Book and worked until 1967, sits astride the river Yare and, having recently undergone conversion, now provides new family homes. At night, the lights shining from the several tiny windows are mirrored on the water, looking for all the world like a living Advent calendar. The bullocks which graze the river meadows take no notice of the comings and goings of the residents, preferring

The mill at Bawburgh

instead to watch the antics of the ducks, and the occasional swans, which dip in and out of the water, rearing their young on the river banks.

Behind the mill, half way up the hill which rises away from the river valley, stands the parish church. During the summer it nestles in a froth of trees and bushes but stands out clearly against a starker winter skyline of leafless branches. It is to this spot that pilgrims have come since 1016, from far and wide, to worship at the burial site of St Walstan, patron of agriculture and farm workers. Once a year, the village still pays homage to the 11th century saint. Parishioners and friends from the United Benefice of Colney and Cringleford attend the annual patronal service in the round towered church of St Mary and St Walstan, followed by a procession down to the well. (The traditional drawing of the curative waters from the well, the final resting place of Walstan's oxen and cart, has unfortunately been curtailed by successive public health condemnations.) A ploughman's lunch follows, usually held in the grounds of the historic Church Farmhouse. It is said locally that however much the farmers need the rain, it never comes until after two o'clock!

Behind the Old Post Office, whose listed buildings date from the 15th century, is the Hall Farm housing development, which incorporates the 18th century Slipper House and dovecote. Both are classified as Ancient Monuments and once stood in the grounds of the now-demolished Elizabethan Bawburgh Hall. During the 1970s, thanks to long-sighted and caring members of successive parish councils, the village managed to retain its character and charm. More recently the pressure to allow increased development has become intense and the debate over the planners' interpretation of 'conservation area' is as vital an issue in Bawburgh as anywhere in Norfolk.

🍁 BEACHAMWELL

Travel west down the quiet road from Swaffham through gentle farmland and dark sinister forests, through remnants of scarlet poppy fields and twisted pines and on until you reach the quiet village of Beachamwell. There you find a large village green surrounded by cottages, a church, pub and former school, a shady tree and a seat.

Beachamwell is an ancient place. In the Dark Ages an earthwork called Devil's Dyke was built, which remained the parish boundary until 1879. Prehistoric tools, Roman coins and Saxon jewellery have all been found in the area.

The Domesday Book, however, mentioned not one, but two villages, 'Wella' and 'Bitcham'. The remains of Wella have been found near the ruins of All Saints' church on the outskirts of the present village. The ghost of Diana and her dogs is said to haunt All Saints' church and certainly owls hoot eerily on moonlit nights.

Two further redundant churches point to a larger population in the past. St John's remains just as a tower standing in the middle of farmland, and at Shingham, woods and meadows surround St Botolph's with its beautiful Norman doorway and pretty green copper roof.

In those days Beachamwell must have been a meeting place, as the stumps of two medieval crosses show where regular markets took place – at the crossroads and on the village green.

Now as ever, the social life of the village centres around the green with its two rows of semi-detached cottages. One was already a shop in 1841 and still serves as the post office. Another was made into a reading room at the end of

St Mary's church, Beachamwell

the 19th century and provided books and newspapers – today the county mobile library calls. The baker also lived close by in the 'bake office' and each year he baked the Bread Charity for the poor. John Motteux from the big house left money for these loaves, but now the church receives the income from the bequest.

At the west end of the green, guarded by cherry trees, stands Beachamwell's fourth and oldest church, St Mary's. The tower was built by the Saxons a thousand years ago. Later generations added the octagonal lantern and the thatched roof. On one of the pillars in the nave is the 'Beachamwell Demon' sticking his tongue out at the congregation. The Norfolk painter John Cotman visited Beachamwell in 1810–11 and an engraving of his view of St Mary's can be found at the back of the church. The school building is to the south of the church. A plaque marks its life from 1835 to 1986.

At the far end of the green opposite St Mary's is the pub which was known as the 'Hole In The Wall'. Apparently, when purchasing ale, drinkers would not go inside the building but would go to a hole in the wall at the side and drink in the open air. Now whether this was just for the farm hands and whether the gentry went inside and sat down is not known.

The Memorial Hall – given to the village in memory of those who died in the First World War – is also next to the green, run by the villagers and the centre of social life.

Working life was centred around and controlled by the 'big house', as almost everyone in Beachamwell worked for the estate until the 1960s when it was sold. Beachamwell narrowly missed becoming a royal estate when King Edward Vll decided against Beachamwell in favour of Sandringham.

Neither the number of houses nor the size of the population has changed much since the 1920s, with the latter about 326 people. Now, however, there is little employment within the village and people travel to neighbouring towns, returning in the evening to enjoy the countryside.

Set deep in Breckland, the land is poor, the climate dryer than the rest of England and winds can whip up the soil into dust storms without warning. Footpaths and bridleways criss-cross the parish allowing ramblers to discover the delights of nightingales singing in thickets and nightjars chucking in forest glades, wild deer wandering across lanes and hares racing over the fields. Spring is heralded by snowdrops in the hedgerows, summer by wild raspberries in the forests and autumn by blackberries along the byways – isolation still has many advantages.

🍁 BEDINGHAM

Eleven miles south of Norwich, the population of the village is 180. The name is of Saxon derivation, 'a place of the people of Baeda'. It is an ancient parish noted in Domesday in 1086 as mostly belonging to the King, but in Saxon times to Hagan, a nephew of King Harold, who was probably dispossessed. There is a field called Hagg or Hagherne, fancifully supposed to have been named for him!

The parish lies in pleasant, open, gentle countryside so little changed from 1066 that Rider Haggard, who owned a farm here, writing in 1901 thought Hagan would still recognise it. The scattered houses originally lay near commons which were finally enclosed in 1843, accounting for the seemingly illogical siting of them. Several are medieval hall houses though Bedingham Hall itself was demolished in the 1870s. Osborne's, 15th century, and Hall

St Andrew's church, Bedingham

Farm, 1660, with its moat, latterly a refuge for wild fowl, are both rewarding buildings. Moat Farm is a late medieval hall house but in this case the name may derive from John Molet, who died in 1471. Nearby the quiet bridlepaths and lakes were replaced by harshly concreted trackways in the Second World War, when the ancient woodland just beyond the parish boundary was a bomb store.

The fine round-towered church, so wonderfully spacious and light, has a Saxon tower and tower arch while the rest is largely 13th century. In the east window of the north aisle there are noteworthy stained glass panels, the gift of the patrons of the living, King's College, Cambridge. The size and beauty of St Andrew's almost certainly owes much to the fact that in 1226 Hubert de Burgh granted it to the Priory of Our Lady at Walsingham, one of the richest in Europe. The canons of the priory may well have influenced life in Bedingham until the Dissolution of the Monasteries, when it reverted to the Crown. There is a story that pilgrims on their way to Walsingham were in the habit of resting here. In 1318 a manor was also given to the priory, the house of which stands to the east of the church, appropriately called Priory Farm.

Life here has always been dominated by farming. Like all villages Bedingham, until 1926, had its own vicar; its blacksmith until 1900; its wheelwright, butcher, cooper, shop-keeper and shoemaker; a mill which shut down in 1900; a school active 1863–1906; a post office until 1926 and a public house which survived until the late 1960s when it was converted to two private houses. The curious name of the latter, the Triple Plea, is explained in a song reputedly sung by habituees:

'Let mankind live in peace and love,
The lawyer's tricks they need not prove,
Let them forbear excess and riot,
They need not feed on doctor's diet,
Let them attend what God does teach,
They need not care what parson preach,
But if men fools and knaves will be
They'll be ass-ridden by all three.'

The records show that Bedingham people have always been independent and never very feudal in outlook, though with a very marked sense of community.

🍁 BEESTON

Beeston is a quiet village in west Norfolk, half way between Swaffham and Dereham. It has a 14th century church, St Mary's, on the outskirts and a school, post office and public house in the centre, the school accommodating 50 pupils. It has been mainly a farming community, with 48 houses dating back to the 1600s, including the pub, the Ploughshare. The lanes were adequate back in the days of horses and carts, when the post was delivered by bicycle.

During the Second World War, American airmen were based at the airfield here. Although the runways were in Wendling, the men's sleeping and eating quarters were here in Beeston. The American war memorial was dedicated in 1989, when several airmen came back for a visit.

There were once two butcher's shops and three public houses – the Holkham Arms, the Bell and the Ploughshare, a silversmith, blacksmith and a whitesmith. The bakery is now Bakehouse Farm. A laundry and a games school were also in the village. Where the chapel was is now a small bungalow.

27

Beeston today is not quite so quiet as it was, the industrial part of the village bringing more heavy traffic through, causing damage to roads and verges and making what used to be pleasant walks a danger now to children and mothers with prams. Industries here include a canning factory, wood pallets, Jaguar spares etc. There are also two builders, a riding school and a hang-gliding school operating on meadow land. Farming, however, is still the main life of the village. A hunt still meets here, a colourful sight with around 30 horses.

There is a cricket and a football team, and a social club for the ladies. There is still no street lighting but the centre of the village now has mains drainage. As the water table here is very high the rest of the village will be pleased when they too share that service.

🍁 BELTON

Where to start on a village which has changed so much, particularly in the last four decades? Why, it has even changed its location from Suffolk to Norfolk with boundary changes in 1974 and with it its Parliamentary constituency from Lowestoft to Yarmouth!

Belton folk were mostly farmers and market gardeners, with associated jobs like transport and a sturdy breed who went 'down to the sea in ships'. Until 1959, the railway station was a busy spot. Market gardeners sent, and sometimes queued to unload, their produce to London and Newcastle. Trucks of coal came in for local merchants – four of whom are remembered as they took their sacks to customers. The line to Yarmouth was direct, quick, and relatively cheap, now replaced by slower and more expensive buses.

Passengers going the opposite way, included for years, generations of school children making their way to Beccles' Sir John Leman School at 7.30 am and back at 4.30 pm, to a welcome shout from the porter of 'Belton or Burrer' (Burgh Castle)! The old station site lives on in modern houses named 'Platform 1 and 2'.

Not far away, the site of a Methodist chapel is marked by a bungalow, Chapelfield. The chapel was a centre for meetings and services – especially anniversaries, in which children and adults gladly took part. Methodists now travel to town or join services in All Saints' church.

Names reflect past uses and changes. A short stretch of road called The Green *was* green – with cottages and one of several blacksmith's shops. Another one is remembered as The Forge (now part of a restaurant called The Forge and Feathers) and shows the importance of horses and carts for transport – not just riding for pleasure as our various stables provide today. Footpaths called The Free and The Walk gave short cuts from Station Road (now renamed North and South) to Bell Lane, the church and the King's Head. The King's Head has seen changes from horse-drawn brakes (wagons with seats) and cabs, to coaches and cars. The inn used to boast tea-gardens and a drill hall where there is now a community room.

Neither must the beautiful stretch of common be forgotten. Less open and wild now, it embraces two growing caravan/holiday sites with amenities for villagers as well as visitors.

The school had three classrooms for village children of all ages and a headmaster at the turn of the 20th century was Mr Mills, father of actor Sir John, who was a pupil. During the Second World War, the senior girls had a visiting domestic science teacher seconded from Bungay for two days a fortnight. There was no special room and washing water was often used to scrub gravestones in the adjacent churchyard! The school has now been made into three separate dwellings, the headmaster's house (later the caretaker's) now enlarged to modern executive type. And today's children? They are provided for with those from Burgh Castle with two up-to-date schools – first and middle. Seniors are bussed or cycle to Gorleston. A cycle-track beside a busy road has been laid to help them. A dormitory-type village comes alive at school times when younger ones are taken and fetched by numerous cars, and blue buses tour the roads.

Another famous name must be recalled – one John Ives 1751–76, who is depicted on the village sign (1977). Born at Yarmouth, son of a merchant-landowner, he lies buried at Belton church and in his short life proved himself an antiquarian of considerable promise, writing the *History and Antiquities of the Hundred of Lothingland.*

🍁 BIRCHAM

Bircham, which is on the fringe of the Sandringham estate, lies approximately 13 miles north-east of King's Lynn. It consists of three parts: Great Bircham, Bircham Newton and Bircham Tofts.

For many years much of the land was owned by the Marquis of Cholmondeley of nearby Houghton Hall, but during the 1940s the Sandringham estate purchased some of the land for shooting purposes. In recent years the estate has been selling village houses and parcels of land, thus changing the character of the village as incomers have moved into the many new houses and bungalows.

One approaches Bircham via Bircham Heath, where there are four barrows. These have been excavated and found to contain funerary urns, gold pins, a bronze pin, skulls etc ascribed to the Bronze Age. Near here, the ancient Peddars Way runs across the main road to its ultimate destination at Holme.

Another mile or so brings one to Great Bircham where the village shop, the King's Head pub and the old school nestle around a pretty dell; this is flanked by the phone box, a seat and the interesting village sign. The old school, which was built in 1842 by the then Marquis of Cholmondeley and later extended, provided education for the three Birchams. The Marquis even clothed the school children every year at his own expense. Nowadays, the children go further down the road to a modern primary school which lies in spacious grounds, presented by King George VI. To commemorate the 50th anniversary Her Majesty Queen Elizabeth the Queen Mother visited the school on 13th January 1998 to unveil a plaque and rename it King George VI School. The old school buildings and house are now private homes.

The pub has been renovated in recent years but has retained its splendid original facade. It directly faces the Country Stores, another very attractive white building. Most of Bircham is now red brick but some old cottages were built with flintstone and these – together with the pub and village shop – are what visitors find so attractive.

Just past the new school, as the road curves round on its way to Docking, the war memorial forms the central point of another area of interest. To the left, along the Snettisham Road, the working windmill provides a venue for family outings from April to September. The mill, which was built in 1846, has been restored by its owner to a very high standard, and now provides a place of much interest.

St Mary's church is surrounded by giant limes and both new and old churchyards. The church, most of which was constructed in the 15th century, has a beautiful 13th century doorway approached by a fine north porch. Inside, the lofty nave forms a striking feature, having stone seats around the bases of the slender-shafted pillars.

Outside, at the entrance to the new churchyard, is an iron gate which was donated by Queen Mary (George V's wife) and which came from Queen Alexandra's Rose Garden at Sandringham. In the old churchyard is the first Cross of Sacrifice to have been erected by the Imperial War Graves Commission after the Second World War. This cross was unveiled by King George VI on 14th July 1946. Here lie 66 young airmen and one WAAF, mostly from the Dominions, together with a number of German airmen who had been shot down.

The airmen had been stationed at Bircham Newton, first built for the Royal Flying Corps in 1916 and then rebuilt in 1929 with the present buildings and hangars. It closed in 1960 and was then taken over in 1967 by the Construction Industry Training Board; it is now the headquarters for training and teaching personnel the many aspects of the building trade.

The village part of Bircham Newton is a conservation area situated on the road between Great Bircham and Docking. Around here there are wonderful views and also facilities for private trout fishing. All Saints' church, one of the smallest churches in the county, is a place of dignity and charm; it was mostly built in the 13th century and it is noticeable that there are no windows on the north side – an advantage in the cold weather. The old pews have pricket lights or candle holders which are still used when the occasional services are held.

In the sanctuary is a stone coffin lid representing the figure of a man. Executed with skill, it depicts a Roman Catholic priest in full costume of the High Mass, holding between his fingers a small effigy of a human heart. At the right cheek of the figure the head of a child is sculpted. Conjectures have been made as to the origin, thought perhaps to be part of a sarcophagus. During repairs in 1832 the ground was excavated to find at a depth of three feet eight inches the bones of a man and child, but it was evident that this was not their original resting place. The jaw bone was perfect and contained a full set of teeth without blemish – that of a young man.

At the Tofts end of Bircham there is an ivy covered, ruined church. There is an air of mystery about this bird-haunted place which is attractive to artists and poets alike. Not far from here, on the way back into the main part of the Birchams, lies what was the Primitive Methodist chapel, erected in 1871 with bricks from the now extinct nearby kilns. The chapel has now been converted into a private home.

The village has changed during the course of the 20th century. It used to be almost self-supporting with its forge, mill and bakery delivery, butcher, coffin maker, cobbler, basket maker, taxi service and cottage sweetshops.

Now only the mill in its new guise remains, together with the pub, post office and shop. There is a scant bus service to King's Lynn, Fakenham and Hunstanton, making it necessary for the use of private cars. For those without? We are most fortunate in having a strong bond of friendship in the village, not the least that which comes from the WI and the Meals on Wheels service.

BLAKENEY

A picturesque coastal village, half way between Wells-next-the-Sea and Sheringham, Blakeney can look back on a long and eventful past. Its existence was first noted in the Domesday Book as one of a small group of ports around the estuary of the river Glaven.

By the 13th century Blakeney was prosperous enough for the Carmelite friars to found a friary on the eastern side of the port. There they stayed and prospered until the Dissolution of the Monasteries brought their influence and way of life to an end. Blakeney's ancient Guildhall, at the foot of Mariner's Hill, may well have had some connection with the Whitefriars, whose lands are known to have extended as far as this, but the origin of this small, sturdy building with its vaulted roof and tomblike atmosphere, has never been discovered. Throughout the centuries it has been used for a variety of purposes by merchants, mariners and even, for a time, as a morgue for drowned sailors. Now restored by the Ministry of Works and kept tidy by the Parish Council, it is open for the public to wander in and out, free of charge.

It was the beginning of the end of Blakeney as a port when a local landowner, Sir Henry Calthorpe, built a bank across the Glaven in 1637. Silting up began causing local consternation amongst the merchants and fishermen, so much so that the bank was partly demolished. But too much damage had already been done and when, after the Enclosures Act in 1824, there was more embanking in order to join Blakeney and Cley by road, the channel to both Wiveton and Cley ceased to be navigable. With the coming of steam and larger vessels Blakeney's trade, mostly shipping corn and bringing in coal from Newcastle, dwindled away. The final blow was when the hoped for railway link with the rest of East Anglia never came.

This might have been a mortal blow, but Blakeney was not destined to die.

The harbour was ideal for safe dinghy sailing and there was the charm and interest of the Point, the long promontory of shingle and sand dunes, for many years now under the care of the National Trust. A nature reserve and sanctuary for migratory birds, it is a mecca for those who love the windy emptiness of marshes and grassy dunes, the call of sea birds, the sigh of the sea on the shingle.

Blakeney's fine church of St Nicholas stands well away from the quay on the main coast road (A149). It was built in the 13th century, but rather more than a century later the nave was rebuilt and the present tall, pinnacled tower added. It has a second tower or turret at the eastern end, supposedly to guide ships into the harbour (it is still lit at night) but more likely this was to provide a stair turret as an architectural feature. One's first sight of Blakeney, approaching from any direction, is its church tower.

The post-war years have seen much residential development along the coast road and adjoining roads. As well as a council house estate there are purpose-built bungalows for the elderly who have their own day centre, largely funded by the local community, with a luncheon club, health services and day care provided for the frail and handicapped.

Old Blakeney begins from where the narrow, picturesque High Street winds its way down to the quay, growing steeper all the way. Fine Georgian frontages, cobblestone fishermen's cottages, the Congregational church, a restaurant, a pub, shops and a café mingle harmoniously. At intervals 'lokes' or alleyways lead into yards where cottages huddle together away from the icy north winds. Along the quay, ferries for the Point pick up passengers. Traditional water sports are held every summer and dinghy races are organised by the Sailing Club. A ship's chandler and a marine stores cater for the sailing fraternity; there is a combined post office and general stores and two hotels overlook the sea. Many holiday visitors turn into 'settlers'; most are soon absorbed into village life, playing their part in local activities. Now as well as a large new hall as a centre for most events, Blakeney can boast two hard tennis courts. A caring village, there is the Blakeney Neighbourhood Housing Association to provide low rental housing for local people unable to buy their own homes, and every Christmas 'Twelve Good Men and True', known as 'The Blakeney Twelve', give a bumper Christmas party to the senior citizens of the parish.

In the past 60 years Blakeney has found a new role, but still draws its life and charm from the sea and its tranquil marsh-fringed harbour.

✿ BLICKLING

Many villages owe their origins to settlements around a manor house, and Blickling is no exception.

Sir Nicholas Dagworth (1390) built a rectangular moated house on the site of the present Hall. The villagers of Blickling, like many others, lived in the shadow of the 'great house', but this one grew in magnificence and fame from owner to owner to rival all others. Sir Thomas Erpingham, Fastolf, Geoffrey Boleyn (all one-time owners) were made famous on the London stage by Shakespeare. In 1616 Sir Henry Hobart bought from Sir Edward Clere a dilapidated building, neglected by a spendthrift owner, and his successors rebuilt it in the Georgian style. In 1850 the property passed to the 11th Marquis of Lothian who left the Hall and 4,500 acres of estate to the National Trust on his death in 1940.

Few villages have witnessed the comings and goings of so many of the great and powerful, if not always of the good, or been involved in preparations of such lavish balls and entertainments. For how long was recounted the tale of the great fire sweeping the house in 1874?

The village of Blickling today consists of no more than ten dwellings and an inn (Buckinghamshire Arms), built in its present form in 1700, with a population of 23, although the parish extends to some ten miles taking in scattered farmhouses. Since the 17th century the village has been grouped around the Park gates and the mainly 15th century St Andrew's church with its 13th century south door. Hobart House, once a rectory, was at first a fine farmhouse, hence the address 'Farmyard' given to the two houses (originally one) running at right-angles to the church. Beyond these groupings, on the main road, is the school building with its star-topped chimney and the school house of Norfolk flint. White's 1845 *Norfolk Directory* states that Lady Suffield (second daughter of Hobart, Earl of Buckinghamshire) supported a school for poor children, and mentioned a Mary Varden, schoolmistress. The school house with her Ladyship's crest on the front is dated 1867–8, and as she died in 1850, it might be conjectured that some simple building preceded the present one.

The artists' favourite house is No 8 – a rare survival of the once-numerous 18th century mud wall and thatch cottages.

Silvergate, a hamlet of estate cottages three-quarters of a mile from

Blickling village, has a long terrace of thatched houses, as most were until the end of the 18th century. With a population of some 80 people it is regarded as 'Blickling' for practical purposes.

Coming nearer to our own time, since the closure of the village school the building has been used as a Community Centre for Blickling (with Silvergate) and three other villages. It provides a useful venue for groups of varied ages.

Many dwellings in Blickling and Silvergate are, as of old, occupied by workers on the estate, others are on short leases from the National Trust, so that to a large extent the village is still under the shadow of the 'great house' and its fortunes are bound up with it.

🍁 BLOFIELD

Blofield is a growing residential area still retaining a few examples of 18th and 19th century country-type houses. The village has a long history and is mentioned at length in the Domesday Book.

The present church of St Andrew and St Peter replaced an older building, probably on the same site, of Norman construction, and it is today much as it was built between c1380 and c1440. It is the largest church in what was the Blofield Hundred and it owed its size and importance to the prosperity of the wool trade and the residence of bishops as lords of the manor.

The land is mainly level farming country. Into the 20th century Blofield was renowned for the quality of its market-garden produce and several of those responsible for the highly regarded output are remembered in the surviving names of lokes and lanes in various parts of the parish. In recent years there has been a considerable change to 'pick-your-own' marketing.

The village is now a mixture of old and very modern dwellings with a variety of retail shops surviving from earlier years. There are good road and railway connections with both Norwich and Great Yarmouth, and also Lowestoft. The village remains to this day divided both by the main Norwich–Great Yarmouth highway and a well-defined green belt. The railway line does not traverse the parish, but there is a station at Brundall, one mile distant.

There remain a few of the old footpaths which in earlier times formed the means of communication between the two parts of the parish and neighbouring villages. There are schools in each of the separated communities, the slightly older one near to the centre of old Blofield now much improved and enlarged from its 1877 origin.

There were at least two windmills in the parish, one in Mill Road and the other in Lingwood Road, east of Waterlow, right on the boundary and to which local residents would take their corn for grinding.

There are two post offices, each serving a widely separated residential area. The number of licensed houses has within recent years been reduced to three and a hundred years ago there was in addition a well-stocked wines and spirits off-licence, of which there is some evidence of the extensive cellars. The village supports a number of lively and friendly bodies and associations. Blofield WI was formed in 1918, the oldest one in Norfolk, and to commemorate its 50th anniversary a village sign was presented to the village.

❧ BODHAM

There are three mentions of Bodham as a hamlet in the Domesday Book, and today it is a scattered village on the A148 between Holt and Cromer. It is obvious from the number of farmhouses that the main industry was agriculture. Farming still plays a prominent part, but people also work outside the village.

Until 1926 there was a flourishing foundry, making agricultural and other equipment for the area. After the foundry closed the building was used as a blacksmith's, producing tools for farming and domestic use. Now the building has been converted to private dwellings. A joinery business, started a few years ago, provides some employment for local people.

Much of Bodham and the surrounding land was owned by the Mott, later Mott-Radclyffe, family, and there are still estate cottages and houses with the family's monogram. During recent years there have been several housing developments, but latterly this has been mainly infilling.

The Bodham and Beckham village hall opened in 1986, replacing the old Jubilee Hall, which was financed by money-raising in the village. It is kept very busy with events ranging from line dancing to horticultural shows.

The Red Hart public house has always been an important part of village life. There has been an inn here at least since the 1700s. One family, the Sayers, were licensees for 74 years, spanning three generations. Bodham Stores, converted from an old farmhouse into a village shop and post office, is a valuable asset to the local community.

The former village school, Bodham

There are two churches, the Methodist church, built in 1866, situated on the main road, and All Saints' church which is some way from the village. The first rector recorded here was William de Wendling in about 1268.

Over by the parish church, reached by Hart Lane, is the Marlpit, now a fishing pond providing a pleasant pastime. And for ramblers or walkers Bodham Common contains about ten acres of unspoilt habitat. A playing field and bowling green are situated near the old School House, which is now a factory producing model 'live' steam railways.

🍁 BRACON ASH

Bracon Ash is a village six miles south-west of Norwich, with a population of about 400. The parish church of St Nicholas is built of flint, stone and brick and has a small bell turret with one bell. A notable feature is the Berney Mausoleum, added in the 18th century.

Bracon Hall is a modern mansion built on the site of a much older building, which Queen Elizabeth I is said to have visited.

The village hall was built in 1970 and is open to social club members twice a week, plus special events throughout the year. It is also used for other activities, a baby clinic and various clubs as well as private functions. The village school was closed in 1977 and the children now go to Mulbarton first and middle schools and Hethersett high school. There is a playing field and a bowling green and a thriving bowls club.

🍁 BRADWELL

The village of Bradwell, on the A143 near to the seaside town of Gorleston, is regarded by many as the residential suburb of Great Yarmouth. Before the Second World War it was a peaceful rural village comprising about 500 inhabitants. It boasted an inn, a post office where business was conducted in the front room of a terraced house (later to be moved to a more prominent position with the addition of a grocery business), a mill and a small bungalow shop. Incidentally, the post office was run by three generations of the same family.

The parish church, dedicated to St Nicholas, is about 700 years old, although the present church was actually built in the 14th century on the site of the older building. There is also a Methodist chapel. Although a great deal is known about the Roman fort and later Saxon township at nearby Burgh Castle there is very little to be discovered in history about Bradwell. Perhaps it was just a marshy area except for where the church stands.

Today Bradwell has 10,000 inhabitants and is growing continually. It is cheek by jowl with an industrial estate. The community centre which began life as the village school, a lovely old flint building, is used constantly by the various organisations which have grown over the years.

At the time of the reorganisation of local government in 1974, a delegation from Bradwell, Burgh Castle and Belton (the adjoining villages) went to see the local MP at Westminster to urge that the Norfolk–Suffolk boundary be left unchanged. However, these three villages are now in Norfolk.

Some years ago a new village sign was required and the parish council, co-operating with principals and teachers of the three village schools, promoted a competition for a design. Mr Harry Carter of Swaffham was sent all ideas en bloc, and he combined some of them in his final sketches. There is a horse pulling a plough, a mill, a golden sunrise (an allusion to the village pub) and, overlooking them all, St Nicholas, children's and fishermen's patron.

BRAMPTON

Brampton is a small village with a population of less than 200. It is situated ten miles north-east of Norwich, though not all maps show it. The Romans occupied much of the surrounding countryside in AD 140. Many treasures have been found, some of which are on display in Norwich Castle Museum, and Roman kilns are often unearthed when deep ploughing of the fields takes place.

Within living memory Brampton had the Maid's Head public house, a small shop, a post office, a blacksmith and a well sinker. Now all these, with the infants school, have been closed. There was a second public house, the Cross Keys, which was closed in the early 1900s. The Mack family were the publicans and when it closed Macks lived on there until 1958. There are still members of the Mack family living in the village.

Brampton church, St Peter's, is a compact little building, with a beautiful piped organ. The octagonal brick top to the tower was built in the 16th century and there are some interesting brasses.

The river Bure divides Brampton from Oxnead, which is also a pretty area. Much history is attached to the church and Oxnead Hall, where Charles II was supposed to have been entertained in 1676. Prince Charles, Prince of Wales, visited the church privately in 1990.

BROOKE

The village of Brooke lies either side of the Norwich-Bungay road (B1332), seven miles equidistant from Norwich and Bungay. Its houses are a mixture of the old and the new – the oldest one being Porch House in The Street which was originally the dower house belonging to Brooke Hall, now demolished. There has been some infilling but the majority of new houses are to be found in the Burgess Way/Churchill Place development and to the north of High Green.

Kelly's Directory of 1924 describes 'the pleasant village of Brooke' with its

Brooke post office

'population of 540'. There were three grocers, two butchers, a blacksmith, a well sinker, a boot repairer, a harness maker, a cycle repairer and a baker. Today's services include two grocery shops, the post office and newsagent's, a garage and petrol station, a hairdresser, a farm shop and, in converted farm buildings adjacent to the farm shop, a veterinary surgery, an upholsterer and another hairdresser. Brooke is referred to in the Domesday Book and details of farmers etc living in the area are shown on the 1841 tithe map.

In 1831 the Baptist chapel was built, and in 1924 the Methodist chapel. The village hall was built in the 1970s to replace an old YMCA hut, bought in 1918 by a committee of villagers. An extension was carried out in 1998. The custom of holding a harvest supper originated in Brooke in 1854.

Brooke church has a round tower topped by a handsome golden weather-vane. The tower, one of many in Norfolk, has a Saxon foundation and is built of flints. The church was built c1200. The thatched roof was replaced with slate in 1849. Inside are six bells which are rung regularly. The church is dedicated to St Peter and there are many reminders of this. On entering the porch there is a little statuette to him and inside is a carved wooden figure from Oberammergau. The use of his emblem is to be found on the altar linen and many of the hassocks. The seven sacrament font is badly mutilated and worn but still shows signs of bright colours with which it was once painted.

There is a wall plaque, near the church, to one of England's greatest surgeons, Sir Astley Cooper, who was born at Brooke Hall, son of the local vicar. He was surgeon to several sovereigns including Queen Victoria and is buried in the chapel at Guy's Hospital. There are many interesting gravestones, notably one to Robert Pearce who fought with the 7th Hussars at Waterloo and another to Benjamin Riches, for 45 years a respected servant in the House of Commons, and a stranger who met with such kindness in the village that he asked to be buried here.

Finally, look at the new church room which has been so sympathetically attached to the church on the north side, to provide facilities so essential for modern church life. Brooke is a delightful village of the old and the new blending happily together, with many different organisations catering for all age groups.

✿ BRUNDALL

Brundall is approximately six miles east of Norwich, lying on the banks of the river Yare. From a population of around 300 only 50 years ago, it now contains over 4,000 inhabitants, many of whom work in the city of Norwich. It does, however, still retain the atmosphere of a village and manages to cultivate a very active community life. It is served by both bus and train routes and the level crossing at Brundall station is still manually operated. Its river life is very busy: Broom's boatyard flourishes, among others, and numerous river craft are made and housed on the water's edge. In summer visitors enjoy a stay in one of the small summer houses on the river banks or living on a boat on the Broads.

Fifty years ago Brundall presented a very different picture – that of a much smaller and more rural village. The entrance to the village from the A47 is down Cucumber Lane, so named because on either side there used to be fields covered with glasshouses for cucumbers and tomatoes.

The shops were small and very personal. At the beginning of The Street was a very small garage and then came Chandlers, a large grocery store selling everything. Long's, still the Brundall butcher, sold his own beef fed on the Acle marshes. At the top of Station Road was a general store and post office run by Mrs Merrison. There was one postman named Ernie who knew everyone in the village and where they lived. Where the supermarket now stands there was Miss Butcher's tiny grocery shop, which was situated in the front room of her home with just one sash window for display. More than one customer at a time would cause a squash and so it was politic to wait outside until there was room! There were some lock-up garages adjacent to her shop and this permitted a fish and chip van to park and operate regularly for the benefit of villagers. The Co-op, next to the chemist, served groceries and fresh meat. Three local herds provided milk for the village.

Much of what is now Highfield Avenue was Morse's Rose Nursery and spectacularly good it was, with Mrs Graver in a key position. As many large houses were situated in or near the village there was always a ready sale for her products.

The train was 8½d for a return to Norwich from Brundall. Trains ran frequently and there were porters at both stations and a ticket office. The porter at Brundall Gardens Halt obligingly gave hair-cuts to men between train arrivals. Both stations competed with flowers and shrubs to win prizes for the best-kept railway station. The Brundall level crossing was operated by a man who tended to open it when he thought fit, thus entailing long waits. At night it was firmly closed at 11 pm until the next morning – this sometimes had the effect of stranding people late at night.

Large boats carried cargoes to Norwich – one firm chose names ending in 'ity' and their boats became known as the 'ITTY' boats. Many of the larger ships came from Holland and Sweden and they could only reach Norwich when the tide was high. Many of the skippers would try to beat the tide with the result they skidded on the mud and went out of control. The quay near the present Yacht Club was a notorious spot for this occurrence and had to be rebuilt many times.

River steamers came up to Brundall Halt and visitors came to see The Gardens. These were superbly landscaped and planted by a Dr Beverly in 1880; he also amassed a fine collection of rare birds. The Riverside Hotel offered refreshments and also provided facilities for playing tennis. When Mr Lawrence and his daughter took over the hotel it became a private residence but he generously allowed the villagers to keep boats there, and during the war they were able to swim from the stone steps. In winter the villagers were allowed to skate on the lake in The Gardens and at night would do so by the light of car headlamps.

The Colman family were keen river enthusiasts and owned one of the beautiful old wherries – excitement was always caused by the appearance of the firm's tug called the *Mustard Pot*.

A public car park has been built in the centre of the village where Long's pig farm was situated. In April 1998 a flowering cherry tree was ceremoniously planted by the entrance in memory of Princess Diana.

In 1980 Brundall Parish Council purchased seven acres of what was originally grazing marsh land, formerly part of the flood plain of the river Yare. This is now being made into a nature trail, together with land from the Brundall Gardens adjoining it.

Children from the village school, funded by the Broadland District Council and supported by the Parish Council, have collected acorns from very old oak trees in Brundall which will be planted as seedlings for the Millennium.

🍁 BURGH CASTLE

In 1974 the village of Burgh Castle became part of the county of Norfolk. Until then it had been since time immemorial a Suffolk village. When, in Saxon times, the East Anglians called themselves the North Folk and the South Folk it was the river Waveney which became the recognised boundary between the two counties. The village of Burgh Castle, then known as Cnobheresburg, stood on the extreme north-eastern tip of a spur of land known as the Island of Lothingland, which jutted into Norfolk as far as Yarmouth. When in 1974 the local authorities decided to straighten out this section of the county boundary, Burgh Castle, together with several other Lothingland villages, found itself in the county of Norfolk.

Not half a mile from the village centre of Burgh Castle stands Gariannonum, one of Britain's best preserved relics of the Roman era in these islands. Here, where the cattle can be seen grazing on the water meadows and old drainage mills dot the landscape, stretched the wide estuary of Gariensis Ostium. Along the staithe below where now the pleasure craft are moored, lay the Roman galleys waiting to be refitted and sent out again to guard the coast from raiders from the Continent.

Three hundred years later, an Irish missionary named Fursey built his monastery within the shelter of the north-east corner of the Roman walls, bringing Christianity for the first time to this part of East Anglia. Fursey's buildings were of wood and plaster, so little of them survived until modern times. In 1958, however, the late Charles Green carried out an investigation on behalf of the Ministry of Works and discovered post holes and some painted plaster to bear out the written evidence of a religious settlement here. It was not until 500 years later that the first church was built and dedicated to St Peter and St Paul. In its round tower dating back to the 11th century can be seen a number of thin Roman tiles indicating that much of the material for its building was taken from the ruined Roman fort nearby. In the churchyard can be seen a Celtic stone cross erected in 1897 in memory of St Fursey.

Burgh Castle has been influenced very much by its riverside environment. In the early days the river provided almost the only means of transportation to the rest of the region. No main highway passes through it, so even now the visitor can go no further once he reaches the church. In its heyday during the 19th century about three different staithes enabled wherries and other smaller craft to tie up, unload and load their cargoes. During this time one of the most important commodities which were dealt with was bricks, which were manufactured at a riverside brickworks located close to where the yacht marina now lies. Besides bricks, this yard also produced cement, the 'clinker' for which was ground at Burney Arms windmill which stands just across the river on the bank of the river Yare. The Burgh Castle Brick and Cement works flourished from the mid 1800s until the early 1920s.

Rural life in early times left very little opportunity for leisure pursuits, but as work became less time consuming such pastimes as fishing and wildfowling became popular. The game of camping, which was a rough and ready early forerunner of football, was played. From the 15th century an aquatic festival known as the Burgh Castle Water Frolic took place annually, gradually dying out until the year 1889 when the last one was held.

The marshy nature of much of the low-lying land makes it ideal for the growing of osiers, that is willows for basket making, and a well known firm of Yarmouth basket makers still grows a small proportion of their raw material here. In recent years a small boat-building industry has developed on the river bank, though no doubt boats of one kind or another have always been built there over the centuries. Over the past 20 years the greatest change in the character of Burgh Castle has been its growth as a holiday centre. No fewer than six holiday caravan camps have developed besides a riverside holiday village and a yacht marina, all adding to the summer population and a large increase in the seasonal traffic.

🍁 BURGH ST PETER

The village of Burgh St Peter lies approximately six miles north-east of Beccles in the valley of the river Waveney. At this point the Waveney, flowing in an easterly direction, turns north to eventually reach the sea via Breydon Water. Thus the village is surrounded to the south and east by the river and the marshes. This corner of Norfolk is further isolated by the A143 road leading to Great Yarmouth, which bisects the area ensuring that the three villages of Aldeby, Wheatacre and Burgh St Peter remain quiet backwaters free from passing traffic.

The present day village consists of three areas: the outlying farms which are built on the higher parts of the marshes, the church, inn and cottages near the staithe on the river and the cottages, old mill and former public house around the crossroads some one and a half miles inland. This leads to the conclusion that the village must have been very much bigger at some time.

The church of St Mary, although drastically restored in 1880, mainly dates from about 1200. Its great length in proportion to its width is because the nave and chancel are under one continuous roof, which is thatched with local reed. After a fire in 1996 the roof has been renewed and looks as good as ever, but funds are still needed to repair damage inside the church. The strange looking 'stepped tower', a local landmark for river traffic, was built about 1790 onto an older base. A story is told that a son of the then rector, Samuel Boycott, had travelled in Italy and seen a tower of this design. The lower part contains the vestry reached by a narrow staircase, there is no access to the higher sections. Church registers date back to 1538 and the list of rectors to 1301. The ruins of the ancient priory church of St John used to stand in the field to the west of the church, but of recent years all visible traces of them have disappeared.

Although a quiet and peaceful place in which to live, the pace of 20th century life has not left the village unscathed. The shops and the public house have closed, and so has the school, which was built in 1877 just inside the parish boundary with Wheatacre and served both villages. In its time the school educated over a hundred pupils at a time, aged from five to 14. The school house was attached and occupied until the early 1970s.

The King's Head pub at the crossroads is now a private house, and old people's flats and bungalows have been built on the site of the old forge opposite. In spite of the fact that the school has closed the village continues to grow with new building in infill situations. The village hall, an old Methodist chapel, has been modernised and is well used by local organisations from the pre-school playgroup to the Wednesday Club for the elderly. Aldeby Bowls Club have their green next to the village hall and on the parish field opposite an extensive play area, including a five-a-side football pitch, has been installed for young children.

At the staithe on the river Waveney where the ferry operated, within living memory, to carry people across to enable them to walk to Oulton Broad, many changes have taken place. The Waveney Inn situated by the water was always a favourite place for boats to moor when travelling between Beccles, Oulton Broad and on up to Reedham and beyond. Now the complex has been altered and consists of a large marina, shop, the inn with its purpose-built carvery, a caravan site and the Nordic Leisure Centre with swimming pool and gymnasium. These facilities are used by local people as well as holidaymakers.

Now that the agricultural industry is not so labour intensive many 'incomers' leave the village each day to work in nearby towns. This has not reduced their interest in village affairs and indeed they contribute to the sense of community which makes this village such a pleasant place.

🍁 THE BURNHAMS

The Burnhams are a delightful group of villages spread along the valley of the little river Burn, close to the north Norfolk coast. Burnham Market, the largest, has an attractive village green surrounded by Georgian houses and cottages, and dominated at the western end by the church of St Mary Westgate, with a fine flintwork tower. Its importance in the Middle Ages is shown by the old verse:

> 'London, York and Coventry
> And the Seven Burnhams by the Sea'

Burnhams Westgate, Sutton and Ulph (named after a Danish Chieftain, brother of King Canute) make up Burnham Market itself. Burnham Thorpe, birthplace of Nelson, is situated a mile and a half to the south. Burnham Norton lies to the north on the edge of the reclaimed salt marshes; its lovely Saxon round-towered church, of which the chief treasure is a painted wine-glass pulpit, is isolated on a hill much nearer to Burnham Market itself.

Burnham Overy, half a mile east, has another beautiful and unusual church with a square central tower surmounted by a bell turret, and an old water mill which, unusually, has also a windmill beside it. Both mills, together with adjoining farm buildings, have now been converted into houses. Overy Staithe, a small seaport in the past and now a popular place for sailing, is on the coast. The Burn runs out to the sea here and its creek winds out from the harbour between lavender-covered salt marshes, emerging into the sea between sand dunes which stretch away to Holkham in the east and Scolt Head island with its bird sanctuary to the west. The tower windmill at Overy is a landmark for miles and nearby on the river is a very picturesque water mill with a row of old cottages beside it, both mills being the property of the National Trust and both now converted into residential accommodation.

The seventh Burnham is Burnham Deepdale, two miles west. In the Middle Ages the Burn ran out to sea here and has since changed its course. Now it is quite detached from the other Burnhams and is joined to Brancaster Staithe. It too has a charming little round-towered church and a splendid Norman font.

To return to Burnham Market: very many changes have taken place in the last 50 years. In those days a cattle market was held every Monday, accompanied by an auction on the village green – the auction is still held occasionally during the summer months. In those days we had a railway station; one could travel to Wells and go by train to Norwich or to Heacham and get through trains to London. Many small industries flourished. There was a blacksmith's forge, a foundry, a shoemaker, three bakeries and at least five pubs of which only two remain, the Lord Nelson and the Hoste Arms, named for one of Nelson's captains. In the 19th century the main crop of the surrounding agricultural land was barley and there were several maltings in the Burnhams, most of which have been converted into dwellings.

Burnham's most famous historical figure was, of course, Nelson, son of Rev Edmund Nelson, rector of Burnham Thorpe and also for several years of Burnham Norton. There are many relics of the great Admiral in Thorpe church and memorabilia at the Lord Nelson inn at Thorpe. Nelson's daughter Horatia lived with her aunt and uncle, Mr and Mrs Bolton, at Bolton House in Station Road and was married in Westgate church. Nelson was not the only famous mariner who came from these parts. Captain Woodget of the *Cutty Sark* was a native of Overy Staithe, and is buried in Norton churchyard.

Burnham has changed greatly in recent years. Many of the old cottages have become holiday homes and a number of retired people have settled

Gatehouse of 15th century Carmelite friary, The Burnhams

permanently in the village. Much building has taken place on the outskirts, most of it tasteful and not too intrusive, including a fine new doctors' surgery. Many of the old shops now sell antiques, gifts and smart clothes, but the basic essentials still remain. In 1994 a new, beautifully appointed Methodist church was built on the site of the old one in Station Road.

Inevitably the village becomes very crowded in the summer months and the Hard at Overy is crammed with cars and the creek with sailing boats and windsurfers. But it remains a friendly place; newcomers soon settle in and there is plenty going on. There is a Flower Show and Carnival in July, a Craft Fair on the green in August, and also in August there is a first class concert every Saturday evening in one of the Burnham churches.

A County primary school which draws in pupils from the surrounding villages was built in the 1950s in Friar's Lane, opposite the ruins of a 15th century Carmelite friary, of which the gatehouse has recently been restored.

When the summer is over and the visitors have gone Burnham reverts to its old self, surrounded by the fields and the wide skies and the salt marshes. It is a mecca for bird watchers as the great flocks of wild geese arrive from Siberia. From the same quarter come the great north winds which, when they coincide with the spring tide, can cause disastrous flooding as in 1953 and in 1978. And when the winter is wet and the water table rises the Goose Beck flows through the market place, channelled through the greens but crossing the road in the centre and having to be forded, to the great delight of small boys on bikes. It finally disappears into a culvert which discharges into the Burn. Just another thing which makes Burnham different and a fascinating place in which to live.

🍁 CAISTER-ON-SEA

Ceaster, Castra, Castre, Chester are all names referring to the village of Caister-on-Sea dating from Anglo-Saxon times. Caister-next-Yarmouth was an established name until 1927 when the Parish Council formally applied to become Caister-on-Sea.

Late in the 1st century AD a small settlement was founded by the Romans. By the 2nd century a Roman camp or fort had been established on rising ground on the estuary. Large vessels transferred their cargoes of wine, glassware and pottery, imported from the Rhineland, onto smaller boats which carried the goods to Norwich or on to London.

49

Medieval Caister was divided into two ecclesiastical parishes, one called St Trinity, where the Holy Trinity church dates from the 13th century. Five of its rectors died from the Black Plague. At the other, St Edmund, the church fell into ruins, but a chapel of ease was built close by. This area is known as West Caister.

The Fastolf family were major landowners in the 1300s. John Fastolf, after a brilliant military career, was knighted and built Caister Castle. When he died his property and land were inherited by the Paston family, famous for the 'Paston Letters'. Caister-on-Sea still has a lord of the manor who has rights to the fore-shore.

Since 1281 beacons, and much later lighthouses owned by Trinity House, have guarded the Caister coastline. The lighthouses were the first on the British coast and forerunners of modern lighthouses. Beach Companies, groups of local fishermen and beachmen, were formed in the late 1700s for the purpose of salvaging from wrecked vessels and saving life. The first lifeboat stationed at Caister in 1845 was manned by these men. The Royal National Lifeboat Institution later took over the responsibility for this service, but the lifeboat station was closed in 1969. The lifeboat tradition was then carried on by the unique and privately run Volunteer Rescue Service.

Tragedy hit the village in 1904 when there was a lifeboat disaster and nine crewmen died (they included husbands, uncles, brothers, cousins). From this disaster the famous saying came, 'Caister men never turn back'. A memorial stands in the cemetery paid for by public subscription. Beachmen were finally given 'notice to quit' by the lord of the manor, and their company shed and look-out was dismantled. The company disbanded in 1939.

In the early 18th century a causeway was built to link Caister with Yarmouth. The population increased in the 1850s when the Yarmouth fishing industry expanded. Families from Winterton-on-Sea moved into the area and their surnames of Haylett, George, Brown and Woodhouse are commonplace in the village. Men were employed in Yarmouth on drifters and trawlers, many becoming captains and officers in leading shipping lines. Women gained employment from making and mending nets or as domestic servants.

Sarah Martin, the prison reformer, was born in Caister in 1791. Her parents died when she was young and she was brought up by her grandmother, Mrs Bonnet, a glovemaker. Sarah trained as a dressmaker. From the age of 19 she spent her spare time at the workhouse and the prison in Yarmouth, reading the Bible to inmates and teaching reading and writing. She lived in near poverty and was buried in Caister churchyard at the age of 52.

In the 1900s, a mast was erected in the High Street and was the first wireless, telephone and telegraph communication to lightships.

Transport had made access to the coast easier and in 1906 Fletcher Dodd opened his 'Socialist Camp', the forerunner of the modern holiday camp. His aim was to provide holidays for city dwellers. They were housed in tents with very basic amenities. With the influx of holidaymakers, tea rooms, guest houses, caravan and camping sites proliferated.

The 18th century manor house in 1930 became a 36 bedroom hotel with a nine hole golf course. Continual sea erosion caused the hotel to collapse into the sea eleven years later. The sea also claimed a row of ten houses in a nearby area called The Warren.

A gas supply was brought to the village in 1925, followed a year later by an electricity supply. The sewerage system was connected in 1931 and people were pleased to see the demise of the 'honey cart'. A sea defence scheme completed in 1958 provided work for the unemployed.

Great Yarmouth has been the main source of employment over the past 40 years. We have seen the decline and end of the prosperous herring fishing industry. Subsequently employment was centred on Grouts silk factory, Birds Eye Foods (both factories have closed), STC Components and Hartmann Fibre. The North Sea gas and oil exploration brought jobs and prosperity, but prospecting in the area ended after ten years leaving behind mainly service industries and an expanding heliport at Caister which transports men and equipment to oil rigs. Caister now stands a dormitory village of Yarmouth, and unfortunately history and tradition are vanishing under the modern needs of housing, transport etc.

🍁 CANTLEY

Cantley is situated on the east bank of the river Yare approximately half way between Norwich and Great Yarmouth. It is a straggling village with just over 200 houses, two pubs, a church, a school, post office and general stores, a railway station and a village hall.

Cantley is mentioned in the Domesday Book, although it was then spelt Cantelai. The population was then 140 persons and this had only increased to 257 by 1891; it is now 600–700 with most of this increase occurring during the

51

1960s. The great flood of 1607 caused considerable damage to the parish and was followed by a deadly plague which drastically reduced the population for some while.

The church of St Margaret was built in 1142 of flint. It consists of a nave, chancel, south transept and porch, and a square tower. The list of clergy goes back to 1270 when Rev Stephan de White was the incumbent. The village school was built in 1871 by William Gilbert for 50 children.

Village life used to centre on The Street (now School Lane). Here could be found a post office, a carpenter, a blacksmith and the school, the latter being the only survivor. Various other businesses have come and gone. Salt evaporation tanks were mentioned in the Domesday Book. Of a meat processing factory, only the well remains. A boatbuilder operated at the staithe but only a sunken wherry can be seen today.

In more recent times can be found two large employers, British Sugar and the Cantley estate. Both were founded by a Dutchman, Van Rossum. He came to the area in 1910 and introduced sugar beet as an arable crop. The beet was shipped to Holland for processing. Once he had established that the crop could be grown, he built England's first successful beet-processing factory. He chose Cantley because of its good river and rail links. The factory was closed during 1916–1919 as beet seed came from Germany. The factory now processes some 7,000 tonnes of beet per day during the 'Campaign', which runs from September to January.

The Cantley estate was formed by larger companies buying smaller farms and land around the village. This has recently been split into smaller parts again, and the immediately surrounding land has been bought by a consortium of farmers. Modern production methods have meant that the number of farm workers has declined, but there are still a few villagers who work on the land.

The village hall was built on land donated by Van Rossum and is used by many local organisations. The village sign was erected in 1977 to commemorate the Silver Jubilee of Elizabeth II. It was carved by a local craftsman and depicts the three churches of the parish, the wherry, a pheasant, a grebe, sugar beet and the river Yare.

There is a legend that a headless horseman rides at midnight from Callow Pit to Cantley Spong, a distance of one mile. Many of the older residents avoid that stretch of road. Another legend tells of a pot of gold at Callow Pit near Southwood. It is at the bottom of this dark pool and is guarded by an evil presence. No one has yet retrieved it despite numerous attempts!

🍁 CASTLE ACRE

Castle Acre is a rural village four miles north of Swaffham, with an adult population of just over 700. It is unusual for Norfolk in that it is constructed on the side of a valley and unique in having not only a large Norman castle and earthworks, including a fine bailey gate, but also the ruins of a Cluniac priory, sometimes described as the finest in Southern England. The village is situated where the ancient Peddars Way crosses the river Nar.

William de Warenne, one of the Duke of Normandy's most powerful supporters and also his son-in-law, was given Castle Acre, as part of a huge estate, at the time of the Conquest. It was his son, the second Earl of Surrey, who founded the priory in c1090. Recent excavations show that at first William de Warenne built a country house on the site of the present castle. It is likely that the troubled political times which followed made the building of a fortified castle desirable, though the defences were never put to the test. At the same time a walled Norman town was laid out and constructed between the castle and the priory. This forms part of the present village and the outlines can be clearly seen. The parish church of St James the Great, begun in the 13th century, was built outside the town walls, probably on the site of an earlier Saxon church.

Until the dissolution of the monasteries in the 16th century Castle Acre received many visitors as it was on the route to Walsingham, the famous medieval shrine. But on 22nd November 1537 the last prior Thomas Malling surrendered the priory to Henry VIII with the manor lands attached. The castle had long since been left in a ruinous state and this together with the priory lands and its manor were granted by Henry VIII to Thomas Howard, Duke of Norfolk. Unlike many other villages Castle Acre retained a number of freehold, ie privately owned, properties in the centre of the village and while the majority of the farmland was eventually acquired by the Holkham estate starting in the early 17th century, many houses remained apart. For this reason it was known as an open village and when, in the early 19th century, there was a need to house an ever increasing number of displaced people the freeholders saw a chance to build numerous small cottages and rent them out to those seeking a refuge. It was during the 19th century that the well known gang system was started. These were farm workers, mostly women and children, pulling weeds and clearing stones on the neighbouring farms. With a shifting population, many evicted from previous homes for poaching or suspected of being troublemakers, and all seeking work, Castle Acre acquired a reputation as an unruly and unpleasant place and in 1843 became the subject of a Parliamentary report.

A hundred years ago the population was twice that of today. Then most people worked on the land, although Castle Acre always had a number of industries. There was a foundry, a tanner's, a brick kiln, two corn mills, two smithies, a saw mill, a wheelwright and a saddler's. Despite being so close to Swaffham, Castle Acre was a centre for shopping and services for a large area. It even had a theatre, in Drury Lane. Today the majority go out of the village to work, though the remaining shops, two grocers, a butcher, post office and garage do well, serving not just the villagers but also the many visitors. As in previous times, Castle Acre continues to support many small businesses besides.

The centre of the village, the Norman town and Stocks Green, most of which dates from the 15th century, is a conservation area. The Parish Council lease the greens and commons from the Holkham estate and there are many good walks to be had in and around the village. The priory, castle and bailey gate are in the care of English Heritage.

❧ CASTON

Caston is a small village, with a population of about 420. It can be found 20 miles south-west of Norwich and approximately four miles south of Watton.

In the 1920s one could hear the blacksmith's anvil ringing and could smell the newly baked bread from two bakeries. There were three shops to choose from, also three public houses. The post office continues two mornings a week in the village hall and the only business remaining is the Red Lion public house. Several houses in the parish relate to the past, namely the Old Duke's Head, the Old Bakery, the Old Forge and the Old Post Office. There has been an Old Rectory for as long as villagers can remember. As the rectors continue to move into smaller and smaller houses, the 'old rectories' grow in number. One has been renamed The Curatage to avoid confusion for the postman.

The church of the Holy Cross stands by the village green. This is an extremely well kept building with a hammer-beam roof. It is a lovely little church and is always full for the harvest festival and the carol service. The

Holy Cross church, Caston

church overlooks Church Farm, which dates from 1500 and is thought to have been a refectory at which pilgrims of medieval times received hospitality. The old school borders the green and the new school at the end of The Street nearest to Griston is well attended. Caston is justly proud of its village green which is kept in excellent condition. In 1988 the local MP Mrs Gillian Shephard presented Caston with the Best Kept Village award.

The windmill stands three quarters of a mile from the green on the road to Watton. It is almost into the neighbouring village of Griston for it is on Caston's border. Once it ground corn for the farmers and it was a pleasing sight to see the mill sails turning merrily on a windy day. For some years now the mill has been without sails, which gives it a decapitated appearance, but it is hoped that one day it will be restored.

This is an agricultural area, and was once very self-contained, most of the inhabitants being either employed on the farm or in the local trades. Now the small businesses have gone and although the farms remain, they are often worked by just the farmer and his sons. This means the people of the village find work in the nearby towns. So the countryside changes, but the old fashioned friendly atmosphere still pervades. One could not go far without meeting someone with a cheery smile passing the time of day.

CATFIELD

Catfield village school now caters for four to eight year olds and there has been an addition of a sports field next door to the school. At eight the children travel to the middle school in Stalham in a bus provided by the long established transport company. There are also lorries available for haulage in this mainly farming community. The mill has closed which used to produce animal feeding stuffs and a modern factory has taken over the site. A new industrial estate has developed over recent years with small and large companies busy producing and repairing.

All Saints' church has had repairs to the tower and a new bell. There are now sheep grazing in the churchyard. The old rectory has been sold and a modern one built to the west of the church. Flower festivals with craft displays and concerts have been held annually for the last few years and visitors come along to enjoy coffee or tea in open gardens for charity.

There have been many newcomers to the village moving into the three bungalow developments. Recently the council has provided terraced bungalows for the elderly and disabled people and a terrace of modern houses for young families. There has been a return to tradition with cottages built on farmland and in the same area extensive barn conversions.

The Methodist church has celebrated over 150 years in Catfield and has built an extension with a schoolroom. They have a lively Sunday school and the village also has a team of church bellringers and hand bell ringers.

Three shops have closed but there is still a post office and general store. The Crown is a meeting place for darts and pool teams and we have a large playing field with changing rooms for football players.

The poet and hymnodist William Cowper spent some time here when his uncle was rector and wrote, 'Of all the places in the earth, I love Catfield'.

🍁 CHEDGRAVE

Chedgrave lies some nine miles south-east of Norwich, mainly north of the river Chet, which takes its name from that of the village, having once been known as the Loddon. The erstwhile town of Loddon is on the other side of the river, though the boundary between them is not obvious. It follows an older, more winding, course of the river, so adjoining properties may fall in different parishes.

The church, All Saints', stands in a prominent position on one of the highest points in the village, with a thatched tower at the north-east corner of the building. The lower part of the tower is probably 11th century, and both doors and the nave display Norman work. The medieval font, sketched by John Sell Cotman, was replaced by something more modern in the 19th century, which again was replaced by something more ancient a few years ago!

The coloured glass in the east window is generally, but incorrectly, said to come from Rouen Cathedral. In fact it was part of a large consignment purchased by an enterprising Norwich cloth merchant during a lull in the French Wars in 1802 from a dealer in Rouen. The Chedgrave glass, or some of it, has been traced to Steinfels in Germany.

Until the end of the 19th century, Chedgrave consisted of little more than a church, two farms, a public house, a baker, various trades and shops, and a few houses. Some of the outbuildings of Langley Hall fell within the parish, including a couple of almshouses and the estate laundry. It is amazing that it appears to have maintained a population of over 300 in less than 40 houses throughout the 19th century, and there was a substantial village school. The 18th century manor house, 'a neat mansion' according to Kelly's 1845 directory, and the Old Rectory, a gentleman's residence of the 17th century, later enlarged and enhanced, are examples of the larger houses of this period, and can be seen from the road through to Loddon, as can also Soane's ornamental 18th century gates to Langley Hall.

The break-up of the Langley estate in 1953 led to the development of the village, with estates of bungalows and chalet bungalows, raising the population to nearly 1,000.

The coming of Wood, Sadd and Moore and the wherry traffic to the Chet in 1884 brought more employment and prosperity to the parish, as did the opening of Cannell's seed firm a little later. After the wherries had gone, the pleasure boats began to come, though it was a few years before the hire boat industry reached its peak. The Chet is tidal as far as Chedgrave, and new large moorings have been cut at this extremity of the Broads' navigable waters.

The school closed early in the 20th century, though the last rector only departed in 1997. The police station has returned to Loddon. Many authorities find it more convenient to treat Loddon and Chedgrave as a single entity but Chedgrave has always maintained an independent personality. It still has its own public house, a thriving group of shops, and regular bus services to Norwich and Lowestoft. There are few empty premises. Even the redundant police station has been found a new role by St Matthew's Society as Baynard House (after a Norman landowner), with roses around the door.

✹ Cley-next-the-Sea

It comes as a surprise to the modern visitor that William White, in his 1845 Norfolk directory, described Cley-next-the-Sea as a 'small town and port' with 'sailing packets to London and Hull once a fortnight'. He listed four inns and public houses, two beerhouses, three each of bakers, butchers, grocers and drapers, and shoemakers, and also four tailors, along with half a dozen mariners and other tradesmen and professional people who would have been resident in any small community 150 years ago.

Cley has a long history which goes back well before 1845, but its importance gradually declined when reclamation of the coastal marshes was begun in the 17th century, and it is now a small village, more or less L-shaped, with around 500 permanent inhabitants. The sea, three quarters of a mile away, is kept at bay by a high shingle bank and the area between village and sea is an expanse of part salt, part fresh marsh.

The river Glaven, which was originally tidal and which brought to Cley its prosperity as a port, is now a slow-flowing river never more than 20 ft wide and only navigable by the smallest of boats. It is largely silted up and is gradually being narrowed by the growth of *Phragmites australis*, the Norfolk reed which is cut in winter and sold for thatching.

St Margaret's church, which looks over the green and the Glaven valley towards Wiveton, dominates one end of the village. The square tower, dating from the 13th century, is the oldest part, but during the following two centuries rebuilding and enlargement resulted in the grand church of today.

Dominating the centre of the village and situated on the edge of the river stands Cley windmill, which was built as a corn mill at the beginning of the 19th century and last functioned in 1919. At present it is run as a bed and breakfast establishment but is open (for a fee) to anyone who wants to climb to the top and enjoy the extensive views.

However, the windmill and church are by no means the only interesting buildings in the village. A mixture of brick and flint and colour-washed houses give character to the main street. The old Custom House, a brick building now privately occupied, still stands. Around the corner, past the only pub remaining in the centre of the village (the other one is near the church), is Whalebone House, formerly a shop, the outer walls of which are decorated with sheep vertebrae.

Over 400 acres of marshland on the eastern side of the village was bought by the Norfolk Naturalists Trust in 1926 and, under the paternal wardenship of Billy Bishop for 41 years, and now of his son Bernard, the area has become a bird reserve of international importance.

Today the population of Cley is divided between the true 'Norfolk Dumplings', those who have lived and worked most of their lives in the area, and the 'foreigners' who have retired to, and love, the Norfolk coastline with its brilliant light and wonderful sunsets and who are at the same time prepared to brave the northerly winds which sometimes blow for months at a time.

Most disturbing is a north-west gale coinciding with a very high tide. The wind banks the water up against the land and prevents it from flowing seawards on the ebb tide. Then at the next high tide the water level builds up even higher until it overtops, and sometimes breaches, the sea defences, flooding both the marshes and the village. Older Cley inhabitants still tell gruesome stories of the night of 31st January 1953, when the sea flooded many parts of eastern England. A flood wall was built subsequently and the shingle bank was strengthened but on dark tempestuous nights people living in the lower-lying parts of the village become apprehensive and listen for the flood-warning siren.

🍁 COLBY & BANNINGHAM

Colby and Banningham lie about three miles north-east of Aylsham. The two villages are often treated as one for administrative purposes and the boundaries between the two are difficult to define. This is a mainly arable area, the chief crops being wheat, barley, sugar beet and potatoes.

Colby covers an area of 1,121 acres and Banningham 938 acres, and the population of the combined villages was 540 in 1996. The churches of St Giles at Colby and St Botolph at Banningham are built of flint in the Perpendicular style, and each has only one bell.

Banningham has one public house, the Crown, standing near the church and village green. Colby and Banningham Jubilee Hall, in Banningham, was originally built as a reading room but has since been made into a village hall and extended and modernised to include a club-room and bar. The post office and general store serves both villages and this too has been recently modernised and up-dated. Several new houses have been built in recent years, both in the main part of the village and at the lower end, near the North Walsham road. At this end of Banningham a garage and petrol station occupies premises which were once another public house, the Bridge Inn. There is a Wesleyan Reform chapel which is no longer used, and there was at one time a corn windmill, a brick kiln and a smithy.

The recently extended village school, in Colby, serves four villages and caters for about 90 children. Near the school, a Wesleyan Methodist chapel has been converted to a private house, and at the other end of Colby a Wesleyan Reform chapel is still in use.

🍁 COLTISHALL

Coltishall is about seven miles north of Norwich on the B1150 North Walsham road. Situated on the north bank of the river Bure, it is known to many for the long stretch of riverside moorings, by the green and pleasant Lower Common. With two good pubs and a large car park extending to the river bank, the whole area has always been popular with anyone wishing to enjoy river activities. In winter the common is sometimes visited by flocks of wild geese.

Away from the river, a walk up the village street gives clues to the fact that Coltishall is a very historic place. There has been a settlement here for over 1,000 years. The thatched church was dedicated to St John the Baptist in 1284, but the structure includes evidence from much earlier periods: Roman tiles, thought to have come from a nearby Roman villa, and two small Saxon windows, high on the north wall.

There are some lovely old buildings in the village streets, some with the curved Flemish gables of the William and Mary period. The 'Old School House', opposite the church, was built in 1744, paid for by the friends of John Chapman, 'Brewer of Coltishall' who died in 1719, leaving instructions in his will for £10 to be set aside annually to teach reading, writing, and 'arithmetick' to ten poor lads from the village.

The boat building yards in Anchor Street became famed throughout Broadland for their skill in building the huge wherries that, with their cargoes of malt, grain, timber, reeds, coal, and local-brewed beer, were the mainstay of the river trade for many years. They sailed upstream to Aylsham, and downstream to Yarmouth. With the coming of the railways and motorised transport, river trading and wherry building gradually declined. The boatyard in Anchor Street began to build more private sailing yachts, and later motor cruisers. There are no boatyards or maltings in Coltishall now, only the names survive to add local colour to the tasteful conversions of the old buildings, and the new houses and bungalows built to provide desirable residential areas.

There are still a few old cottages at the end of Anchor Street and beyond them a footpath leads over fields and water meadows, on a delightful walk to Belaugh.

With the famous RAF Fighter Station still in operation a few miles outside the village, Coltishall has changed again and moved with the times. The close proximity of the river Bure has made it very attractive to the tourist trade. It is also a very pleasant place to live. A splendid new school has been built for the children of Coltishall and Horstead. Many residents now work and shop outside the village, but there is a warm community spirit, a blend of the old with the new. Several families have been settled in Coltishall and Horstead for generations the same names are repeated on the two war memorials. The descendants of these well known local names and their families will carry them on, alongside the many new names, into the next millennium.

🍁 CORPUSTY & SAXTHORPE

When King Henry III gave Saxthorpe to his half-brother, William de Valence, the village passed from the Crown into the ownership of one of the wealthiest and most powerful families in the country. Aylmer de Valence's residence in Saxthorpe was Mickle Hall, the whereabouts of which is uncertain. He founded a chapel dedicated to St Dunstan, which had its own chaplain, and which stood at the eastern end of Post Office Lane. In about 1315 Aylmer de Valence gave part of his estate to Simon de Creping, who built a large moated manor, Lound Hall, near the Briston Road.

Lound Hall and Mickle Hall eventually came into single ownership and in the 17th century were bought by the Earle family of Heydon, who were friends of Oliver Cromwell. Corpusty church and rectory were acquired by the same family and by the end of the 18th century most of Corpusty and Saxthorpe was owned by the Earles of Heydon. Subsequently they came into the possession of the Bulwer family.

For much of the Middle Ages, the wool trade brought great prosperity to Norfolk. The fulling mill on the western edge of the village, close to the boundary of Briston parish, was busy soaking, cleansing and twisting newly made cloth.

Fourteenth century bricks and much medieval pottery have been found near the fulling mill. The present water mill beside the Norwich road was built at the end of the 17th century and later two post mills were built in Corpusty. One was the White Mill on Mill Hill, taken down in 1902, and a Black Mill behind Mill Villas.

In Saxthorpe, an agricultural foundry, founded in 1800 by Thomas Hase, an engineer, employed about 20 men as blacksmiths, carpenters, wheelwrights and moulders. It finally closed in 1962. A mineral water factory which claimed royal patronage was opened in Corpusty in 1864 by James Pinchen and gave employment to several men and women. John Pinchen, brother of James, started a bakery in the same yard.

The Midland and Great Northern Railway reached Corpusty in 1883 and employed about a dozen men. Sadly, it closed in 1959. The village was partly flooded in 1912, when all the bridges over the river Bure were washed away, due to continuous rain for three days. The railway lines were suspended over the river at Blackwater, the bridge having collapsed.

Many young men of Corpusty and Saxthorpe lost their lives during the First World War. There are 38 names on the war memorial in the church, from a population of no more than 600. It was said that the percentage of dead was higher than any other village in England.

Today a small and enthusiastic group are holding money-raising events for the refurbishment of the New Village Hall. This hall was formerly an Adventure Centre owned by Suffolk Education Committee on the site of our former railway station, now sold back to the parish, which seems very fitting and it will be used by our own village groups.

❧ COSTESSEY

Costessey is situated to the north-west of Norwich, just off the A47. There is still some 13th century work to be found in St Edmund's church, though much of the building now dates from the Victorian restoration and the top and lead spire of the tower were added in 1930.

The medieval Hall in Costessey Park fell into ruins long ago, though not before it had been added to in the 1800s. The poet Edward Jerningham built the Gothick chapel in about 1800.

There is a curious story connected with Costessey Woods and St Walstan's Well, once a place of pilgrimage for farm workers whose patron saint St Walstan became. He laboured in the fields at Taverham, despite having been born a prince, and became known for his saintly manner. In 1016 he was warned of his imminent death by an angel but he carried on making hay in the fields, unafraid, until the moment came. His body was carried across the river Wissey on a bier drawn by oxen, and it was said that their hoofprints remained visible on the water for many years afterwards. As they carried him through Costessey Woods, a spring gushed out where the oxen had paused to rest, and this became known as St Walstan's Well.

The WI in Costessey have long been a part of village life. Formed just before the Second World War, they kept the Home Guard well fed and took in mothers and children forced out of the bombed cities. The evacuees in turn helped with the fruit picking in the village, with which the WI made pounds and pounds of jam for the war effort.

❧ CRINGLEFORD

Cringleford is a large, pleasant village three miles south-west of Norwich at a natural crossing of the river Yare. Despite being so near Norwich it has, so far, managed to keep a distinct identity.

The most picturesque part of the village is centred around the ancient bridge. The medieval core, plus its additions, replaced a timber bridge washed

Coaching pump at Cringleford

away during a disastrous flood in 1519. Queen Elizabeth I would have passed over this bridge on her visit to Norwich and the Duke of Norfolk; likewise Robert Kett and his men on their march to Norwich in 1549. In 1901 two men were killed when their threshing machine plunged into the river from the bridge.

St Peter's church, which stands on a rise above the river, contains Saxon remains, including small double-splayed windows and the remains of a finely decorated cross now built into the fabric. Until the Reformation a chapel dedicated to St Ethelbert stood to the east of Cringleford Hall. Pilgrimages were made there. Another church stood a mile along Cantley Lane at the deserted medieval village of Canteloff.

The mill house, rebuilt in 1795, is all that remains of the mill which was burned down in 1916. A mill was recorded on this site in the Domesday Book. The fish pools which stretched from the mill to Earlham were invaluable to the Great Hospital, Norwich, which has held land in Cringleford for 700 years, providing fish and wild fowl, as well as pheasants, hares and partridges from the surrounding meadows.

Farming was formerly the main occupation. The village contained four farms, one of them, Hill Farm of 220 acres, being operated as a working farm as late as the 1970s. The farm houses and buildings of all four farms have now been converted for residential use, and the surviving farmland belongs to farms outside the village or to the John Innes Institute. In the church is the crook which belonged to the last shepherd working in the village. One shepherd, Mr Curson, worked on the same farm for 50 years, and claimed that his family could trace a connection with the village back to 1250.

During the 18th century a few of the larger houses, including Cringleford House and Hill Grove, were built. Ford End, formerly the George Inn, was modernised and Mill House rebuilt. In the 19th century a few houses were built for workers, and large houses for Norwich businessmen. Oaklands was built for Frederick Harmer, the clothing manufacturer. This firm finally closed in 1990. He was also a well-known botanist and geologist, being partly responsible for the first geological survey of East Anglia. The Pattesons, of the brewing family, extended Cringleford House. In 1911 Mrs Stanforth Patteson gave the Patteson Club to the village as a working men's club and reading room for agricultural workers and servants. This is still a social centre.

There was expansion between the wars, especially of Tudor-style houses designed and built by Archie Rice, and again in the 1950s and the 1960s. The first estate built by a national company came in the 1980s. The toll house on the bridge and the pump on the green near the village sign, given to the village by the Afternoon WI in 1970, indicate the importance of the A11 as a turnpike road. In 1974 the A11 bypass funnelled traffic between Norwich and London away from the bridge and the centre of the village. The opening in 1992 of the southern bypass, taking the A47 trunk road between Great Yarmouth and the Midlands through the western outskirts of Cringleford, has been followed by proposals for extensive new housing development, accelerated by the construction, started in 1998, of the new Norfolk and Norwich Hospital in Colney, just over the parish boundary.

The village is particularly attractive in spring and summer and the residents take pride in its appearance, as evidenced by Best Kept Village awards on a number of occasions. Recreational activities and pastimes are well catered for. Today's residents are fortunate in having the services of a village post office cum general stores and a thriving primary/middle school. It is hoped that the distinctive character and identity of Cringleford will survive the major changes projected over the coming years.

CROMER

We hear much today of the crumbling coastline and the need for better sea-defences but this is the 'old, old story' in this region. The prosperous town of Shipden, situated seaward of Cromer, slowly slipped into the sea and disappeared in the late 14th century. A large rock, several hundred yards out to sea from the pier, can sometimes be seen at very low tides and is known as the Church Rock, the remains of the church of St Peter, Shipden. Naturally legends have arisen that the bells can be heard to chime in stormy weather (or do they herald disaster?).

Old Shipden and then Cromer (or Crowsmere as it was known) were quite prosperous, with annual fairs and markets. Two of its men became Lord Mayor of London and one, Sir Bartholomew Rede, founded a school to teach 'gentlemen's sons, poormen's sons and other good men's children of Cromer'. The school continued until 1895 and the Goldsmith's Charity still exists to help young Cromer people to further education.

Cromer was becoming known as a holiday resort by the early 19th century and is mentioned by Jane Austen in her novel *Emma*, but until the coming of the railway in 1877 it was mainly patronised by the gentry.

The poet and journalist Clement Scott helped to popularize the region by discovering 'Poppyland' and writing in his newspaper of the profusion of poppies, and also discovering the ruined cliff-edge churchyard at Sidestrand. This was commemorated in Scott's poem *The Garden of Sleep*. Cromer profited from Scott's work by making Poppyland crockery and Poppyland perfume. The sea claimed the 'Garden of Sleep' in 1915.

One of the best known features of Cromer is the pier, built in 1900, replacing a series of jetties. The Pier Pavilion is one of the few remaining buildings which still features an end-of-the-pier concert party in the summer season and this is well patronised. In 1990 the amusement arcade was destroyed by gale force winds and it was decided not to replace it as there were plenty of these in Cromer. Instead, in 1995 shelters were built in the centre of the pier. In November 1993, a platform called Tayjak I which was being used by Anglia Water north-west of Cromer broke loose and was swept into the pier, breaking it in two and also damaging breakwaters. Reconstruction was completed in May 1994.

In 1998 the Lifeboat House was removed from the end of the pier and a new, larger house and new slipway constructed, to be ready to house a bigger, more modern boat. Speaking of Cromer lifeboat brings memories of its most famous coxswain, Henry Blogg, who three times won the Gold Medal of the RNLI, and four silver medals, as well as the George Cross and the BEM. His rescues are famous and have been well documented. Off duty, he was a man of few words who made a living hiring deck-chairs and beach huts on the East Beach, but he knew the seas round Cromer better than anyone and the dangers faced by the local crab fishers, several of whom were his relatives.

Still visitors come to Cromer, mainly by their own transport now, and not by the railway. They mostly stay in self-catering flats or caravans now instead of in the former seaside lodgings in the cottage homes or hotels. A few of the 19th century hotels still survive, such as the Hotel de Paris. Cromer church tower reaches to a height of 160 ft, the tallest in the county, and there is another landmark here, the lighthouse sending its beams out to the shipping, though it is now radio controlled and unmanned.

🍁 DENTON

Denton is a rural community in South Norfolk. The name, meaning 'the village in the hole', is derived from the fact that the original settlement was built in the valley around the church. After the great plague of 1665, however, the villagers moved up the hill to settle around Well Corner. The availability of water was of prime consideration in choosing a settlement.

To the north of the village, a Saxon motte and bailey castle was built which had a track by which the cattle and livestock could be driven to safety inside the castle should marauders be sighted. The Danes and Vikings made use of the Waveney and Yare to sail inland to pillage. There is little to be seen nowadays, save a mound surrounded by a ditch, but the site has been acquired by the National Trust. Nearby are Hangman's Hill and Misery Corner – grim reminders of the rough justice dealt out in former times.

The flint church of St Mary the Virgin was probably another sanctuary in time of pillage. Part of the original round Norman tower collapsed in the 16th century and was repaired as a square tower. The beautiful east window in the chancel contains stained glass of many periods, the oldest believed to be from the 14th century.

The United Reformed church was built in 1821 on the site of another building which was thought to have been the oldest chapel in Norfolk. The church at one time possessed an old oak chair upon which, it is reputed, Oliver Cromwell once sat. In 1986, the churches united to form 'The Church in Denton'.

The village sign, depicting a horse-drawn plough, was the gift of Denton WI on the occasion of their 50th anniversary. The shield shown on the sign is believed to be the arms of the D'Albini family – the first lords of the manor of Denton.

The local school was closed in 1978 and the former public houses the Watch-house and the King's Head are now used as private residences.

The people of the village have always extended a genuine welcome to newcomers, engendering a community spirit of which they are rightly proud.

🍁 DENVER

Over 50 years ago Denver was a village surrounded by agricultural land. It had three shops, a separate post office, seven public houses, a blacksmith, a shoe repairer, a butcher and a carrier's business. It also had a passenger/goods station with a junction to Stoke Ferry off the main King's Lynn/London line. Denver is no longer a stopping point, and has not been for many years.

Over subsequent years Denver has seen many changes. Quite a lot of agricultural land has been used for housing development, for estates such as Nightingale Walk, Nightingale Close, Brady Close and Denver Hill.

The construction of the A10 bypass relieved the village of the heavy traffic which had to negotiate dangerous bends at Denver Hall corner and the church corner. More recently the A1122 southern bypass of Downham Market cut the village in half and the Boundary Commission allocated all the properties on the north side of this bypass to Downham parish, although it had to remain as the old ecclesiastical parish of Denver. With this change the population was cut drastically. Although the boundaries have been changed the friends made earlier still remain loyal to the village.

Denver now has only one public house in the village although there is another one at the sluice. The post office is incorporated with the village stores and there is still a butcher's business.

The cricket club, which was formed at the beginning of the 20th century, is still in being. Denver Mill, which was owned by the Harris family, is now in the care of the Norfolk Windmill Trust. The school is over 100 years old and the building itself has not changed. A large extension has been added at the rear. The children in earlier years left at 14 whereas now they leave at eleven for Downham High School. St Mary's church stands in the centre of the village and has been a focal point since 1300.

✤ DERSINGHAM

Dersingham is a large village between King's Lynn and Heacham. There are lovely views out over the Wash and towards the beautiful woods of Sandringham.

The imposing church of St Nicholas is reached by an avenue of cypresses. It dates from the early 14th century, with later Perpendicular additions, and there are some interesting items to be seen inside, such as the magnificently carved wooden chest and the painted screen. Just outside, to the north-west, is a fine carrstone and red brick barn, dating from 1671, which belonged to Dersingham Hall.

The old school is now Dersingham Youth Centre and is used for many village activities. There is a modern junior school, and a middle school in a beautiful setting up Dodds Hill on the Sandringham estate.

✤ DITCHINGHAM

Ditchingham is a real border village lying on the Norfolk bank of the river Waveney which divides Norfolk from Suffolk. This location makes it a bit of a 'no-man's-land' as so many of its residents owe their working and social allegiances to the little market town of Bungay on the Suffolk bank. A Bungay directory of the 1840s calls Ditchingham a 'Suburb of Bungay', but the hard core of those who have lived in Ditchingham all their lives, and their parents before them, refute that allegation vigorously.

Ditchingham is not a pretty village. It has no village green or thatched cottages, or even a village pond. Until about 1938 it had a corn mill, commemorated in a horseshoe of terraced council houses euphemistically called Windmill Green, the green being a modern patch of mown grass in the middle. These houses and the three rows of old people's bungalows opposite were designed by the firm of Tayler & Green soon after the Second World War and won architectural awards. There are now large areas of housing and bungalow development mostly lived in by retired people from out of the area.

Like so many villages the centre of Ditchingham has moved, leaving the large and lovely 15th century parish church of St Mary stranded a quarter of a mile or so away, with a scatter of cottages, the one-time pub The Three Bells, several farms and the two big houses of the parish to keep it company. Of these, Ditchingham Hall is an imposing Georgian mansion with pedimented facade and a lake and parkland boasting the usual claim to 'Capability' Brown. The other house of any size is Ditchingham House, also Georgian but of squarer more modest dimensions with estate and farm of about 400 acres. This was the home of the celebrated Victorian novelist and traveller Sir Henry Rider Haggard from his marriage in 1880 until his death in 1925. His grandson still owns and farms the estate. Sir Rider was knighted in 1912, not for his writing, but for services to his country on Royal Commissions on coastal erosion, reafforestation and the study of agriculture here and in Denmark. His fascinating diary *The Farmer's Year* written about his Ditchingham farm and estate in 1898 is still some local farmers' bedside reading.

Apart from farming, the main occupation of Ditchingham residents takes them over the river to Bungay to the printing works of Richard Clay, but recently more small businesses have started up in the village which has helped restore the feeling of self-sufficiency that, alas, so many villages are losing. We have always had and still have a post office-cum-stationery store, a pub and a Church of England primary school and there is a good grocery shop, and for builders, electricians, taxis, tyre service and high class cabinet making, we can now call on our own residents.

An unusual feature of Ditchingham is the location of the Anglican Convent of All Hallows. This was founded in 1855 and the House of Mercy, Cottage Hospital and a school for girls followed. The founder and first warden was the Rev William Scudamore. He and his son the Rev Charles Scudamore were between them rectors of Ditchingham for 90 years. The school alas has now closed, but the buildings are used as a religious conference centre and retreats and study courses are held there. The hospital is still run under the administration of the convent and now specialises in post-operative care and terminal cases, and the quality of the care given is widely known and appreciated. It has maintained its independence with the help of many loyal supporters, but the amount of Council help it will get in the future is a matter of great anxiety.

A new village hall was built in the 1970s and this is in constant use. Ditchingham WI has been going, without a break, since 1918, one of the earliest in the country.

A very comprehensive Parish Newsletter, subsidised by the Parochial Church Council, was begun in 1961 by the then rector and Miss Lilias Rider Haggard, daughter of Sir Rider and a well known writer herself. Sadly they both died in 1968, but the magazine has gone from strength to strength and proved a vital force in keeping all parishioners aware of what goes on in the village, both spiritual and temporal, and has linked people of varying interests and backgrounds into a lively and caring community.

🍁 DOCKING

There has been a village on the site of present day Docking since Roman times, when the Roman legions were stationed at Branodunum (Brancaster) five miles down the road on the coast. The village grew up in Saxon times on a crossroads leading to Fakenham, King's Lynn, Heacham and Ringstead and Hunstanton. It was known as Dry Docking because of the lack of streams, although today it boasts no fewer than five ponds. In the 1700s a well was sunk to provide domestic water for the village, which was in use until water was piped into the village in 1936.

A church has stood on the site of the present parish church since Saxon times. The church is dedicated to St Mary the Virgin and the church registers date from 1588. In 1838 the church was renovated and in 1875 it was enlarged by the addition of a north aisle, organ loft and Lady chapel. It is a very large church for a village of this size and is something of a landmark as it can be seen on the horizon for miles around.

Docking, in this modern day, is a very self-contained village, with a variety of shops and services. It has often hit the headlines as being the home of the Seal Rescue Unit, and several villagers gave a helping hand.

Docking is one of the many Norfolk villages which has received an influx of mainly retired folk from other parts of the country, who find the peace and beauty of the surrounding countryside very much to their liking. The people of Norfolk, in their quiet way, are very hospitable to strangers, and none more so than in Docking – a very good place to live.

🍁 DRAYTON

Standing in the centre of the village it is easy to see why the first settlers chose this spot. The green river valley, sheltered on three sides by gentle uplands, would have been an ideal spot and the stream running through the centre (now piped underground) could supply their animals with water. The Romans were here. In 1849 labourers digging trenches found their pottery and a small ampulla or flask came to light later. There are signs that Angles, Saxons and Danes came plundering this peaceful farming community from AD 450 onwards. Legend has it that a fierce battle was fought between Saxons and Danes on a field by the river, called Bloodsdale to this day. Burial urns unearthed in 1848, one containing a dagger, give colour to the story.

A church was built on the present site of St Margaret's during the reign of Richard I and the first rector appointed in 1198 when Hermanus de Draiton, lord of the manor, presented his son Peter to the living. However, as the font is thought to date from 1150 and the graveyard from 1160, there may have been an earlier church, perhaps a Saxon building.

Throughout the 13th century the lordship was in the hands of the Bellomonte family. One erected the weathered cross now on the village green. On the pedestal is an inscription in French, promising a pardon for the sins of all who pray for the souls of William de Bellomonte and Joan his wife.

Until his death in 1459, Drayton and Hellesdon formed the great estates of Sir John Fastolf, who fought against Joan of Arc in the French wars. When he died he left his vast wealth to a kinsman, John Paston, who fought many battles with the Duke of Suffolk to keep his lands. While John was away, his wife Margaret dealt with the situation and there are letters showing how she vigorously repulsed the Duke's onslaughts. One letter she wrote described the lodge and the church being broken into and treasures stolen. The lodge referred to now belongs to the NHS Trust.

Drayton had a railway station from 1882 to 1959 on the Midland and Great Northern line, used during the First World War for troop movement. It is now an industrial site. Before the war was over, Drayton had its own hero. Harry Carter, son of a railwayman, was awarded the VC, the Croix de Guerre and the MM. In the early 1920s Mr R. G. Carter started his building business, now well known in the district and controlled by his grandson. The lychgate to the church is in memory of R. G. Carter and the many good works he did for the village, and the playing field was given in memory of his wife.

Many large houses have disappeared. Drayton Hall is now a Christian centre and Drayton Wood a day care centre. A new home for the elderly has been built on School Road, and a larger doctor's surgery in the same area. Much building has taken place over the last few years as the population has increased.

❧ EARSHAM

Earsham is situated in the south-east of the county, within the Waveney valley, where the river forms the boundary between Norfolk and Suffolk.

The surrounding low, rolling landscape is mainly pasture, with small areas of woodland which once covered a much greater extent. Most of the land is now owned by the Earsham estate and farmed by about seven tenant farmers.

In medieval times the land was held by the Bigods and later by the Dukes of Norfolk. Important for use as a hunting reserve, there would have been wildfowl on the marshes and deer in the forest. Indeed one of the oldest remaining houses in the village, which dates from the 16th century, is reputed to have been built as a hunting/shooting lodge. Temple Bar House is a timber-framed, wattle and daub structure with massive beams and narrow Tudor bricks in the footings and in the inglenook fireplace.

The original site of the village was near a mill beside the church. The old road ran along the valley above the floodplain, crossed the river at a ford and continued into the nearby market town of Bungay. There was certainly a Saxon settlement at Earsham. Evidence of Saxon burials was uncovered in a field opposite the church and it is also recorded that Vikings sailed up the river Waveney to attack the village.

The village of 'Ersam' and its mill is mentioned in the Domesday Book. Successive mills continued to operate on this site until the early 1980s. Up until the 1850s the Waveney was navigable as far as Diss and supplies were thus carried to and from the mill and similarly coal was delivered to the village.

The church of All Saints is believed to stand on the site of a Roman encampment. It is largely a 14th century building with more modern additions; part of the nave walls may be Norman. Unfortunately a number of the carvings on the 16th century seven sacrament font were mutilated, probably by Puritans, but the Flemish glass in three of the windows survived. Earsham Hall lies on the outskirts of the village. The main part of the present Hall was built in 1710, but an earlier building is known to have existed.

During the Second World War much of the Earsham estate was closed to the public and was used for the storage of bombs and other armaments for the USAAF in East Anglia. There were eight airfields within twelve miles of the village. Beside the now closed railway line a nearby area was used as a marshalling yard for unloading the bombs and fuel. Now all that remains are the hard standings and some of the concrete tracks.

In the mid 19th century the railway linking the main London/Norwich line with Beccles and Lowestoft was opened. This line ran along the edge of the village and remained open until 1953 for passengers and until 1967 for freight. It now forms the A143 bypass which was opened in 1987.

The village school was founded in 1877 and is happily still in existence, though now as a first school. In 1878 the village had four public houses, three shops, three smithies and a smoke-house. When the last shop and post office closed it was jokingly suggested that the pub should sell stamps. The idea was taken up and now a room in the pub opens as a post office in the mornings. The former shop premises have been converted to a private house where the owners have set up a playgroup. A community shop at the village hall opens for two hours every Thursday afternoon and has become a much appreciated social occasion. The village hall, rebuilt in the 1960s, was originally erected, together with the war memorial, to commemorate those men from the village who lost their lives in the First World War.

The village sign is surmounted by an otter, which reflects the proximity of the river and the site of The Otter Trust beside it. Here the animals can be seen in their natural habitat, and the Trust has provided the base from which otters have been reintroduced into other rivers.

🍁 EAST HARLING

East Harling lies in the south of the county near the Suffolk border, about nine miles north-east of Thetford. It is surrounded on three sides by Breckland farms and to the west lies the edge of Thetford Forest and the scattered hamlet of West Harling. There is archaeological evidence of Bronze Age settlement in the area but the village on its present site is probably Saxon in origin. Records show that its population rose during the 18th and early 19th centuries to around

Church of St Peter and St Paul, East Harling

1,100 in 1851. Numbers then steadily declined. However, the trend was reversed when the nearby town of Thetford was developed in the late 1960s as a London 'overspill' town. As a result of this and helped by the provision of a sewerage system, much development has taken place in Harling in recent years and about 2,000 people live in this delightful village. A thriving community, its several shops, school, medical and other services also supply the needs of smaller villages around.

The village is centred around Market Street and Square and White Hart Street and this part has been designated a conservation area. The houses and shops are mainly Georgian with a few more recent buildings. The Swan Inn and the Nag's Head are the only two remaining public houses. Some 13 buildings have been identified as having been inns or ale houses in the past – hopefully not all in business at the same time! Amongst the modern buildings, the new surgery with its flintwork turret is prominent. A modern Sports and Social Club has been built on the edge of the recreation grounds, and the old school converted to provide a village hall.

The loveliest and architecturally most important building, the parish church dedicated to St Peter and St Paul, is situated on the outskirts near the river Thet.

On the site of older buildings, the present church dates mainly from the 15th century and is in Perpendicular style with a lofty west tower topped by an elegant spire. Inside it is light and airy, described by Sir John Betjeman as 'a riot of splendour!' In the Lady chapel can be found the marble tomb of Sir Robert de Herling, for 40 years lord of the manor. He was a great soldier and was one of 'the happy few' who fought at Agincourt. Afterwards he remained in France, dying during the siege of Paris in 1435. Sir Robert left instructions that he should be buried at 'Estherlinges' as he would have called it, but as it was not possible to return him straightaway, the story is told that his body was stewed and the bones kept until they could be safely brought back to England! At his eventual burial, Sir Robert's remains were carried into the church on the back of his favourite charger. The church was enlarged and beautified during the 15th century, mainly by Anne Herling, daughter of Sir Robert, and her first husband, Sir William Chamberlaine.

Anne Herling married three times. Her second husband was Sir Robert Wingfield, Controller of the Royal Household, and it was through him that Edward IV granted a charter to East Harling in 1474 to hold a weekly market and two fairs a year on the Feast Days of St George and St Edmund, each lasting three days. These markets and fairs became important in the district, with regular sales of livestock and provisions. Following the coming of the railway in 1844 which transported stock and goods to Norwich for sale, the Harling markets rapidly declined and became obsolete although annual sheep sales continued into the early years of the 20th century and are remembered by some of the older inhabitants. The carved wooden lamb on the village sign is the only reminder left today of these sales. The area around the war memorial, named Cheese Hill, is the site of the old provision market.

🍁 EAST RUDHAM

The village of East Rudham lies approximately 15 miles from King's Lynn and seven miles from Fakenham on the A148. In the centre of the village is a green which belongs to the parish. At one time it had a pond on it. There are two other pieces of common land, both of which were once ponds. One is now a garden and the other a children's play area.

The village was on the pilgrim route to Walsingham and close to Coxford Abbey, which was active from the 13th to the 16th centuries, and so was once larger and more important than it is today. The population now is about 550, having been about 900 in the 1850s.

The land in the village was originally owned mainly by the Townshend family of Raynham, whose connection with the village goes back to the 13th century. Over the last 200 years the ownership has changed and houses and land are now owned by the council, the farms or privately. Four farms in the village provide some employment, as does an agricultural engineer, a garage and the shops, but the majority of people go out of the village to work.

The school, which was built in 1858, has a roll of 50 pupils at present. When it was built for pupils up to the age of 14, the average roll was 144. The reading room to the north of the A148 was built by the Townshend family in the 1880s for the village. It has had many uses including serving as a canteen for soldiers during the Second World War, and is now a private home.

The village has a post office and general store, a butcher's, a mobile fish and chip shop, two public houses, a garage and individual craftsmen and women working in pottery, woodwork and silver. In the past the village was practically self sufficient, with about 40 businesses including an antiques shop which was visited many times by Queen Mary, 'Pinchers Pop' was produced in Rudham before being transferred to Creake. A veterinary practice started in the village in 1837 by William J. Bower on the south side of the green still continues, although the surgery has moved approximately 100 yards to the east. The splendid Rudhams' Village Hall, serving both East and West Rudham, was built in 1992.

The church of St Mary had a major restoration in the 1870s after the tower fell down, but has old foundations and parts date from Norman times. An Augustinian priory was founded at Rudham in the 12th century and later moved to Coxford when the abbey was built by the De Cheney family in the early 13th century, and although not a very large or wealthy community, it was an important one. It also had a hospital for 13 poor people and it is believed the Anchorage in East Rudham was where the anchorite of Coxford lived. In the 16th century the lands and manors passed to the Townshend family, and the abbey buildings were used to provide material for the building of Raynham Hall in the 1690s. There are some remains of the abbey situated behind the farm at Coxford on the south side of the A148.

🍁 EAST WINCH

East Winch, a once peaceful rural village, is now bisected by the busy A47, along which traffic rushes from the Midlands to Norwich and Yarmouth. It is situated in the rolling country between King's Lynn and Swaffham.

The church of All Saints stands well, on rising ground south of the winding main road. It is noted by travellers for its two-faced clock, illuminated after dark, and for its graceful proportions. Perpendicular in style, it dominates all approaches to the village. Sir William Howard, founder of the family of the Dukes of Norfolk, is buried with many members of his family in a mortuary chapel, now the organ chamber. The moated remains of their manor house can be found on the south side of the village.

Walter Dexter, illustrator of the delightful water-colours of the resorts which were displayed in pre-war railway carriages, lived in the village, and is buried in the churchyard.

The vicarage near the church no longer houses a vicar and presently the priest in charge is resident in Gayton and has the care of five parishes.

Sir William Lancaster, founder of the Prudential and a great local philanthropist, bought East Winch Hall in 1906. The late cartoonist Sir Osbert Lancaster, of Maudie Littlehampton fame, in his book *All done from Memory* refers to his arrival at East Winch station to visit his uncle. Sadly the station was closed in 1968, depriving the village of easy access to Norwich.

The station was well used, both for produce and passengers. It is reported that in 1981 as many as 12,000 people arrived on the Great Eastern trains for the steeplechase races organised by the West Norfolk Hunt Club. In 1905 the meetings were moved to Fakenham, together with the grandstand and railings. An airstrip for light aircraft, close to the route of the old line, is used during daylight hours. Adjacent to the airstrip is the RSPCA Norfolk Wildlife Hospital. Opened in 1993, it is now an integral part of the village and has put East Winch firmly on the map.

Of the three public houses once boasted by the village only the Carpenters Arms remains. The main industry of the village is agriculture. The soil is mostly of a sandy consistency and there are extensive carrstone quarries. The mixed farming of previous generations has been replaced by intensive arable.

East Winch Hall is no longer a private residence but is occupied and well maintained by an international chemical company.

The common, administered by the Norfolk Naturalists Trust, is situated south of the A47 and the Swaffham side of the village. It extends to 80 acres and is noted for its bog areas and rare plants. Some residents still own grazing rights which are now taken up as it has recently been fenced and gated. The track though the common has become a tarmac road used by gravel lorries and local traffic.

A new housing estate has ensured the continuation of the village school, which was threatened with closure.

🍁 EGMERE

Although Egmere, a deserted village, is little more than a remnant of a medieval past, it is worth visiting, as one of the most peaceful places in the county.

Take the B1355 from South Creake to North Creake, and having passed the great threshing barn of Manor Farm, an unmistakable feature, turn right onto the Walsingham road. After some three miles, you will see, on a slight rise, the tower of ruined Egmere church. By about 1600, this church was in use as a barn.

From the rise, one may trace the village street of one of Norfolk's most readily recognised former vills. The mere is in a hollow, and at a time when the water table was higher, it drained to nearby Waterden Bottom and then to the river Burn. In the 1850s, Egmere Farmhouse was rebuilt as the centre of a designed complex, with barn, stables, cattleyards and stackyard.

🍁 ELSING

Elsing is one of the many farming villages in Norfolk; it lies about 15 miles north-west of Norwich on the banks of the river Wensum.

The church of St Mary was built by Sir Hugh Hastings in 1347 and it is his memorial brass, to be found in the chancel, that is so widely known. The church too is remarkable for its very wide pillarless nave. Sir John Hastings, a descendant of Sir Hugh, built the manor house, which is now known as Elsing Hall, sometime before 1477.

It has been said Elsing was once a dying village, losing the chapel in 1979, the school in 1983, the shop in 1986 and more recently the post office. Elsing Mill, which still stands on the river Wensum as a private residence, was once much used by the local farmers for grinding their corn. The last rector left Elsing in 1971, the following year the then Bishop of Thetford, the late Aubrey Aitken, came to live in the rectory, which is now also privately owned.

The WI raised the money for and designed the village sign, which was carved by the late Mr Harry Carter, and was given by the WI to the Parish Council. The wooden seat nearby was also given to the village by the WI, on the occasion of the marriage of the Prince and Princess of Wales.

❧ ERPINGHAM WITH CALTHORPE

Just three miles north of Aylsham and seven miles west of North Walsham lies the village of Erpingham. The mile or so that separates it from the main Norwich/Cromer road also protects it from the ever-increasing traffic, and leaves it still a pleasant rural backwater.

The village gave its name to the Erpingham family who were landowners here. The most famous, and the last, of the family was Sir Thomas Erpingham who became a figure of national as well as local fame. Described as a 'chivalrous knight' he accompanied the Duke of Lancaster to Spain in 1399, and fought in all the wars of Henry IV and Henry V. William Shakespeare immortalised him in the play *Henry V*.

His greatest memorial in the village is the church of St Mary the Virgin. Standing isolated on Gallows Hill and surrounded entirely by fields, it is a splendid and picturesque sight from whichever approach brings you to it. Its building was begun by Sir Thomas, and completed after his death. The church contains a fine brass of Sir John Erpingham, father of Sir Thomas, who died in 1370.

The church is well-maintained and cared for, inside and out, and well worth a visit. It looks solid and unchanging, but the church and its tower seem to have been waging a battle with the parishioners over the centuries. Sir Thomas Browne, writing in 1665 about a thunderstorm in Norwich and elsewhere, and of the fireballs that accompanied it, says, 'about four days after, the like fulminous fire killed a man in Erpingham church, by Aylsham, and beat down divers which were within wind of it'. Again in 1721, one of the four statues which stood on the corners of the tower fell during a storm killing one of the congregation and injuring two others. Sometime prior to 1840, part of the tower fell through the roof, destroying the baptismal font, and finally, in April of 1888, lightning struck the tower and hurled several heavy stones through the roof. Perhaps it is safer to go to Calthorpe church, in the adjoining village, which has been officially linked with Erpingham since 1935.

There are one or two interesting features in Calthorpe as well. Approaching the village from Erpingham, there are several allotment strips on the right hand side of the road, together with Townland Farm on the opposite side, which are still administered by the Townland Trust (known to be in existence in 1887) which gives annual gifts of money to local pensioners. One of the few wartime bombs in the area fell opposite the church and partially destroyed a nearby house. There is also a small pottery now established on the corner of Aldborough Road.

Erpingham village has not changed much over the years, although some new houses are appearing now. The population in 1861 was 423, and today is about 488. The two windmills and the water mill have gone. There is a general store, although at one time there were three shops, one of which incorporated a barber's shop, and there is one public house. The school still survives. A flourishing restaurant exists in what was previously the other public house, and a boat building firm has recently moved into the village.

Following the closure and departure of the large national breweries from Norfolk, the village boasted the largest private brewery left in the county. This was attached to the Spread Eagle Inn, but success has caused it to outgrow its premises and it moved to Woodbastwick. Although fewer people now work on the land, the atmosphere is still that of an agricultural community, and hopefully will continue that way.

🍁 FELTWELL

Years ago it was always claimed by Feltwell folk that theirs was the largest village in Norfolk. Methwold also laid claim to the title, but since they had a regular market, they were dismissed as being really a small town! The village has grown enormously since the 1950s, with four new housing estates and much private housing, but there are no new amenities and no council housing has been built for at least 30 years.

You used to be able to buy anything you needed here, apart from furniture

– lino, rugs, footwear, clothes, glassware and crockery, books, jewellery etc. Mrs Darby's clothes and fancy goods shop was a veritable Aladdin's cave, it was so full. There also used to be a cinema, but that died with the advent of bingo and TV, and four pubs have also been lost.

For several years after the Second World War, RAF training planes were stationed here, followed by a WAAF officers' training section. Then the RAF left and it became a satellite of the American Lakenheath base. Now the Deep Space Tracking Station has been built here. Unfortunately, with tractors pulling huge trailers full of carrots and sugar beet through the village and the container lorries from the docks coming to the camp, tranquil village life seems to belong to the past.

❧ FINCHAM

Fincham is a parish of rich farmland, with its attractive village set along the main road from Downham Market to Swafflham, with a population of approximately 700.

Travelling from Downham Market, the first house in the parish is Rose Cottage, the front facing towards Downham displaying the plaque of an insurance company. A short distance along the King's Lynn road is Playter's Hall, which was probably the site of one of the ancient manors, perhaps Grandcourt's or Brother Hall. It takes its present name from an owner in the 17th century.

Coming back towards Fincham, Talbot Manor is situated on the corner of Lynn Road, once renowned for its orchids and rare plants. This collection of rare plants is now housed at Fincham Manor in the safe keeping of Mr Hugh Mason, the son of the late Mr M. Mason who collected the plants.

The rectory is old and well built. It consists of three storeys with high pitched roofs and gables. By a date on a large central chimney, it appears to have been built or rebuilt in the year 1624. It presents a handsome front to the north and is situated with its garden and glebe lands on the south. The parish church of St Michael stood west of the rectory, but was levelled to the ground during the 18th century as it was falling into decay. The rectory has now been sold and a new one built on the site of St Michael's.

Outside the Old Rectory is the village sign, which depicts Fincham Hall with the De Fincham family dressed as in the 16th century. It also has the

Fincham coat of arms and the Women's Institute crest, together with an orchid representing Talbot Manor gardens.

The Swan Inn, the only public house left in the village, is also a very old property. It claims to have entertained Royalty years ago when they visited the area for the shooting season.

The beautiful large St Martin's church stands high in the centre of the village and was completed about 1460. On the floor of the church are several large black stones dedicated to members of the Fincham family buried here. Their brasses have been stolen, except one small effigy of a woman in her shroud. The arms of Fincham are on the doorway of the rood loft stairs. The ancient font of St Martin's church belonged originally to St Michael's. It was brought here on the destruction of that church in 1744.

Opposite the church is a green area which was once the village pond. It is now known as the Peace Garden in remembrance of those who died in the Second World War. Church House stands in the shadow of the church and dates back to 1750. It was originally a farmhouse.

Fairswell Manor was one of the 13 manors of the village which existed in the 12th and 13th centuries. Its site was on the road leading to Stoke Ferry. Moat House is a very impressive building in Queen Anne style, situated on the Stokeferry Road, and gets its name from the moat surrounding the property. Fincham Hall was a considerable manor, which gave its name and residence to the Fincham family for about 500 years, occupying the chief position of the village.

The airfield to the east of the village shatters the quietness of the community when the aircraft take off to distant countries.

🍁 FRAMINGHAM EARL & FRAMINGHAM PIGOT

The area covering the Framinghams lies between the B1332 and the A146 in gently undulating country. Some say it was originally owned by the Earl of Norfolk Roger Bigod (or Bigot) and, when divided into two villages, named Framingham Earl for the Earl and Framingham Pigot for his cousin Reiner Picot.

It is essentially a farming area, but is interspersed with woodlands and there are some interesting walks along quiet country roads and tracks which are well marked as public footpaths. The old gravel pit at the five-way junction has been renovated and renamed The Dell, and has received a Norfolk Society award for conservation.

There is a small village green outside Framingham Earl post office, on which has been erected the village sign depicting a knight in armour. Each village has a church. St Andrew's, Framingham Earl, part of which dates back to the 12th century, is very well worth a visit. St Andrew's, Framingham Pigot is Victorian with a steeple at the side and both churches and their churchyards are kept in immaculate condition by the parishioners.

The villages are well served by three good pubs; The Feathers free house and restaurant in Framingham Pigot on the corner of Fox Road and the A146, The Gull situated nearby on the A146, and the Railway Tavern in Framingham Earl. All these have generous car parks. The modern Framingham Earl high school serves a large catchment area and caters in the evenings for a wide range of courses and activities.

✸ FRITTON

Fritton is a pleasant village about eleven miles south of Norwich with a 70 acre common surrounded by fine oak trees. At one time the village had a school, shop and public house, but these are now gone.

St Catherine's church has a fine rood screen, dating back to the 1500s. The screen was given by John Bacon, who with his family is portrayed on one of the panels. There are also two wall paintings, discovered in 1850, of St Christopher and St George.

We are proud of our fine common, which has many visitors in the summer months, especially to hear the cuckoos.

✸ FULMODESTON

Outwardly the changes to the village since the end of the Second World War are not dramatic. The post office remains but the village store no longer bakes bread. One of the most noticeable and, some would say, sad losses is the school. Soon after the war there were some 60 children in education but numbers diminished and in 1984 it was closed. It was not lost, however, as the building was purchased and converted into a village hall now used extensively by all age groups. In more recent years the council has built six retirement homes for the elderly.

The Hastings Arms public house has now gone, but the same building is now The Red House, a small hotel or guest house, while the second public house, the Star, closed some time ago. The railway through Thursford was unfortunately a victim of the Beeching closures and even the very limited bus service has ceased. The inevitable result was that the motor car has become not a luxury but an absolute necessity.

Farming remains the dominant occupation but changes have taken place, notably a swing from six individual farms to only two, whilst the main acreage is in the hands of Lord Hasting's Astley estate.

The parish and Methodist churches still provide for the spiritual welfare of the village, but the Anglicans have become one of a group of six parishes served by a single rector.

🍁 GARVESTONE

It is possible that the very first ancient inhabitants of Garvestone founded their settlement in the Tanners Green area of the village. It is here, even today, that one of the oldest houses in this Breckland parish can be found.

In the Domesday Book, Garvestone was known as Gerolfestuna. The village takes its name from the river Yare which winds through the parish and was originally known as the Gar or Ger. St Margaret's parish church has a fine tower, built in the late 14th or early 15th century. The main body of the church dates from the first half of the 14th century, although the south aisle and nave windows are from the Tudor period. The interior of the church is very plain, even the font which dates from the 16th century.

When Rev Robert Key came to Garvestone in 1831 his first impression was not good. 'I found its inhabitants in the deepest, grossest ignorance. I could not find one God-fearing man or woman in the place. One dark, dismal mantle covered the whole and the Devil had it all his own way!' It was in response to this that Methodism came to the village and the chapel was built in 1864.

In the mid 1800s the 800 acre parish had almost 400 inhabitants. A poor house was built with the income from land rental charges, and today the charity trustees still distribute funds in the village. There was then a grocer and draper, a shoemaker, a blacksmith, a miller, a tailor and a wheelwright. There were also four pubs at that time; the King's Arms, the White Horse, the Windmill and the Wheatsheaf. The Wheatsheaf closed in the 1800s and the Windmill in the 1920s. The White Horse closed in 1899 when Rev Alpe purchased the inn, its land and other buildings. It was rumoured that the main reason for his purchase of the land was to prevent pheasant shooting taking place on Sundays.

🍁 GAYTON

Gayton lies on a flat plain, approximately seven miles to the east of King's Lynn. The name Gayton was derived from a British word 'guy', which was associated with water, and Gayton certainly has more than its share of springs. To the north of the village the ground rises to the lime kilns, also known as the 'chalk pits'. Here chalk was once excavated and burned in the kilns to produce lime.

Gayton Hall was built in 1766, as a shooting box in the first instance. In the reign of George V the Hall was often visited by the King and Queen Mary for shooting parties. They would be attended by several servants employed mainly from the village. During the First World War, local children would take a basin and queue at the back door of the Hall for twopenny worth of dripping. Two local residents remember this well and declare the dripping 'bootiful'.

The main road running through the village past St Nicholas' church was an old coach road between King's Lynn and Norwich. The Rampant Horse, one of the original five pubs in the village, was used as an overnight stop for prisoners being taken from King's Lynn to Norwich prison. Evidence of this remained in one of the rooms with iron rings set in the wall which were used to secure prisoners. Opposite is the village hall. This hall was erected by the Ancient Order of Shepherds in 1887 at a cost (inclusive of land) of £390, and has been known ever since as the Jubilee Hall.

The school stands near the church. On St Valentine's Day, during the lunch break, the school children would run and skip around the village singing 'Old Mother Valentine' and would be given an orange each at Lattice House shop. At the mill each would be given a hot penny which had been heated on a shovel in the bakery oven.

The mill is the focal point of the village even though the sails are no longer in place. Two sails were removed in 1921 and the other two in 1925/26. The mill ground wheat for bread making and ran a bakery. This provided villagers with bread and local housewives would often take trays of dough and cakes there to be baked in the ovens after the baker had finished his work for the day. For this service they were charged ½d per tin. Local farmers would have their grain ground into cattle feed.

In the early 1900s there were many small businesses. There were three general stores selling everything, a post office, cobbler's, draper's, butcher's, barber's, a wet fish shop and a garage which incorporated a blacksmith's, undertaker's and builder's.

Today sees great expansion within the village with several housing estates and therefore an increase in population. The businesses have moved with the times and reflect the changing needs of the villagers.

🍁 GREAT ELLINGHAM

Great Ellingham is quite a large village with a population of 1,125, situated two and a half miles from Attleborough. On approaching the village travelling from Attleborough, the church of St James, dating from the 14th century, comes into view, standing serenely on high ground with a spire and the familiar gold weathercock.

The school built in 1896 is thriving with an attendance of 153, with children attending from neighbouring villages and Attleborough. There is also a school providing private education for children of under eight years of age.

The recreation centre is used by all the organisations in the village, also the Breckland Astronomical Society. The Scouts have their own premises, built on the recreation ground and used by the Scouts, Cubs and Brownies.

During the 1970s two new private estates were built, and in recent years Peddars Way Housing Association have built a small estate by purchasing glebe land adjacent to the old coal house which still stands on 'Coal House Corner'; this was used to store charity coal, which was then distributed to the needy in the village. The charity still continues to this day, but is in cash form.

'Ye Olde Thatche Shoppe' and bakery provides for everyone's needs, baking fresh bread and cakes on the premises. There are also a post office, timber mill, scrap metal yard, the very popular and well known Tropical

Butterfly Gardens and Nursery, and several small businesses. There were originally four public houses: the Pig and Whistle which closed many years ago, the Queen's Head (known locally as 'The Swamp') and the Chequers closed more recently, leaving only the Crown remaining, with its excellent restaurant, function room and beer garden. There was a bakery at the mill house, and the mill is still standing though sadly not in use. There were also once three blacksmith's shops and a harness maker's.

During the Second World War there was a local aerodrome, known as 'Deopham Green' though most of the land was in Great Ellingham. In May 1992 a memorial was erected to commemorate the 452nd USA Bomb Group which was stationed at Deopham Green, on this occasion and many others we have had the pleasure of welcoming and entertaining our American allies.

🍁 GREAT HAUTBOIS

Great Hautbois is a hamlet adjacent to Coltishall: a left turn from Coltishall High Street, which is on the B1150 North Walsham road. There has been controversy from time to time over the origins of the name, but it has always been pronounced 'Hobbies', and that has Saxon meanings. It is situated on the north bank of the river Bure, and probably on an ancient thoroughfare, because in the 13th century there was a hospital here, attached to a religious house, and giving care to travellers and the sick and needy. The old round-towered church of St Theobald is in ruins, but as it stands on a slight incline, it can be seen from across the fields, through a screen of trees. The churchyard is a very peaceful place, and in spring, snowdrops and daffodils flower amongst the old gravestones.

In 1864 the old church was replaced by Holy Trinity church, built at a cost of £1,230 by the Rev Girling, Rector of Coltishall, mostly from his own finances. In the early 1900s, Rev Girling sold the Great Hautbois estate to the Patteson family. Here grew up Beth and Phillipa Patteson, both committed to the Girl Guide movement. When the Patteson sisters died, they left their house and estate to the Guides. The house is now a training and activity centre with modern facilities, owned and managed by Anglia Region of the Guide Association. The estate is used for camping and outdoor activities by Guides and other youth organisations. In part of the original estate, Norfolk Guides have built a modern building which is used for pack holidays, and called 'Patteson Lodge'.

The rest of Great Hautbois consists of farms and a few houses. One of the farms is popular for fruit and vegetable picking in the summer. The road continues to Little Hautbois and leads to RAF Coltishall, a large self-contained camp, and very much part of Coltishall.

🍁 GREAT MASSINGHAM

Every visitor to Great Massingham is first aware of its two ponds lying at either end of a large green. One is a favourite spot for fishermen who often share it amicably with a pair of swans. Between them on the open green there was once a weekly market held on Fridays and an annual fair originally held on 28th October each year. Although the market has long gone, a fair is still held each year when the bumper cars and candy floss stalls draw the crowds.

The second thing to catch the eye is St Mary's church with its splendid and very tall tower which is visible for miles around. In past days when great heaths and sheep walks lay to the south and west of the village, it must have been as valuable to travellers as a lighthouse is to sailors. Around the green is a selection of houses typical of the area, many of flint crowned with red pantiles, as is the Rose and Crown, with its seats outside on the green well patronised on sunny days. Opposite stands what was the Swan and this in turn is not far from the Fox and Pheasant and around the corner was the Royal Oak. Massingham inhabitants must have been very thirsty! Now these three pubs have closed, as has the small fish and chip shop and all but one of the shops.

There is a second part to this village and that is along the side road to Weasenham where there is yet another pond, more wide, open grassy areas and some very attractive houses. Beside the largest of the central ponds is Abbey Farm, a late Georgian building. As its name suggests it is on the site of a former monastery, but not in fact an abbey but an Augustinian priory founded in the early 1200s. A few pieces of masonry survive in and around the farm, but that is all. The abbey lands included Hartswood, long cleared but commemorated in the name of a field and a tiny remnant of what was once there. Its presence can still be traced by the woodland plants which grow in the hedgerows around it.

Beyond it lies Peddars Way. Southwards it marches towards Castle Acre crossing Massingham Heath, home, more than a thousand years before the Romans came, to flint miners who dug the black stones from the chalk before

89

knapping and shaping them into tools and weapons. To the naturalist this open area was famous for its stretches of heather studded with tiny islands of chalk-loving plants on the anthills, but it was all ploughed up in the 1940s and is now covered with waving barley.

In recent years new houses have been built, some infilling spaces and keeping the close pattern of buildings around the green, others in developments to the north of the village. The recovery in population has happily meant that Massingham has kept its post office cum general store and village school, the last something it has possessed since 1676 when a free school was founded by Charles Calthorpe and held in the room over the church porch, a far cry from today's warm and comfortable classrooms!

🍁 GREAT MOULTON

A village twelve miles south of Norwich, Great Moulton is spread over agricultural land, which has probably been settled for more than a thousand years, possibly deriving its name from the Norse 'Mula Tun'.

There were originally two Moultons, Great and Little. Both with a church, but that of Little Moulton fell into disuse in the 16th century, and was subsequently demolished in 1570. The remaining church of St Michael is probably of Saxon foundation but medieval rebuilding and a thorough Victorian restoration have obscured any definite evidence. Many period features remain, notably the 15th century font, the fine set of Commandment Boards, and an unusual Benefaction Board detailing a gift by Samuel Hammond to the poor made in 1762. A Salem Evangelical chapel opened in 1890 to serve the surrounding district, it is now part of the Rural Ministry. A new chapel was completed in 1990. The hundred year old, corrugated iron chapel was carefully rebuilt for display at the Stowmarket Rural Life Museum.

The former rectory, which is featured on the village sign, was built by the architect W.J. Donthorn in 1831. This is Donthorn's only surviving unaltered classical building, made distinctive by its sharply profiled and squared stucco on the south and east front and its three storey tower.

The Coronation Hall in Great Moulton is used as a joint village hall, by the parishes of Aslacton and Great Moulton. Social activities, Women's Institute and playgroup are all shared by the two parishes. There is no railway station but the main London to Norwich line runs right through the village. The Fox and Hounds is both village public house and restaurant, and Great Moulton has a well stocked shop and post office.

🍁 GREAT RYBURGH

Great Ryburgh lies about four miles south-east of Fakenham off the A1067 to Norwich. The village has grown with additional houses being built in the centre, where a farmhouse and buildings once stood. However, there has been a decline in amenities such as the loss of the 'Bottom Shop' and the closure of the Crown public house, which was bought by the Maltings and turned into offices, which in turn led to the disbandment of the Bowls Club. Although we still have a Cluster school the authorities have been looking at sites here and in Stibbard, our neighbouring village, to build a new school to accommodate the increase in school-age children.

The police house and the nurse's house in the early 1970s were occupied by their own professions, but were sold and are now privately owned. The foundry closed, the buildings being turned into industrial units which are occupied by small businesses. The granary also became redundant, then was used as a factory. The Mill House, home of the Smith family for many years, was in the 1970s turned into a nursing home and had a 14 room extension built in 1988.

The youth club used to meet in the rectory barn until 6th June 1977, when on this particular day, part of the barn collapsed whilst celebrations were taking place in the village for the Queen's Silver Jubilee. As one approaches the eastern end of the village there is a new set of traffic lights, followed by the renovated church barn which had stood empty since its collapse in 1977, giving a much better impression as one enters the village.

🍁 GREAT & LITTLE SNORING

Great Snoring is a small village seven miles inland from Wells-next-the-Sea. Over the last century the population has declined to its level today of less than 200. At one time there were three shops, two pubs, a school with a resident head teacher, and a rector, a blacksmith and carpenter. Milk was delivered by pony and cart from dairy farms in the village. Sainsbury's had an egg-packing station here from 1936.

Between the wars football and cricket played an important part in village life, on a pitch provided by the farmer. After the Second World War, during which time the meadow was ploughed up, a ladies cricket team was formed as well. Today there are no pubs but a social club and adjacent bowling green. The school has closed and the younger children go to school at Little Snoring. The shop/post office has closed but the butcher and baker deliver to the door. There is public transport provided by Age Concern and the community bus.

Unlike Great Snoring, Little Snoring's population has increased tenfold and still supports a school, pub, post office and shop, and also an engineering works.

St Andrew's church is an architectural gem with many unique features. Nearby the old parsonage house was once a lepers' colony surrounded by a moat. The first Norfolk Agricultural Station was created at Jex Farm in the early 1900s. Little Snoring also had a cock-fighting pit.

In the early 1940s the airfield was constructed and used by Bomber Command. Villagers were allowed to visit the camp cinema and attend dances. Recently a playing field has been sown and land is being made available for a village hall.

🍁 GREAT WITCHINGHAM

Great Witchingham is situated ten miles north-west of Norwich, with the busy A1067 Norwich to Fakenham road passing through the village, which includes the hamlet of Lenwade.

The gravel pits that have been dug out are now used for game and coarse fishing and are a very attractive feature of the village. The river Wensum flows to the south of the village and is flanked on one side by a now unused corn mill and on the other by the public house called the Bridge Inn. Both are interesting buildings and have been well kept up.

Great Witchingham has two churches, All Saints' Mission Church, now called St Faith's, which was built in 1888 at a cost of £600 and stands parallel to the main road, and St Mary's, which stands to the north of the village, built between the 13th and 15th centuries. At one time there were also two chapels but these have now been converted to dwellings. The village Memorial Hall was built in 1921 as a tribute to the men who fell in the First World War and stands today next to the village school.

The Midland & Great Northern Railway line which ran from Melton Constable to Norwich had a station at Lenwade from 1883 to its closure in 1959. The old railway line now forms part of Marriotts Way, which is a walkway and cycle track from Norwich to Aylsham.

On the northern outskirts of the village lies Great Witchingham Wildlife Park. Opened by Philip Wayre in 1961, this covers an area of some 50 acres and has a varied collection of animals and European birds which are housed in natural surroundings. Conservation is one of the main aims of this delightful park and many species have been saved from extinction and returned to their native countries.

Another interesting building is Great Witchingham Hall at the south of the village. This is an Elizabethan building which stands in pleasant parklands with the river Wensum running through the grounds. It is now the headquarters of Bernard Matthews' turkey organisation. Some villagers are employed in the modern factory which adjoins the park but many people travel to Norwich for their daily employment.

In the 1883 records there are listed amongst the tradesmen a blacksmith, harness maker and saddler, basket maker, carriage builder and wheelwright to name but a few. Sadly all these crafts have virtually disappeared but there is a post office and general store, a butcher's, a newsagent's, a cafe, a craft shop serving light refreshments, two petrol stations with garage service and an excellent pub that now serves meals.

HAPPISBURGH

Happisburgh (pronounced 'Haisbro') was once a very small agricultural village situated between Great Yarmouth and Cromer, on the coast. It is now fast becoming a well known holiday resort. During the past 40-odd years many changes have taken place; the population has grown and over the last decade many houses and bungalows have been built. Many would say that 'Haisbro' ain't what it used to be'.

The magnificent church, St Mary's, was built in the 14th century and during the Second World War it suffered damage when all the windows on the south side were shattered. Hill House public house stands high on the cliff top and in years gone by has had many notable visitors. There is also a very large country house, the biggest in the village, built in 1900 of flint and brick with a large thatched roof. Almost opposite to this magnificent house stands the village school, which dates back to 1861.

Another feature and attraction in the village is the famous red and white striped lighthouse, which became the responsibility of the Happisburgh Lighthouse Trust, formed to prevent its closure by Trinity House. This was the only lighthouse in the country to be run privately.

Happisburgh is split in two, Upper Happisburgh where the church is, and Lower Happisburgh which runs into Eccles – another holiday village which many years ago lost a lot of its buildings, including the local church, into the sea. Remains of this 'lost village' as it is known, can be seen at low tide.

🍁 HARDINGHAM

There have been many changes in Hardingham village during the last 30 years. Although the school had been open for 110 years it is sadly closed now, and lived in. The railway which was used for both freight and passengers was closed in 1967. Villagers can remember the days when the farmers carted their sugarbeet to the wagons to be taken to the local factories. Some travelled by train to school in East Dereham and incoming trucks of coal were sacked up by Cordy and Son and delivered locally. A single track is occasionally open and the aim is to runs daily trains from East Dereham to Wymondham once again.

The village sign depicting the old mill which sadly burnt down was erected in 1981, donated by the WI. The film titled *The Shuttered Room* which starred Alan Bates was made at Hardingham Mill and featured the disastrous fire. The Railway Tavern, the village pub, has closed and was an antiques store for a while. There is still a village shop that sells most things but the post office closed in 1977. There is no public bus service with the inhabitants having to get into Hingham for a connection. More recently a post bus service has provided a lifeline with a daily service to East Dereham.

Farming around the village has changed due to large machinery, the hedgerows having been grubbed out to make the fields larger. Crops have changed and are lemon-yellow fields of rape and the bright blue of linseed. Sugar beet and cereals still feature strongly here, though. Many of the lovely farm buildings have been pulled down to make room for larger buildings to house the machinery. Footpaths are generally good and walkable.

The church of St George with the old rectory nearby is situated two miles from the village centre and stands very regally on a hill top.

The village has about 300 inhabitants. The Memorial Hall which was built in memory of the local dead in the 1914–18 war has recently been extended and refurbished. This is used regularly for meetings, playschool, arts and craft afternoons, the cricket club during the summer and also the annual village fete.

🍁 HARDLEY

Nestling on the edge of the marshes near the point where the river Chet flows into the Yare, lies the old village of Hardley. There are a few new dwellings, but most of the population live in the centuries-old cottages and farms which line the village street. The street itself peters out as a rough track leading down to the marshes and dyke. At one time the Norfolk wherries came up this dyke loaded with coal, but now it is a mooring place for sailing dinghies.

Keen walkers can follow the footpath along the river bank to Hardley Cross. This ancient cross stands at the meeting point of the rivers Yare and Chet and marks the boundary of jurisdiction between the river authorities of Norwich and Great Yarmouth.

On the higher ground overlooking the street and marshes stands the village church with its round Norman tower and 15th century nave and chancel. Entering by the south door, one gets the feeling of time having stood still. Here are the old wooden pews untouched for centuries. Some poppy heads, some box pews, and on the north side an arrangement of pews in three sides of a square. Perhaps this is where the servants from the Hall sat. Hardley Hall, near the church, was built in the 16th century with flints said to have been taken from Langley Abbey.

Alongside the river Chet is an area of flooded marsh, Hardley Flood, currently leased by the Norfolk Naturalists Trust who have set up two hides there. It is an important site for winter wildfowl. Hen harriers hunt regularly over the reserve and a great variety of spring passage migrants can be seen. Access to the reserve is along the footpath on the north bank of the river Chet.

🍁 HARDWICK

Hardwick is a small village in south Norfolk, lying five miles north-west of Harleston and 13 miles from Norwich. It is mentioned in the Domesday Book.

Hardwick was once divided into two parts – Boughton Manor and Barret Manor. Both were united in the ownership of Sir Peter Gleave who was MP for the City in 1627. His grandson fought for Charles I in the Civil War.

The oldest building in Hardwick is the church of St Margaret. Sir Thomas Richardson, Speaker to the House of Commons from 1620 to 1622, was baptised here. He declared that the use of the rack to obtain a confession from an alleged murderer was illegal. There used to be a rectory, but after the churches of Hardwick and Shelton were united it was uninhabited, and it fell down in the 1820s. In the 14th century Hardwick had a hospital, and as it was dedicated to St Lazarus it may have been a leper hospital.

The original Hardwick Hall used to stand on the island surrounded by the moat, next to the present Hall. The Gleave family owned the Hall in the 17th century, and during the Civil War two companies of Royalist Foot were billeted there. It is thought that Cromwell's soldiers used the church as barracks.

There are still many old houses in the village. Most of them were built by use of a timber frame filled in with wattle and daub and roofed with thatch. Unfortunately, there are no longer any thatched dwellings remaining.

Chapel Lane was named after the Wesleyan chapel that used to be there, and Mill Road after the post mill that used to stand next to Mill Cottage, but was burned down. A Second World War aerodrome was built on the outskirts of the village and was used by the USAAF for bombing raids on Europe.

🍁 HARPLEY

Harpley is a small village, with a population of about 350, set amidst undulating farmland. Its western boundary is marked by the ancient trackway Peddars Way. Long and round barrows in the parish indicate human activity in the area during Neolithic times. A few thousand years later Harpley or Herpelai is mentioned in the Domesday Book.

The main part of the village lies either side of Nethergate Street which runs from the main Lynn/Fakenham road, the A148, to the Massinghams. The rest of the village forms a rough square round fields and woodland. Some of the land still belongs to the nearby Houghton Estate which for several hundred years was the principal landowner.

The houses of Manor and Lower Farms were standing in 1720, but they, like other buildings in the village, were altered in Georgian style at the beginning of the 19th century. Parts of the Rose and Crown pub date back to the 15th century. A council estate was built after the Second World War and Harpley Court, flats for the elderly, during the 1970s. A few private homes went up in the 1960s but most of the new houses date from the 1980s.

The large flint and stone church of St Lawrence stands on high ground opposite a belt of woodland. While the church dates from the 14th century, the first record of a rector is 1154. The church has a medieval rood screen, alas repainted in Victorian times, and ancient pews with curious creatures carved on their ends. The weathervane on the tower glistens real gold in the setting sun; it was painted with gold leaf by the late Charlie Mountain, village blacksmith. He also made the wrought iron village sign with a pheasant, a hare and a sheaf of wheat.

The one and only shop is open seven days a week. Next door is the chapel. Sadly, it ceased functioning in 1996 when the last trustee died. Opposite are six almshouses built in 1850. With curved Dutch gables, they stand on three sides of a courtyard.

A little further down Nethergate Street is the village hall opened by Lord Fermoy in 1930. Behind the hall is the bowling green, unused for 40 years, but restored in 1997 by members of the bowls club. During the winter the club moves inside the hall and plays short mat bowls. Alongside the bowling green is a small playground with swings and a climbing frame.

Harpley combines with Houghton each year to enter the Inter-Village Games. In 1996 the enthusiastic teams of more than 40 villagers from the two parishes won the class for Small Villages.

The old brickyard which had become a wilderness of undergrowth and nettles is to become a nature reserve and picnic site. The footpaths in the village offer a variety of walks, across fields and past woods.

Lower Farm in Back Street is the only locally-run working farm left. The main crops grown are wheat, barley, sugar beet and linseed. For many years Hall Farm had a large dairy herd but it has now been sold. Some of the barns and outbuildings were turned into rural workshops. The largest firm in the village is Harpley Engineering which makes agricultural machinery. A family firm, it has developed from the village smithy. A computer firm is based elsewhere in the village and a plumber also carries on his business from Harpley. Most residents travel to King's Lynn for work.

The village school was established in 1845 in a house at the foot of School Lane. The current building was put up in 1907 and in the autumn of 1998 it had 40 pupils on the register.

The old windmill, standing on high ground to the east of the village, was used as an observation post during the Second World War. The top and sails were removed and never replaced. The mill house is now a private home.

❧ HEACHAM

Heacham lies on the Wash, to the south of Hunstanton. It has grown quite considerably over the past few years from the quiet village it once was.

The parish church of St Mary is 13th century, with later additions, and there is still a remnant of original wall painting on the west arch. A brass over two feet high on the west wall commemorates a knight of 1485.

Heacham today is of course famous for its lavender, the perfume of which scents the air for miles around in the summer. The industry is centred on 19th century Caley Mill, which stands on the site of a mill recorded in the Domesday Book in 1086. Norfolk Lavender is famous the world over and it is grown here in all its variants of colour, a wonderful sight spreading over nearly 100 acres.

The village sign recalls the Red Indian princess Pocahontas. She married John Rolfe of Heacham Hall after saving his life and that of other early colonists in Virginia. She came to England with him in 1616, but sadly she died at Gravesend as she was about to sail home a year later. Heacham Hall itself no longer exists.

Many shops have been lost over the past few years and the only big store now is Coley's in Station Road. The entrance into the High Street has been enhanced by the demolition of some derelict properties which have been replaced with an attractive development of cottages. In the High Street can be found a greengrocer, a flower shop, two butchers, a post office, a card shop, a cycle shop, a furniture shop, a high class restaurant and an off-licence. This is all old property and it still looks like a village street. It is a friendly place and Heacham people live amicably with the many newcomers to the village.

🍁 HEDENHAM

The little village of Hedenham, with its population of just over 100, spreads across the main Bungay to Norwich road as it has done since Roman times, when it was a small settlement centred on the rich seam of brick-making clay, still much in evidence to those who garden on the south side of the village. The highway connected the important Roman strongholds of Bungay and Caister and it is reasonable to suppose that the brickfield supplied both these early towns. Certainly, a Roman kiln was discovered close to the road in 1858, but Norfolk weather soon took its toll, though not before several members of the community had made sketches of it and recorded it in any way they could. Brick-making continued in Hedenham right up to the 20th century.

When the Normans came, the village was recorded in the Domesday Book as being of much the same size as it is today. It was given by the Conqueror to his nephew. The lovely old church of St Peter is first recorded as having a rector in 1245. However, the small lancet windows in the north wall were common in the late 12th century and the church is situated on a sharp rise above the stream, along which ran the ancient pack-horse trail, so some form of building could well have existed before that. The heavy oak, iron-studded door has a sanctuary ring, rather useful in the days when sheep-stealing was punished with hanging, and an escort to the coast and banishment at least gave you an option on life. If one stands by the font and looks up towards the altar there is a clear indication of the old belief that the aisle and the chancel should be off the straight in order that the demons cast out during the service of baptism should not be able to find their way to the communion table.

If a village clusters round its church, the same could be said for the local hostelry. The Mermaid is said to date from the time when carriages superseded travel on horseback and, as it is a rather substantial building for a village of this size, it could well have served as a staging post, being the accepted 'eleven mile stage' out of Norwich. The distinctive name is derived from the 'Mermaid attiring herself in the sea. proper', the Garney family crest; the family, along with the Richmonds and the Bedingfelds, being the changing owners of our village over the centuries. In the early 18th century, thanks to the clay soil, the gardens surrounding the inn were renowned for their strawberries and their collection of roses.

🍁 HEMPNALL

Hempnall, with a population of about 1,300, is situated ten miles south of Norwich on the B1135. At the time of the Domesday survey it was called Hemenhale – 'homestead in a hollow'.

It has had a chequered history, having been granted a charter to hold fairs and having a gallows and a ducking pond. St Margaret's church suffered a fire and damage by Cromwell's soldiers. It was renovated by the Victorians and now, with the pews removed, is able to be used more freely to serve the village.

Our most famous visitor was John Wesley who walked here from Norwich to preach in 1759. Sam Head, a higgler and innkeeper of dubious repute, was converted and went home to Deopham and turned his pub into a chapel. The WI depicted this visit of John Wesley on the village sign they erected in 1977. The Wesleyan chapel was built in 1895, replacing an earlier building destroyed in the Great Gale earlier in that year.

In 1979, the Queen Mother came to open the Mill Centre for Day Care, a converted windmill, used mainly by disabled and elderly people.

Hempnall village sign

100

There is a modern, well used and equipped village hall, on the playing field, which caters for clubs and sports organisations enjoyed by this busy village. We are fortunate in having a good general shop, a butcher's shop and two public houses. The school is a thriving and happy place and we have amenities which are the envy of many villages. Hempnall is a good place to live!

🍁 HEMPTON

Hempton lies about a mile to the south-west of Fakenham. It consists of a collection of Victorian cottages and post-war housing. Its main feature now is its enormous green, a favourite dog-walking place; it is the home of many rabbits and skylarks, one or two pheasants when the season is over, and a barn-owl beating its way over in the twilight.

It is hard for the passer-by to believe that this large empty space was once the site of one of the most populous and popular sheep fairs in England. In the 13th century King John granted to the canons of Hempton Priory three fairs to be held annually. The sheep fair was on the first Wednesday in September, and it is recorded that in 1848 between 5,000 and 6,000 sheep were penned. The last sheep fair was held in September 1969, when 1,026 sheep were offered for sale. The cattle fairs were held on Whit Tuesday and in November. The cattle were enclosed on what is now known as the Bullock Hills – an emerging oak wood. Here were sold steers walked from Scotland, known on their journey as 'Hemps' because of their destination. Local farmers would buy them, feed them up, and send them on with drovers to the London markets. At the November fair, horses were sold.

Behind a row of cottages on the eastern side of the village lies the site of Abbey Farm and before that of Hempton Priory. In the reign of Henry I a hospital was built for travellers which soon developed into an Augustinian priory dedicated to St Stephen. Because it stood at the head of a causeway across marshy ground beside the river Wensum, all goods coming from the south had to pass the priory and could be confiscated from time to time. The prior became a very powerful man and was lord of the manor at the time of the dissolution.

Before the coming of the Normans a church dedicated to St Andrew, thought to be Saxon, stood in what is now known as Church Meadow. It is mentioned in Domesday as having an acre of land, but by 1623 it was in ruins. WI members and their families collected flints from the site which were then built into the base of the village sign which they presented in 1974.

The Domesday Book records that there were four freemen farming about 60 acres between them. The lord of the manor at that time was William, Earl of Warren, who had married William I's step-daughter Gundreda. The present lord of the manor is the Marquess of Townshend, whose Victorian forbear gave the land upon which Holy Trinity church and its vicarage were built in 1856. There was a National school in the church room from 1858 to 1874.

In living memory Hempton has had a pork butcher, a village shop and post office, a busy blacksmith, a brickyard, a windmill, a watermill, an inn and two pubs. Of these just the Bell remains. There was also the village laundress who dried her linen on the green and bleached it on the whin bushes.

🍁 Hemsby

Hemsby is a coastal village, settled and named by Danish invaders. The village lies in the East Flegg Hundred, which comprised 24 parishes.

The people living in the village have generally been concerned with farming and fishing. Many a boy leaving school would go fishing in the herring season and work on the farms during the rest of the year. Those who were away in Yarmouth market on Saturday selling their produce could leave their pies and puddings at the bake office in School Loke on Fridays. These would be put in shelves on either side of the massive chimney holes and there they would be slowly cooked so that the people could have hot food on Sunday. The charge for this service was about a halfpenny to twopence per container.

There are several old houses in the village still in occupation, very much renovated and altered but still very interesting to look at. Perhaps one of the most interesting is 'Homestalls', which was occupied by the Beech family for 162 years until the death of the last local member, named George, who was a truly memorable 'character' to be seen about the village.

Hemsby continued in its own rural lifestyle, the seasons dictating not only the work of the men but the games and pastimes of the community, until after the Second World War, when the earlier 20th century trickle of camping holidaymakers became a flood of people coming to the holiday camps which proliferated all over the country. Suddenly in a very few years it seemed that the whole nature of the village changed. But Hemsby has always maintained its 'heartland' and the centre of the village is still the hub of village news gathering and giving; people still find enjoyment in local things.

🍁 HEYDON

Heydon is a small village set amidst farmland and woods about twelve miles north of Norwich. The main part of the village clusters around a green. The church of St Peter and St Paul stands guard to the north of the green beside the park gates which are the main entrance to Heydon Hall.

Overlooking the green is the Earle Arms, a picturesque whitewashed village pub. Visitors flock here from far afield on a sunny Sunday to have their pints and crisps sitting on the green. The village shop also faces the green. The village blacksmith attends his forge most days, his main work being shoeing horses. A life size model of a horse which Mr Barber has created from old horseshoes stands proudly outside.

The population of Heydon is about 200 and, as well as farming, people are engaged in widely differing occupations. The farming is mixed but mostly arable. Mr Aves of Dairy Farm used to raise the most succulent of turkeys for local Christmas dinners.

Crofton Hall farmhouse, now a private residence, used to be a guest house. One of the highlights of their Christmas programme was to have the village carol singers visit them on Christmas Eve. Carols are sung all around the village and the outlying farms and cottages, and money collected for charity. Several families offer drinks and mince pies so a very convivial evening is enjoyed. A big barn at Crofton Hall has been converted into a cabinet making and joinery workshop. Wood grown on Heydon estate has been used in some of their products.

The serenity and beauty of the village have great appeal to film-makers and TV cameras, over 30 productions having been partly filmed here.

🍁 HICKLING

Historically, the village of Hickling is a collection of small settlements forming an ecclesiastical parish situated between the lowland heathlands of north-east

103

Norfolk and the marshlands bordering the North Sea. Most of the older village houses are near the north-west corner of Hickling Broad, a large expanse of reed-fringed shallow water over a mile long.

The Broad was formed by the flooding of medieval peat diggings, the source of fuel supplies for the many religious houses surrounding Norwich. The area is now a nature reserve of international importance administered by the Norfolk Naturalists Trust. It is a haven for birds migrating between Africa and the Arctic, and rarities such as the swallowtail butterfly and the Norfolk hawker dragonfly still survive and breed here. The Broads Authority was created in order to conserve the unique character of the Broads, in danger of being lost owing to environmental and population pressures. Earlier the nucleus of the nature reserve, based on the Whiteslea Lodge Estate, was a world-famous wildfowl shoot to which both kings and cabinet ministers came for sport. The area is also renowned for the quality of its fishing. The world record weight for a pike has been held for many years by a locally-landed fish.

Hickling Broad is also well known for good sailing, windsurfing, canoeing and other water sports which attract visitors from far and wide. In the holiday season the population doubles from 1,000 to 2,000. Artists are also attracted by the clarity of the light and diversity of subjects, and Hickling has in the past been home to several internationally known wildlife painters.

Despite its remoteness Hickling was bombed in both world wars. Damage and injury were, fortunately, minimal, and the events accepted stoically by a local population used to the hard life of those gleaning a living from the marshes and farmland. An important local crop is reed, in demand worldwide as a roofing material due to its excellent quality.

In 1185 the de Valoins family financed the construction of Hickling Priory by the Augustinians. Little trace of the priory survives today, but parts of the outer walls can be seen incorporated in the buildings of a farm. The Augustinian canons started to build a new parish church, St Mary's, in the 13th century. In 1875 many of the original features were removed during a Victorian restoration, resulting in the present austere interior. The church tower is visible for miles across the marshes and dunes bordering the sea.

Gone are the fairs connected with King John's charter of 1204 and the other festivities that were held in the aisles on feast days. However, a restoration of the bell tower and rehanging of the peal of bells (the tenor weighs 20 tons and was cast in Norwich in the 15th century) has given people a new place to meet as well as to worship. Who can resist the call of those ancient bells across the marshes on a still winter's night?

HIGH KELLING

Situated in north Norfolk, two miles from the delightful old market town of Holt and four miles from Sheringham on the coast, High Kelling came into being about 100 years ago, although at that time it was not known as such and was merely a large rural area of the village of Kelling, boasting only two pairs of houses.

In 1901 Bramblewood Sanatorium was built, then Kelling Hospital in 1903 – both for tuberculosis patients, the pinewoods and proximity to the sea being particularly beneficial to the sufferers and the remoteness of the area ideal because of the degree of infection of the disease, then rife in this country. Some 20 years later, Pineheath Hospital was built for child victims of the malady. The other building existing at the beginning of the century was Home Place, later known as Thornfield Hall, a magnificent private residence with distinctive 'butterfly' wings, one of only three such buildings still surviving in Norfolk.

In 1916, a group of people purchased land here with a view to forming a self-supporting community, and became known as the Co-operative and Land Crafts Guild. They at first lived in tents, and later in wooden huts. However, the venture seems to have faded out.

A chapel was built in 1924 for the use of the patients and staff of Bramblewood Sanatorium and Pineheath Hospital, with lovely Japanese-style gardens. Queen Mary visited the area in 1934, and some delightful photographs of the event exist. In 1955 the sanatorium was closed, tuberculosis by then being virtually eliminated from this country. Pineheath became a geriatric hospital, and Kelling a general hospital. Over the years, bungalows and some houses were built, until at the present time there are about 200 homes, although apart from some infilling which has taken place, no further expansion is envisaged.

The chapel was offered to High Kelling residents, who purchased it for £500, the first service being held in November 1955 by the rector of Holt. Now smart blue upholstered 'pews' replace the wooden chairs, and All Saints' church, in its lovely woodland setting, has its regular congregation. The hospital staff, who had looked after the gardens, found the Japanese gardens too difficult to maintain and in 1966 these were replaced by shrubs and grass.

A post office and shop was established at Bullens' Corner. It was known to exist in the 1920s, and continued under a number of owners until approximately 1954. When this business closed, the post office was transferred to the hospital shop at the entrance of Kelling Hospital, which was originally managed for the benefit of hospital and visitors, selling chocolates, sweets and teas. The tenancy has continued since then under private management.

Having acquired a church and conscious of the fact there was no village hall to serve the community, these hard-working people raised money from whist drives in their homes, coffee mornings, fetes and many other fund-raising activities, bought a piece of land, and then designed and built an attractive hall. All work, with the exception of the roof, was carried out voluntarily by the residents, many of them retired. In 1969 the hall was completed and now a great variety of activities are carried on.

Having, like Topsy, 'just growed', High Kelling is not in the true sense of the word a village. There are no through roads, and the largest part is situated to one side of the A148, so apart from a few visible bungalows on one side of the road, and the High Kelling signs, the unsuspecting traveller drives along the A148 from Holt to Sheringham, scarcely aware of its existence. Part of the area lay in the parish of Holt, part in Bodham and part in Kelling, but after many years of campaigning, High Kelling proudly became a political parish within one boundary in 1987, while remaining in the ecclesiastical parish of Holt.

🍁 HILGAY

Hilgay, situated on the banks of the river Wissey south of Downham Market, has a population of approximately 800. It is a lively village with three shops and several thriving businesses, and it is surrounded by rich arable farms. The river Wissey, once used for barges carrying cargoes from King's Lynn to Stoke Ferry, is now popular for holiday sailing.

The primary school is set on the lovely playing field in the centre of the village, and there are now over 60 children on the books.

All Saints' church is approached by a beautiful long avenue of holly hedge and mature lime trees. The rector and parishioners are presently raising money for the roof restoration fund. Many social activities take place in the village, and an active village hall committee holds monthly auctions for funds. The well known Hilgay Silver Band, with a 100 year tradition, has a thriving youth section, who have recently won several awards in national competitions.

The Wood Hall estate was at one time the home of Captain George William Manby, born 1765, who developed his idea of a mortar and rocket apparatus for throwing a line from shore to ship, which has been instrumental in saving many lives.

There is one public house today, the Rose and Crown, where once there were six in the village. Many new houses have been built in recent years, including a warden-controlled grouped home for the elderly, Willow Lodge. Before 1920, the village was self-sufficient and people all worked locally but now, with the ease of travel, people work farther afield in King's Lynn, Cambridge etc, and prefer to do so in order to live in this pleasant and friendly place.

HINDRINGHAM

Hindringham, situated in the hinterland of the north Norfolk coast, is a very ancient village. From its high land a blue ribbon of sea may be glimpsed four miles away at Stiffkey. Seven miles by road will lead you to Holt, or Fakenham, or Wells-next-the-Sea. The older houses are mostly built in brick and flint and are pleasantly arranged within the village's five ancient manors. The main street now runs from north to south between Binham and Thursford, but in earlier days all roads crossed from east to west following both the stretch of Roman road now a farm track and the valley of the little river. Much evidence has been discovered of continuous settlement since the Bronze Age. One of the very first written records in East Anglia is a mention of Hindringham in the will of a Saxon bishop of North Elmham. The largest manor in the village was that of the Dean and Chapter of Norwich and rents from the village helped to pay for the Cellarer's expenses.

The church dedicated to St Martin has a very high tower and stands on a rise in the centre of the village. There is no record of the building of this church but the first priest, John of Dudlyngton, was instituted in 1301 by the patrons, the Prior and Convent of Norwich. Foundations of an earlier church lie in the adjoining churchyard. The lofty tower arch and windows date from the 15th century.

107

South of the church on the corner of Blacksmith's Lane and Pound Hill was a walled triangle of land which formed the village pound, where straying animals were held. Across the main street on another corner with Emm's Lane were two almshouses for widows and a small wood of willow trees known as the Osier Carr, used for basket making. This area was purchased in August 1910 and the church institute, later to become the village hall, was built; the willow wood is now a car park.

Very little changed in the village until the mid 20th century. Families who had farmed in the village since the time of Elizabeth I continued to live on the same farms. Many names such as Spooner, Lake, Daplyn and Long appeared over and over again in the village records. The village was almost completely self sufficient. A list of occupations taken from the census returns shows a high proportion of the male population working on the land, often as many as 20 men on one farm. Apart from farmers and stewards there were shepherds, horsemen, stockmen, thatchers, poultrymen, and the inevitable 'back'us boys'. There were for most of the century two windmills, both brick towers. Most trades were represented – blacksmiths, bricklayers, carpenters, wheelwrights, shoemakers and a tailor. There was a cordwainer and saddler, even a razor grinder. Many of the girls were servants but also mentioned are two governesses, milliners, dressmakers, also women who worked with their husbands on the land. There were at any time two or three grocer's shops and up to six public houses. Many of the old fields were referred to by names which today hold great charm – Cranes Lane, Crossegrene, Binham Gate, Littlemans Mere.

Since electricity, water and sewerage came to the village in the post-war era, life has changed for its people. Cottages have been modernised and in many cases two or three have been turned into one residence. Agriculture has changed and now there are very few people employed on the land. Many houses are also let as holiday homes, and while this preserves the fabric of the village there is a risk of it turning into a museum piece. It will be interesting to see how the old and new villages blend together in the coming years. Hindringham WI's gift of a fine oak village sign showing the past life of the village, with church, windmill and old Norman chest, was carved by a newcomer to the village.

🍁 HINGHAM

Hingham is an ancient settlement. As early as AD 925 it is recorded as the property of King Athelstan, grandson of Alfred the Great, and it retained many of the privileges resulting from its royal ownership until the beginning of the 18th century, with several charters (1414, 1610 and 1703) affirming them. Clear indication of its former riches is provided by the grandeur of its 14th century parish church of St Andrew, which towers over the Market Place and is a clear landmark for miles around.

Hingham rejoices in having a daughter town in Hingham, Massachusetts. This name was given in 1635 to a settlement founded by Puritan emigrants from Norfolk at Bare Cove on Massachusetts Bay, a few miles south of the present city of Boston. This emigration to the New World of nearly 200 men, women and children from Hingham between 1633 and 1643 is commemorated on the village sign which adorns the green in the Market Place. The sign was designed and executed by Harry Carter of Swaffham in the coronation year of the present Queen and, having suffered the ravages of time, was replaced by a locally-made replica in May 1989.

Among the first emigrants from Hingham were members of the Lincoln family, who owned land in Hingham and Swanton Morley and have many entries in the Hingham parish register. Samuel Lincoln (the direct ancestor of Abraham Lincoln, the famous 16th President of the United States) was baptised in Hingham church. This proud connection for Hingham, which brings many visitors from across the Atlantic, explains why the village hall is named the Lincoln Hall, and why the bust of Abraham Lincoln takes pride of place in the north aisle of the church.

On the eastern side of the market place is one of the finest groups of Georgian buildings in Norfolk. Here is the Admiral's House, probably named after Admiral Sir Philip Wodehouse, who lived in Hingham in the early 19th century, and the great Beaconsfield House, on the corner of Norwich Road.

At right angles to these houses, just behind the north side of the green is Southernwood, a 17th century house which was for 20 years the home of Field Marshal Edmund Lord Ironside until his death in 1959. He was commander of the expedition to Archangel in 1918, Chief of the Imperial General Staff at the outbreak of the Second World War and Commander of the Home Defence Forces in 1940. Lord Ironside is commemorated on a tablet in the south aisle of the church, opposite the Lincoln bust, and in the name of the Hingham industrial estate at Ironside Way.

The windmill was built in 1829 and is a listed building, though now only a four-storey stump. It lost its sails and fantail in 1928 or shortly after, but was worked by oil until 1937. It was recorded in 1908 as worked by wind and gas – which was, no doubt, town gas, since Hingham had its own gas works from 1871 until shortly after the First World War. (The gas company failed several years before electricity came to Hingham.) The watermill, on the Deopham road, has been converted to a handsome residence. As a mill it was unusual in not being sited on a river. The millpond is fed by several nearby springs.

🍁 HOCKWOLD-CUM-WILTON

The two places run from one to the other, nestling in the countryside beside the Little Ouse river, between the Brecklands with its forests to the east, and the Fens with extensive waterways and bogs to the west, such contrasting vistas pleasing to the eye from dawn to dusk.

Wilton, with many flint walled cottages, is recorded on the Ordnance Survey map of Roman Britain as a minor settlement with a villa, bath house and other substantial buildings. The actual earthworks of the Roman settlement are in Hockwold, now overlaid by a field system and adjacent to, but separate from, the earthworks of a medieval village now partly abandoned. Unfortunately the fenland 'Cut Off Channel' was dug right through the area in 1962, and much of what is left now has a protection order placed upon it.

St James' church, Wilton dates from the 14th and 15th centuries. From its old oak roof, lovely rafters look down on the cream-washed nave and chancel, full of light. The chief charm of the church is in its woodwork, from the roof down to the oak chest.

A monument on the north wall is in memory of Canon Hutt and his wife Mary, a much loved and respected parson of the village in the late 1800s. His wife was devoted to the welfare of the villagers. The churchyard is covered in springtime with the snow-white blooms of the snowdrops planted by her and the village children in the early years of 1900. The descendants of the family still live in the village.

A slender cross stands on the village green, known as Cross-Hill. Little is known about it, but it is believed to have been erected in the village as a symbol of a religious meeting place, from which the name Hockwold originated, meaning a religious meeting point in a wood. A crown, not a cross, is visible at the top, the cross having been knocked off when Cromwell's men raided the village in the 17th century.

A red flowering horse-chestnut tree grows in the centre of the green, planted by the villagers to commemorate the Jubilee of King George V and Queen Mary. Nearby is the Red Lion public house with its outbuildings, at that time housing the village blacksmith's shop, although long since gone, the landlord having been the last of the village blacksmiths.

Before the First World War horse breeding was a great business and of course during the war it boomed. Large farm houses and outbuildings with paddocks formed much of the village structure, with farm workers' cottages in the village's two streets and several lanes. Just one street farm remains, other farm houses and rows of cottages converted into modern houses are all residential, the paddocks and pastures being infilled with new houses and bungalows.

There is a marked dividing line for Wilton and Hockwold, a square stone block which has engraved upon it a set of ram's horns. Close by stands the village club, affiliated to the working men's club. Here there is a cricket pitch and bowling green, and on the edge of this is the village sign. A gift to the parishioners through public subscription in 1973–4, made of oak and carved by Mr Harry Carter, the plinth is built of local flints in which an original Wilton brick is embedded. A brick kiln existed in the 1800s.

There are many interesting aspects of the past incorporated in this sign. A scenery landscape of the church of St James and its rare 14th century spire belongs to Wilton. On the right is the now redundant church of St Peter, Hockwold. The stream depicts the Little Ouse, which is the southern boundary of the parishes and the county. In the foreground are carvings of a hare, greyhounds and their handler, to recall the activities of the widely known Hockwold Coursing Club (1920–1939). Below the name plate are three devices. Loaves of bread denote an early charity when six loaves were provided weekly for six poor Protestants. Three beehives recall the 17 mentioned in the Domesday Book and the acorns represent the 'pannage for 200 hogs and 30 goats'. Finally the chequerboard pattern symbolises the arms of the Earl de Warrenne (1086) who held much land in the area.

Hockwold's church of St Peter keeps company with the Elizabethan Hockwold Hall by the wayside. The house has walls of mellowed brick, gables and clustered chimneys. The church is 14th century, with a great array of old windows.

Today the village has many American residents from the surrounding USAF bases. Houses replace the pastures, sadly the pubs and shops are gradually closing. Yet a great community spirit exists from young to old.

🍁 HOLKHAM

The tiny village of Holkham, on the A149 in north Norfolk between Burnham Overy Staithe and Wells, now part of the Holkham estate of the Earls of Leicester, has a history that pre-dates the estate by more than a thousand years. Here lived Anna, described as King of the Angles, whose four daughters were all claimed to be saints. The church of St Withburga, named after one of the daughters who died in AD 743, was restored in the 1870s by Juliana, Countess of Leicester.

Thomas William Coke commenced to build the great Palladian Holkham Hall in the 1730s, in a park enclosed by eight miles of wall. It was inherited by his great nephew, Thomas William Roberts, who took the family name and became famous as the great agriculturalist, Coke of Norfolk. In 1837, towards the end of his life, he was created Earl of Leicester.

The dunes of the coastal area to the north of the main road, known as the Holkham Meals, in the mid 19th century were planted with Corsica pines to stabilise them, and to enable the land behind them to be reclaimed from the sea. There is a prehistoric fort on these marshes, thought to have been used by the Iceni. Opposite the hotel at the main entrance to the park is Lady Anne's Walk, leading to a splendid walk along the beach to Wells.

Towards the end of the 18th century large scale rebuilding of 20 of the estate farmhouses was begun, with the services of the famous architect Samuel Wyatt. The Home Farm, with Wyatt's huge barn, was the setting for the well known Holkham sheep shearings that attracted crowds of visitors, many of whom came to see for themselves the methods that were making the estate famous.

🍁 HONINGHAM

Honingham is a small village eight miles to the west of Norwich, now sleepily bypassed by the A47. Nestling across the banks of the river Tud, it possesses one main street. At the Norwich end stands the village sign erected to commemorate the Silver Jubilee of Queen Elizabeth II in June 1977. This wrought iron sign was made by the village blacksmith and set in a base of Victorian brick and flint, taken from old farm buildings in the village.

As you look down the street from the sign the Old Mill House stands on your left, the old water mill now sadly removed. One or two newer houses only add to the character of the village with its lovely cottage gardens. Over the bridge to the left stand four cottages, these are dated 1853 and 1854 and were built as estate workers' homes. On the right stands the small wooden chapel dedicated to St Paul. You are now in the heart of Honingham. The Buck Inn stands on your left, still outwardly the old coaching inn that it was over 200 years ago, even if it now sports coloured lights. Opposite the pub stands a blacksmith's forge, no longer shoeing horses but producing farm implements.

A shady oak planted in 1897 for the Diamond Jubilee of Queen Victoria stands as a backdrop for the war memorial to the dead of the First World War, placed in memory of 'Curly', namely Headworth Ailwyn, eldest son of Lord Ailwyn the then occupier of Honingham Hall, now demolished. Several 17th century cottages stand around this triangle and to one side the village pump, built to commemorate the Coronation of Edward VII and Queen Alexandra in August 1902. This was the main village water supply until June 1964. Under the pump canopy is the village notice board placed to commemorate the Coronation of Elizabeth II in 1953.

On the high ground stands the new village hall built by the villagers with help from the local builder and his men. This was opened by the last Lord Ailwyn on the 18th June 1983. Below the hall is the bowling green and the children's playground, in front of which stands one of the three original gatehouses to Honingham Hall, dated 1901. Just past the gatehouse in what was originally the Hall drive stands Red House. This is of Tudor structure and was originally used as a dower house for the Hall.

Honingham church is not in the village but stands some half a mile away on the Norwich side. Dedicated to St Andrew, the church is kept locked. The earliest monument in the church is dated 1663 and the earliest stone in the

113

graveyard is dated 1700. There is a 'scratch dial' situated centre left of the top portion of the buttress nearest to the church porch. This buttress has obviously been rebuilt at some time and the stones replaced in a different position as the 'scratch dial' is upside down!

❧ HORNING

From boats to buildings, from fishermen to folk – so Horning has evolved in the last 70 years and encapsulates, in its village life, the growth and changes that have taken place on the Broads. The boat building sheds in the village street have given way to a row of smart town houses. Traditional cottages remain but old and new often serve as holiday homes . . . what lovelier situation in Norfolk than 'the high ground between the two rivers'. And the maltsters and the peat diggers of the past are almost forgotten!

At the turn of the 20th century, until 1911, peat digging was still in its prime. Peat was still used locally for heating and cooking, and Horning residents were allowed to cut 3,000 turfs a year for each cottage, inn and house.

The school plays an active part in village life and celebrated its centenary in 1972. In 1901, the school's new lease had been signed, which specified that the vicar had the right to teach Religious Instruction twice a week.

In 1937, alterations to the Ferry Inn revealed a 'monk's window' in the 13th century gable; it was also discovered that the annual rent for the property, from St Benet's Abbey, was seven shillings and two fat ewes! The association with St Benet's Abbey is celebrated, notably, on the first Sunday in August, when a wherry carries the Bishop of Norwich to take the service there. The Vicar of Horning is still legally Prior of the Abbey, and Horning church, built in 1206, is worthy of a visit.

Today, people come in their hundreds to Horning, particularly for a river trip on the *Southern Comfort*; sailing is a great attraction with the regatta fete as one of the highlights of the village year, the first regatta having been held in 1903. And fishermen must not be overlooked, as many find refuge in the quiet backwaters. Apart from the river, the village has a charm of its own (although the cows are no longer driven along the street for milking!) and has twice been nominated as the Best Kept Village of the Year. In summer, the tourists take over but, as the season draws to a close, the discerning visitor will enjoy the peace and quietude which time has laid upon this little village.

As well as welcoming tourists, Horning cares for its own folk. A boisterous playgroup cares for the under fives, while there are a variety of pursuits including bowls, horticulture and flower arranging. The active church and the grouped homes for the elderly are a living testament to a caring and concerned community. However, whether crossing the village street or perambulating on the village green, ducks still take precedence over people and cars. Oh yes, Horning has its priorities right!

🍁 HORSEY

Horsey is a lovely unspoilt village, situated on the coast of Norfolk ten miles to the north of Great Yarmouth. The parish of Horsey covers an area of 1,800 acres and has a population of approximately 100 people. This figure has remained about the same for hundreds of years and is unlikely to change, as the village now belongs to the National Trust.

There are no shops or public transport, just a public house – the Nelson Head – a post box and telephone for modern facilities! Horsey has a beautiful Anglo-Saxon church, All Saints, which is thatched and has an unusual round tower. There is also a Methodist chapel built in 1958, both places of worship maintaining regular services.

Horsey is probably best known for Horsey Mill, now a famous landmark and popular attraction for visitors. The mill was rebuilt in 1912 and was a water pump for draining the land. It was a working windmill until 1940 when the sails were struck by lightning. Horsey Mere, a beautiful part of the Norfolk Broads, is enjoyed every year by holidaymakers for both fishing and sailing. The mere is surrounded by reed beds which are used for thatching; a number of houses in Horsey are thatched. Reed cutting and farming are Horsey's only industries. The area surrounding the mere is a nature reserve.

Horsey has a lovely unspoilt sandy beach, and walks to the beach, on clearly marked footpaths over the marshes, are most appealing. There is also a large attractive playing field on which Horsey Fete, a most popular annual event, is held.

During the floods of 1938, thousands of acres of land were inundated, with only a hundred acres of Horsey remaining above the water level. Fortunately no one was drowned. However, the effects of the flood were felt for many

The Staithe, Horsey

years. It was four months before the land was drained and seemed back to normal, but it was over five years before the land could be farmed due to the damaging effect of the salt water. The salt water entering the mere was responsible for killing all the fresh water fish and plants. New sea defences were completed at Horsey in 1988.

Legend has it that this part of Norfolk was known as Devil's Country, due to its open wildness. However, Thomas Brograve of Waxham reclaimed part of this 'wild land' to farmland, and built Brograve Mill between Horsey and Waxham. The Devil, angry at this, attempted to blow it down. Although he was unsuccessful, the mill leans to one side, showing signs of the battle!

Finally, Horsey Mere's own legend is that on the night of 13th June the wailing of small children can be heard from the mere. The children are said to have been drowned in the mere many, many years ago on that day.

🍁 HORSFORD

Horsford is now an urban village situated on the B1149 Norwich to Holt road. The lords of the manor of Horsford go back to the time of the Norman Conquest, although they were non-resident until the mid 1800s when Sir Thomas Barrett Lennard, acquired a small farmhouse and converted it into the present manor. He lived there until his death and his nephew, Sir Richard Barrett Lennard, resided there until 1971 when he moved away and the manor was sold, the estate remaining in the Barrett Lennard family.

The church of All Saints dates back to the 14th century and has two lovely stained glass windows, one of which is a memorial to three sisters, Edith, Dorothea and Nona Day, who died of consumption in the 1890s and whose family lived at Horsford Hall for many years and were great benefactors of the village at that time. The Methodist chapel built in the mid 1800s has been extended, and the old school, built in the mid 1800s by Rev Ballance and now the primary school, has retained its character.

The small river Hor, which starts as a spring in the churchyard of the nearby village of Felthorpe, meanders through the village, crossing The Street on its way across country to join the river Bure. The beck as it is called has been the happy playground for many children over the years. Until water was piped to the village in the 1950s residents living in The Street regularly used water from the beck for washing purposes. Farmers also used to fill their water carts from it for their cattle.

117

To the east of the village are the Castle Hills reputed to be the site of an old motte and bailey. There is also supposed to be an underground passage from there to St Faith's Priory. There are several public footpaths in and around the village, some of which take one through the many woods that surround the village.

The village sign was made by the late Mr Carter of Swaffham and was presented to the village by Horsford Afternoon Wl in 1978 on the occasion of their 50th birthday. It depicts the manor, the church window dedicated to the Day sisters and the river Hor.

Until the Second World War, Horsford was a quiet little village but after hostilities ceased in 1945 development began to take place and has continued steadily to the present time. This has completely altered the character of village life as we knew it years ago.

🍁 HORSHAM ST FAITH

Horsham St Faith lies to the north of Norwich on the A140 road to Cromer. An ancient village, it was named Horsham by the Saxons after the Hor stream which runs through the village. The 'St Faith' was added by Robert Fitzwilliam, Lord of the Manor, when in the 12th century he founded the Benedictine Priory dedicated to St Faith.

The Domesday Book recorded two water mills, and later the stream became a source of osiers for basket making. The Flemish weavers brought their skills to the village and by the end of the 19th century most cottages had their own horsehair loom. Items produced included uniforms and upholstery.

The King's Head, dating back to 1614, catered for drovers from as far away as Scotland who brought their cattle to be sold at the St Faith's Fair, which continued until 1872. The Black Swan, which is the only other surviving inn of Horsham's original six, is said to have been patronised by King Charles II.

The priory church was totally destroyed in the Dissolution of the Monasteries. The parish church, which was built beside the priory church, was founded in the 13th century on a possible Saxon site. Although extensively restored in 1874, it retains a 16th century painted screen and pulpit.

The Twining family, well known for their tea, have been eminent benefactors to the village. They founded the local school, which was opened in 1853, to commemorate Richard Twining's 80th birthday.

🍁 HORSTEAD

Horstead is about seven miles north of Norwich, on the North Walsham road, and divided from Coltishall by the bridge over the river Bure. Down the hill past a line of bungalows and houses on either side of the road from Norwich, the first landmark is the old coaching inn, the Recruiting Sergeant, at a crossroad. A left turn here is the road to Aylsham: follow it uphill, passing more bungalows and houses, to the beautiful old church of All Saints, with its tithe barn, used for many local functions, and the enormous 18th century rectory which is a very busy conference house. A walk through the churchyard leads to a piece of common land with river access and a clearly laid footpath.

Back to the Horstead crossroads and the 'Sergeant', a right turn at the war memorial leads to Horstead Mill. The mill, once a working mill producing flour for local bakeries, was burnt down one night in 1963, and is now a crumbling ruin with very little left of the original buildings. Water from the dammed up river still rushes and tumbles through the ruined arches. The surrounding trees and wild plants make a framework for this place of beauty, and a wooden bench is an invitation to sit and watch the swirling water: this is a very popular place, especially with fishermen. The Parish Council has recently purchased the old mill site, with a lottery grant, and will be opening it for use as a public amenity in the millennium year.

Behind the mill a towpath leads along the river bank, to the bridge. On the opposite bank, where cattle graze in the water meadows, the remains of the old lock can just be seen. The lock-keeper's cottage is no longer there. One hundred years ago or more, this part of the river Bure would have been very busy with wherries queueing at the lock, then slowly quanting their way through to sail up river to Aylsham or down river to Yarmouth, heavily laden with farm produce, corn, timber, chalk, marl, and local brewed beer. Now, the lock is the end of navigation for boats coming upstream from Coltishall.

A good walk in Horstead is to continue along the road, beyond the mill, and up the hill. Pause to look over the old ivy-covered wall on the left, for below is the mill-stream and some enormously tall trees with massive trunks, in the grounds of Horstead House. In the spring there are great drifts of snowdrops and aconites. The walk continues up the hill, past the Lodge house. Take the footpath to the left, with distant views of the river at Coltishall, this leads through bluebell woods to Heggats, where there is an old part-Tudor Hall.

119

Some of this area has been known for years as 'Little Switzerland', because of the deep ravines made by the old marl diggings.

Back on the B1150 at the 'Sergeant', with water meadows to the right, and red brick cottages and villas on the left, a plaque on the wall of the first cottage records the water mark where in 1912, after two days of torrential rain, the river Bure burst its banks. The bridge was washed away and flood water rushed into several houses in Horstead and Coltishall. The bridge was rebuilt by 1913, and it is this bridge over the river that marks the boundary between Horstead and Coltishall.

HOUGHTON

Thirteen miles from King's Lynn, on the A148, a turning to the left leads through an avenue of lime trees to a street of white houses. A note in the parish register on 4th July 1729 reads: 'The foundation dug for the first houses of the new Town'.

Originally houses stood round the village church, which stands in the park. However, when Robert Walpole had his grand Palladian hall built (1722–1735) these houses were not a pleasant view for him and they were pulled down, to be replaced by the houses bordering the street. Almshouses, a school and a school house were built in the 1840s. From the road, it is possible to catch sight of some of the white fallow deer that live in the park.

There had been Walpoles in Houghton since Richard de Walpole married Emma de Houghton in the 12th century: their name came from 'the town of Walpole in Mershland in Norfolk'. Houghton Hall was built for Robert Walpole when he was First Minister to George I and George II. Within the park is the late medieval church of St Martin. It is recorded that the tower fell down in August 1727 and was rebuilt soon afterwards. Sir Robert Walpole, his son Robert and his son Horace (the man of letters) are buried in the church.

The Cholmondeley family, who now own the Houghton estate, are descended from Robert Walpole. When Horace Walpole died in 1797, the estate passed through the female line. Robert's daughter Mary had married Viscount Malpas, later the 3rd Earl of Cholmondeley. Their grandson George, the fourth Earl, inherited the estate in 1797 from Horace. He was made a Marquess in 1815. The present owner is the seventh Marquess, David, who is Lord Great Chamberlain to Queen Elizabeth II.

120

Houghton Hall is open to the public on the afternoons of Thursdays, Sundays and Bank Holidays from Easter until the last Sunday in September. Structurally, the Hall is almost as it was built for Sir Robert Walpole (created Earl of Orford on his retirement from government) apart from the stone steps originally at the east and west fronts. These were removed owing to the depredations of the third Earl, who also sold nearly 200 of his grandfather's collection of pictures to Catherine the Great, when she was setting up the Hermitage in Petersburg. The widow of the fifth Marquess had the steps on the west front reconstructed, to their original design, in 1973 as a memorial to her husband. Today, the sixth Marquess's exceptional collection of over 20,000 model soldiers is displayed at Houghton. The original walled garden has been recreated to feature an area devoted to fruit and vegetables, a herbaceous border and a formal rose garden with over 150 varieties.

🍁 HOVETON

The boundary of the two villages of Hoveton and Wroxham meets in the middle of Wroxham Bridge spanning the river Bure. The single track medieval bridge is protected by an unattractive, double track, umbrella type, Bailey bridge, to accommodate the forty-ton vehicles now allowed on our roads. The persistent use of the name Wroxham to cover both villages came about when, in the late 1880s, the Norwich to Cromer railway line was being laid. The station planned for Wroxham was moved about a mile up-line towards Cromer, to its present site, and the decision made to use the already prepared station name-plates – Wroxham.

The Broads holiday trade also began about this time, at Loynes boatyard on the Wroxham river bank beside the bridge, which then encouraged the two brothers Arnold and Alfred Roy to start selling fruit to holidaymakers on the Hoveton side of the bridge. As the holiday trade grew, so did the trade of the Roy brothers, until their business was advertised and promoted as 'The Biggest Village Store in the World', carrying a tremendous variety of stock, and serving a large area of north Norfolk with their fleet of horse-drawn delivery carts, and providing pre-ordered provisions waiting for the holidaymakers on board their boats when they arrived.

During the Second World War the boatyards directed their skills to building for the Navy, such as Motor Torpedo Boats. Post war, the yards boomed into a busy thriving holiday business, until the late 1970s, when a slump occurred due to the cheap charter flight holidays abroad. This put a number of yards out of business, and allowed the developers to get 'a foot in the door' to produce blocks of holiday houses and flats in place of the big boat sheds, completely changing the waterside skyline.

Hoveton has two Anglican churches, both small, simple, peaceful, country churches, and a small, attractive Catholic church. St John's has a 13th century priest's door, and was completely restored by the Blofeld House estate in 1640, the square brick tower being added to the flint church at a later date. The little gem of St Peter's was built in 1624, and replaced a previous church. Catholic St Helen's was built in 1959, on a one acre site amongst many lovely and varied trees planted by the late Mr Bullard of the old Norfolk Bullards Brewery.

There are two schools in the village, Broadland High, built in 1958, which opens its heated indoor swimming pool to the public on Saturdays and during school holidays, and St John's Primary built in 1972 to replace the old village school in the original village of Hoveton, now referred to as the Black Horse area (due to the pub there of that name). The old school was built by the Blofeld family in the 17th century.

The Blofeld estate covers most of the riverside area between St John's church and Crabbetts Marsh (on the boundary with Horning) and includes Hoveton Great and Hoveton Little (or Black Horse) Broads, the latter only open to water-borne public. There is a Nature Trail, run by the Nature Conservancy Council; again, open to water-borne public only on the Great Broad during the summer months. In 1948 Mr T. R. C. Blofeld of Hoveton House gave the parish five acres of land for a playing field and site for a village hall. The WI had approached the Parish Council in 1944 to ask for a hall, and this was finally built and ready to be opened on Coronation Day (2nd June 1953).

Today, besides the large shopping centre, Hoveton has ten boatyards, two industrial estates, a craft centre, a miniature railway, three hotels, and one pub. Now that the proposed Wroxham/Hoveton bypass has been wiped off the map, the village continues to struggle to cope with the influx of several thousand vehicles a day, which causes endless traffic and parking problems.

🍁 HOWE

Howe is situated in south Norfolk, between Brooke and Poringland. Since the Domesday record it has never had more than 100 residents, and there are about 50 on the present electoral roll. It is a small, pleasant village comprising 20 dwellings, seven of which overlook the large green. There are four lovely thatched cottages and three properties converted from farm buildings. The old rectory, which is privately owned, is behind the church. St Mary's is a round-towered church. The nave and tower are dated about AD 900–950, and the chancel was probably added in the 14th century.

The road to Brooke from the green goes through the farmyard belonging to Howe Hall.There is an old red telephone box on the green and a Victorian post box in the wall surrounding the churchyard. A pit on the green shows where the Romans dug sand for the potteries and building works at Caistor St Edmund. The track used by the pack-horses can still be seen. Another pit in a nearby field, the 'Devil's Pit', was the site of a Roman glassworks.

There are three natural ponds around the green, two of which are in private gardens, and two more ponds beyond the church. Being surrounded by woods and open fields and having these ponds, we are visited by a large variety of birds. The banks are liberally sprinkled with primroses in the spring. There are several places where cowslips and later wild orchids may be found, as well as lots of other wild flowers.

The Sewell family, relatives of Anna Sewell, author of *Black Beauty*, were notable residents in the early 19th century. The village has a Sewells Lane and a Sewells House.

🍁 INGOLDISTHORPE

Ingoldisthorpe is a small village which, until recent times, was on the main road from King's Lynn to Hunstanton and suffered many traffic problems as a result. Since a new bypass was built a few years ago much of this traffic has gone which has been a great improvement for all the village.

The village has a long history and excavations along the site of the new road uncovered a number of interesting finds including a complete skeleton of Roman times. Axe-heads and other signs of ancient occupation have been

Church of St Michael and All Angels at Ingoldisthorpe

found in the area but the name of the village may have come from Saxon times; the lord of the village about AD 850 was called Ingulf. Ingoldisthorpe is mentioned in the Domesday Book.

Although the passing motorist sees only modern houses along the flat main road, there is a steep little hill rising to the east and there, almost completely hidden amongst tall trees and surrounding houses, stands the church of St Michael and All Angels. There are traces of Norman architecture but most of the building dates from around the 13th century, with the addition of mid 19th century stained glass windows and pews. The village school was also built nearby in Victorian days by the vicar of that time.

There are records from medieval times of a number of families who held lordships in Ingoldisthorpe. Amongst these is the Cremer family, some of whom are buried in the church. In 1666 Sir John Cremer became High Sheriff of Norfolk, which was a great honour for so small a village, one of the smallest on this side of the Wash.

But when in 1968 a carved village sign was put up by the then joint Snettisham and Ingoldisthorpe WI, it was decided that two ladies should be shown on it, one from the 17th century and one from the 19th. Agnes Bigge, the Elizabethan lady, was the daughter of Thomas Rogerson, at one time parson of the church, and wife of 'Thomas Bigge, Gent'. When Agnes died in 1608 she left £5 for the 'reparynge of this church and for a stock for the relief of the poor of this town for ever Ten pounds'. By 1858 the value of this bequest had declined so an area of common land was enclosed to give the allotments and the recreation ground which we have today.

The Victorian lady was Mrs Tylden, who inherited the manor from her brother, Dr James Bellamy, President of St John's College, Oxford. Mrs Tylden died in 1928 at the age of 105 and so is remembered by a good many still living. She is remembered as a benefactress of the poor and was held in great respect, villagers would bow to her carriage as she passed. She entertained Queen Alexandra at the manor and photographs show her as a figure somewhat reminiscent of Queen Victoria. Mrs Tylden was responsible for the building of the church or parish hall which is the meeting place for most village activities.

Ingoldisthorpe did not see as many changes during Mrs Tylden's lifetime as have come since. The manor has gone, burned down after becoming an hotel. Once the village was almost self-supporting with brickyards, coal shipping and numerous other trades and crafts people. Now most people work at Lynn or Hunstanton or have come to enjoy their retirement in a pleasant area.

❧ Intwood-cum-Keswick

These two small villages lie a mile apart, south-west of Norwich, over the river Yare. Both have churches with pre-Norman round towers. For about 400 years they have been one joint parish, and at times before that the manors have been held by the same families, eg the Greshams, and also the Hobarts (Sir Henry Hobart started the building of Blickling Hall). The land is used for farming, mainly arable with marshland grazing near the river, and there is some woodland.

Intwood All Saints' church has been in almost continuous use, though altered and repaired, notably in the 15th century and in 1602 (at the expense of Keswick church) and again in Victorian times. The Hall, originally Tudor, and reputedly haunted by a 'Grey Lady', was rebuilt in Georgian times, and finally the exterior was changed to Victorian brick. Walled gardens from the Tudor days still survive.

The few houses at Intwood are near to the church and Hall, and vary from early thatched dwellings through Victorian brick, to a converted barn and a modern Georgian-style rectory. Most were formerly occupied by estate workers, though no longer so, and the rectory is now let privately, as the parish is one of a group. At the old cottage nearest the church is the second-oldest well in the county, Saxon, and pre-dating the church. It still supplies all Intwood's water, now by electric pump. Below the church is a ford, now covered except in times of flood, the stream being a tributary of the Yare.

Keswick All Saints' church has a more chequered history. In 1602 Sir Henry Hobart, owner of both manors, had it dismantled except for the tower, and materials and furnishings used to refurbish Intwood church. Later the Gurney family, owners of the Keswick estate since the mid 18th century, had it partly rebuilt as a family mortuary chapel. This was smaller, as the ruins of the original chancel show. Since the 1930s it has been used regularly for services, and a small apse was added in 1964 as a sanctuary, incorporating the war memorial.

Keswick has two Halls, the Old Hall being Tudor in origin but altered considerably since. The 'new' Keswick Hall was built by Hudson Gurney, nearby, in 1817, the architect being William Wilkins (designer of the National Gallery in London and Downing College in Cambridge). Later enlarged, it was taken over by the Army in 1940. After the war, Mr Quinton Gurney, Chairman of the College Governors, leased it to Norwich Training College (bombed-out in the city), later known as Keswick Hall College. In 1981 this merged with the University of East Anglia, but by 1986 the site was sold to private developers, and is now a residential and office complex, set in pleasant parkland.

There is a village reading room (1887) now used for meetings and events. The stables of the Old Hall, former farm buildings at the Low Farm and Hall Farm and others including the old estate laundry have been converted to housing. Thatched houses (one the former rectory and one-time gamekeeper's house) and others of varying ages from Victorian to present day, including council houses, make up the remainder of the village, mostly on the higher side of the road, away from the marshes.

Keswick had a water mill on the Yare for many years. The present weather-boarded and pantiled building, over 200 years old, once had two water wheels but latterly electricity was used. Flour milling was given up earlier, but stock feed was produced until 1976. The mill is now converted to a private house, the mill house and cottages are still lived in, and there is also an old square brick dovecote nearby. Also in that area, chalk has been quarried for agricultural use, and gravel extracted until recently. In times of heavy rainfall, the Environment Agency controls the sluices at the mill, and may allow the marshes to flood temporarily.

KENNINGHALL

A walk down Church Street into Kenninghall Market Place takes you through all that is best about this village; its lively present, its past, its people.

As you enter from the Fersfield direction, you are treading a path once used by kings and queens, dukes and princesses. For Kenninghall Palace, part of which still stands to the west of the village, was once the seat of the Dukes of Norfolk, and was where Mary Tudor learnt that she had become queen.

You pass farms and smallholdings, for the village is still a thriving agricultural community, mainly arable farming, but also intensive pig production and battery units for egg production. There is also a large dairy farm where the cows are seen grazing contentedly in the fields.

Carving in Kenninghall church porch

127

Entering the village itself, you pass terraces of 18th and 19th century cottages. On the south side of Church Street are houses and cottages with long strip-like fields and gardens running down to the beck, the stream which flows through the village and under the Market Place. Fine timber-framed houses, pretty brick cottages and plainer colour-washed terraces whose exteriors hide the sturdy clay lump construction lead on to the Red Lion pub.

Then you see St Mary's parish church, with its tower dominating the village skyline. In the church porch is a carving of a riderless horse, believed to be Saxon. Next to the church is Church Farm, mentioned in the Domesday Book.

The Market Place is the centrepiece and meeting place for the whole village. Surrounding are Turner's Garage, an antiques shop, the village's other pub, the White Horse with its pleasant beer garden, and another general shop and post office. Roads radiate from the Market Place. The Quidenham road takes you past a disused chapel and the new health centre. Another road heads towards Garboldisham, and passes the Dean's Farm egg packing station, which provides work for many local people.

A brief walk through Kenninghall gives you but a glimpse of its life and vigour. Behind the scenes is a friendly, caring community that encompasses people from all walks of life.

❧ KETTERINGHAM

Ketteringham is a small village with under 200 inhabitants beside the busy A11, six miles south-west of Norwich. It is mainly agricultural, the land now owned by four farmers, one of whom has a large dairy herd.

Until 1958 it was all a private estate; the men working on the farms, the estate and in the Hall gardens. The Hall is a large Tudor mansion set in a lovely park beside a lake which eventually runs into the river Yare at Cringleford. It was the squire's residence until after the Second World War. The last family to live there were the Boileaus, who had fled from France during the persecution of the Huguenots by Louis XIV. At each entrance there are lodges and gates with their crest 'The Pelican in her Piety'. In 1874, Sir John Boileau erected a drinking fountain for horses at the junction of Newmarket and Ipswich Roads in Norwich in memory of his wife Lady Catherine, but the statue of a mother

128

and child now stands in the grounds of the Norfolk and Norwich Hospital, as it was removed to make way for traffic lights. Lady Ethel Boileau kept racehorses and wrote several books. The Hall was bought in 1958 and was used as a preparatory school for boys and then as Badingham College.

St Peter's church is mentioned in the Domesday Book – the first vicar listed is Hubert de Chediston, 1326. There is a beautiful Flemish oil painting *The Wedding Feast at Cana* on the 16th century reredos. There is also a three decker pulpit and some fine monuments and brasses. The tower fell in 1608 but was rebuilt the following year, and it now houses six bells and a clock. A gallery was erected in 1841 by Sir John Boileau. It is a church full of history.

In 1943, huts were erected for the servicemen of the United States 8th Army Air Force, as Ketteringham Hall was used as the headquarters of the American air bases in Norfolk. Hethel was the nearest aerodrome, where the Flying Fortresses were based. There was no electricity until 1952 and water had to be drawn from wells and pumps, but after the Americans left, the huts were used by squatters until the Council took them over for housing and then the whole village was connected to the private water supply. Now there is mains water.

In 1976, to commemorate their Golden Jubilee, the WI gave to the village a sign depicting oxen pulling the plough, with the Boileau crest embedded in the base. It was carved and erected by Mr Eric Pleasants, husband of a member, and unveiled in 1979.

There are three public footpaths signposted. One crosses the busy A11 and another was a short cut to Hethersett station, from where sugar beet, coal and flowers used to be transported by rail. It is no longer a stopping place for trains.

The village has grown over the years, several new houses and bungalows have been built, a few old ones pulled down, but some pretty thatched houses still exist. The laundry used by the Hall years ago has been renamed the Dower House, and the smithy building belongs to Forgestone House. South Norfolk Highways Department is situated on the outskirts of the village, and there is a small business called Ketteringham Motor Services, but most of the working people have occupations out of the village these days.

🍁 KETTLESTONE

Kettlestone is one of the smaller villages of north Norfolk, situated about three miles north-east of Fakenham. The discovery of flint axes, arrowheads and

Roman coins in recent years suggests that there has been a settlement here since very early times.

The present parish church dedicated to All Saints dates from the late 13th century. An outstanding feature of the church is its fine octagonal tower, which still contains part of the old Norman tower. Sir Thomas de Hauville was lord of the manor at the time it was built and as Keeper of the King's falcons could well have used the tower as a vantage point from which to observe the performance of his birds. The original building was a single pile with a thatched roof. Then came the addition of the chancel and the Lady chapel in the late 14th century, and it was probably in the late 16th century that the nave roof was raised to its present height and the thatched roof was replaced by lead. Much of the building became seriously dilapidated over the years and a large-scale restoration scheme was undertaken in Victorian times.

The village has been a thriving community over the years. A toll house once stood at the crossroads on the old Wells–Norwich turnpike between the village and the main Fakenham–Cromer road. Kettlestone once had a mill which stood on high ground in Holbrigg Lane. It must have been a very prominent landmark, being known locally as 'Kettlestone Lighthouse'. There was a smithy which survived until after the Second World War, a public house called the White Horse, a little school, a Methodist chapel and various village shops. Sadly, these are now no more, but despite this the village has grown in the last few years more rapidly than ever before in the number of small housing developments.

The population of Kettlestone has fluctuated. It must have been much greater in the mid 19th century than it is today, as it was recorded then that 40 people, mainly young couples with small children, emigrated from Kettlestone to Canada to escape the poverty and depression that followed the Napoleonic Wars. Various trades and professions were included in the party: a wheelwright, a baker, a shoe-maker, a carpenter, a bricklayer and a farm bailiff as well as labourers. They must have been greatly missed. The emigrants hired horses and wagons and left for King's Lynn on 16th June 1856. They were accommodated overnight at the Ship Inn, Gaywood, and next morning made their way to the docks where they boarded a ship named *Eliza Little*. Tucked away in the north-east corner of Hudson's Bay in Canada is a small inlet known as Kettlestone Bay. More than likely the emigrants named the locality after their old home.

KIRBY CANE & ELLINGHAM

Kirby Cane and Ellingham, although so close that visitors find it hard to know which village they are in, have their own identities in many ways. They are situated in the Waveney valley, four miles from Beccles and three miles from Bungay, surrounded by fields, woodlands and marshes. The river Waveney winds through meadowlands, attracting many artists and fishermen.

In Kirby Cane a row of houses known as Kirby Row, built of ancient rosy red bricks, are designated as scheduled buildings. Beyond the Row is the Memorial Hall presented by Mr J. R. Crisp of Kirby Cane Hall in 1921. The Hall is the centre for most recreational activities for both villages.

The parish church of All Saints has one of the embattled round towers often found in Norfolk and Suffolk, also a fine Stuart pulpit and Norman doorway. Kirby Cane also has a Methodist church built in 1849 and united services are regularly held there.

Some old place names are still in use, ie Pewter Hill, Hungry Hill, Sheep Walk and Wash Lane. The soil is ideally suited for growing cereals, beans, peas, sugar beet, apples and soft fruits.

Ellingham school was first opened in 1865 and was supported by voluntary subscription. Pupils paid two pence per week and provided their own books. In 1897 a school site was gifted by Mr Henry Smith of Ellingham Hall and with contributions from family and friends the money was raised for the cost of a schoolroom and a school house. A flagpole was erected in 1902 to commemorate the ending of the Boer War. The playing fields opposite the school have also been provided by the Smith family.

St Mary's church, Ellingham is on the outskirts of the village, part 13th century with a fine Norman tower. The adjoining rectory was sold in the 1970s and is now a school.

Ellingham mill on the banks of the Waveney is now converted along with its adjoining buildings and granary into charming dwellings with attractively laid out large gardens down to the river. The area is the most picturesque in both villages.

There is a public weighbridge and grain store. Many farms in the villages have fine houses and barns. There is one, Church Farm, which is mentioned in the Domesday Book. Situated in a central position for both villages is an excellent family run stores and post office. A mobile library comes every

131

month, newspapers are delivered, and a mobile butcher comes twice a week. The last train from Ellingham station was on 3rd January 1953, and there is now only a limited bus service to Beccles, Bungay, Lowestoft and Norwich.

The opening of a bypass has taken the heavy traffic out of both villages, making them quieter, and this with the lovely surrounding countryside and friendly communities make Kirby Cane and Ellingham pleasant villages in which to live. In June 1993 a village sign was erected for Kirby Cane at the entrance to the village, paid for by local residents.

🍁 KIRSTEAD

Kirstead, seven miles south of Norwich and with a population of 200, is a small village which lies to the east of the main Norwich to Bungay road, with a sprinkling of houses the other side of the road. The name derives from Kirkstead; 'kirk' being the Scandinavian for church.

The church is St Margaret's, dating back to the 13th century, but of the original building there is little surviving. With its thatched nave, tiled chancel and bellcote at the west end, it must have been a satisfying place of worship, but in 1864 a Victorian architect set out to improve it. The doorway, c1190, survives but the rest was drastically swept away, rebuilt and restored. The Stuart altar table was retained and there are a number of memorials to long gone parishioners. One may regret what was lost but it must be stressed that it is still a building that offers a warm welcome to anyone going in. Hanging up is a list of incumbents from 1377.

The village, set in farmland whichever way you look and criss-crossed by a network of pleasant narrow lanes, has no shop, no school (one built in 1901 closed in the late 1940s), no hall and no public house, for all these the people look to nearby Brooke, but it has a wealth of fascinating houses.

Kirstead House, 1654, was for nearly 250 years the residence of the Whall family. The tombstone of Robert Whall who died in 1720 is the oldest in the churchyard. The last of the Whalls died in 1929.

Langhale House (Georgian) is a reminder that there was once a hamlet of that name with its own manor and church. In the garden is some remarkable topiary. The Clock House, on the main road, is so-called because on the outside wall is a clock placed there by the squire, Mr Palmer-Kerrison, to assist the driver of the carrier's cart with his timekeeping as he travelled daily between

132

Kirstead Hall

Norwich and Bungay. Two listed buildings are Windetts Cottages and Walnut Tree Farm, both 16th century. Until 1965 the gabled Green Man House, c1700, was the village inn but it is now a private house.

But Kirstead's jewel is the Hall. According to the Domesday Book the earlier manor house on the site belonged to Bury Abbey but in 1539, at the Dissolution of the Monasteries, Henry VIII sold it to Thomas Godsalve, one of his civil servants. It is his grandson, Robert, who gets the credit for the present building. Tucked away off the beaten track the red brick, gabled Jacobean front is strikingly beautiful. There is even a priest hole. Since 1964 it has, along with the dovecote, been most sensitively restored.

🍁 LANGLEY

This scattered unspoilt village, consisting mainly of old farms and cottages, stretches along the edge of the marshes on the south side of the river Yare.

On the higher land to the east of the village street is Langley Park, which is well known for its beautiful display of daffodils in April. In the park is Langley

Hall, originally the home of George Proctor and then the Beauchamp Proctor family, (whose name was later changed to Proctor-Beauchamp). It is now a private school. The Hall, built mainly of red brick in the Palladian style, was begun by Brettingham (who also built Holkham Hall) in 1740 and completed by Salvin a century later. The lodges on the Norwich road are early works of John Sloane. An ancient stone market cross stands south-west of the Hall at a point where the boundaries of four villages meet. This cross originally stood in a meadow adjoining Langley Abbey, marking the place where the abbey held its weekly market.

A path across a meadow leads to the 14th century church of St Michael, which stands to the north of the Hall at the edge of the park. The church is used mainly by pupils and staff of the Langley School.

The remains of the abbey stand at the edge of the marshes near the river. It was founded in 1195 for Premonstratensian canons, known as 'White Canons' from their white woollen robes. It was these canons who wrote and illuminated the Sarum Antiphoner now in the possession of Ranworth church. After the dissolution in 1536 the abbey church was completely destroyed and the stones used to build dwelling houses in the area. Some of the domestic buildings are still well preserved and used as farm buildings. A fine vaulted undercroft still remains. These buildings are privately owned and not accessible to the public. Stories of ghostly robed visitors to some of the cottages still abound, but as these apparitions seem to be dressed in brown robes with cowls, it seems unlikely that they belong to the Premonstratensian abbey!

The centuries-old Wherry Inn stands near the head of Langley Dyke, a popular mooring place for holiday cruisers. In 1988 an attractive joint village sign was erected on the boundary with its twin village of Hardley.

The marshes are part of the Environmentally Sensitive area and grazing numbers and nitrogen fertilisers are strictly controlled. There are some areas of special scientific interest, where rare marsh orchids grow. The buses from Loddon to Norwich, three each way, run daily except Sundays, stopping on request, making this village more environmentally friendly in these days of commuters.

🍁 LETHERINGSETT

The village of Letheringsett, situated in the Glaven valley, has a history dating back to the Domesday Book and beyond. There was a watermill here at that time, and a church. The present St Andrew's dates from about 1300 and has some interesting features. The 16th and 17th century stained glass came from Catton Hall in Norwich, and there are also a few pieces of a rare Easter Sepulchre to be seen.

The most important family in the village were the Hardys, now the Cozens Hardys, who have been here since the late 1700s. In 1957 Basil Cozens Hardy wrote a history of Letheringsett, taking extracts from the diary of Mary Hardy from 1773 to 1809. She told of a great storm in October 1793, when several ships were driven aground at Weybourne and Cley. In June 1795 a particularly cold day cut all the vegetables, and in November there was an earthshock which was also felt in Fakenham and Holt. In January 1799 a labourer called James Beckham was killed in a snow drift of over 14 feet at Saxlingham.

The saw mill was built to plans drawn up in 1857, and there was once an inn called the White Horse. The bridge over the river Glaven was built in 1818 and is said to be the flattest in Norfolk as it rises only 16 inches, the river being 15 feet wide at this point. To this day it carries all the coast traffic. William Hardy did not like the road so close to his house so he knocked down the public house and made tunnels under the road, still in use, so that he could get to his house and gardens.

In 1901 Justice Cozens Hardy bought the village a manual Merryweather fire engine from the London Fire Brigade. The fire station was a shed near the public house which up to 1896 was a carpenter's shop. In 1932 the fire engine was handed over to Holt. A fire in 1936 destroyed a weaver's shed which had been built on the site of the old brewery (it had ceased to function in 1895), and also the village clock. The clock is believed to have been made by Johnson Jex, the village blacksmith, who was an inventive genius and who lies in the churchyard.

Letheringsett is not far from the coast and smugglers are known to have been active in the area between about 1787 and 1882. Whisky and gin were often brought in from Weybourne and Salthouse.

❧ LEZIATE, ASHWICKEN & BAWSEY

Once these three little parishes a few miles east of King's Lynn had each its own church, but on Faden's map of Norfolk of 1797, only Ashwicken's was not in ruins. It still stands, but in virtual isolation, since it is said that because of the Black Death the village around it was destroyed.

Nowadays this group of parishes consists largely of modern houses on or off the busy and dangerous B1145. The population may be up to 900, living in four or five unconnected roads, which with its history perhaps explains the lack of an obvious centre such as a pub, a shop or a green with a pond, as one expects in a 'village'.

This area of rolling and wooded countryside has had its industries, possibly an ancient ironworks, a brickworks, and certainly more recently large excavations for sand, which have been delightfully landscaped, providing a number of lakes.

A matter of concern to all is the area of the B1145 known as the Bawsey 'bumps', scene of a number of fatal road accidents in recent years. Otherwise the peace of this region is disturbed only by low-flying Tornados now and then.

❧ LINGWOOD & STRUMPSHAW

Lingwood and Strumpshaw merge, but each has its own identity and attraction. They are situated off the A47 between Norwich and Great Yarmouth.

Strumpshaw, surprisingly, has a 'hill' from which you can see Norwich and out towards the sea. Its church of St Peter has a thin tower and a chancel built in about 1300. The screen is 15th century and beautifully carved, with much of the original colour.

However, Strumpshaw's most important asset is the RSPB sanctuary at Strumpshaw Fen, on the river Yare. Marsh harriers can often be seen here and there are also interesting marsh flowers, such as the marsh helleborine. There are observation hides and the sanctuary is run by a warden, who will conduct parties round the Fen, or one can wander at will.

Lingwood, to the north, has a modern shopping centre and a delightful pond stocked with ducks! The village hall, first opened in 1940, is kept very busy with the number of village activities. Lingwood's church of St Peter is mainly 14th century, though the tower and chancel are older. Some of the pew ends have carved poppy heads.

❦ LITTLE BARNINGHAM

One hundred years ago the population of Little Barningham was 219, more than double its present population of 93. One hundred and fifty years ago the population was 259, and the village boasted four farmers, a blacksmith and wheelwright, a shoemaker, a bricklayer and a rabbit merchant. In their leisure time the men from the village played quoits on the land behind the forge, or called at the little cottage at Dog Corner where they could obtain home brewed ale. There were also two shops in the village, and in the reign of Edward I the village had a market and fair.

Nowadays there is one farm in the centre of the village and another at Barningham Green, a mile from the village, on the road to Edgefield. In the centre of this very compact village there is still a post office. There is always time for a joke or exchange of news, a seat for the weary, and in winter an oil stove spreads its distinctive comforting atmosphere. A weekly bus service allows villagers to spend a couple of hours in Sheringham or Norwich.

The houses lie on either side of the street, which runs from east to west. The church, at the eastern end, is on a steep hill, from which one can look the full length of the street to the rise at the far end at Dog Corner, where the road from Saxthorpe and Corpusty to Matlaske forms a crossroads. At the foot of Church Hill a short lane leads to two well restored cottages, and a house which was once two cottages and now lies empty awaiting modernisation. Old cottages in the village have been well restored. Laurel Farm is no longer a working farm but it and the barn have been sensitively restored. Normally used as a garage, the barn occasionally houses charity events.

Little Barningham has had a church on the hill site since Saxon times, and the list of incumbents in the present St Andrew's commences in 1320. In the church, immediately below the pulpit, there is a box pew which was 'Built at the cost and charge of Steven Crosbee, Anno Domini 1640' and was 'For couples joyned in wedlocke'. A later inscription carved on another panel tells us it was 'Repaired and enlarged at the cost of John Thomas Mott, AD 1867'. On the corner of the pew there is a skeletal carving of Father Time, in a shroud and bearing an hour glass and scythe. A further carved inscription tells us: 'All

137

you that doe this space pass by, as you are now even soe was I. Remember death, for you must dye and as I am soe shall you be, prepare therefore to follow me'. The church is well looked after and has a regular congregation.

In many ways Little Barningham is almost a hidden village – tradespeople from the small market towns nearby invariably have difficulty in locating it for the first time. Little traffic passes through except for local people visiting friends or on their way to nearby villages, and they have to keep an eye open for wandering guinea fowl.

🍁 LITTLE ELLINGHAM

Little Ellingham is a small village situated in the middle of a triangle of roads connecting Attleborough, Hingham and Watton, being approximately one and a half miles from each of these minor roads.

Until 1997 the village had one of the largest duck processing factories in the UK, but the factory was then reorganised to produce prepacked meals. Factory workers are brought in from other areas, and most inhabitants now work outside the village.

Farming is the other main industry. Formerly there were about 20 farms and smallholdings. These have now been merged into larger units, so that today approximately only half this number operates. Before mechanisation a blacksmith's shop which fronted the village green was a favourite meeting place for the old characters, who exchanged their news and views around the forge. Standing on this site now is a corn store.

Dividing this parish into two sections is the 30 acres of Goose Common. Parishioners have rights to cut the gorse growing there for fuel. The herbage is let for grazing. With rents from other charity lands, it provides money for needy residents, plus an education foundation from which young people can obtain grants. A grass area at Church Avenue has been procured as a village enhancement area, where children can play near their homes.

St Peter's church stands in the middle of the village, of flint construction with a square tower forming the porch. The nave was destroyed by fire in 1867. It was rebuilt by public subscription and reopened in 1869. The Prince of Wales, later Edward VII, headed the list of subscribers by donating 21 guineas. The windows and doors not damaged by the fire are unusual. They have medieval carved heads on the mouldings, both inside and outside the building.

138

The school opposite the churchyard closed in 1970. Once a church school, it was bought by the parish for a village hall. Still hanging in prominence are the Honour Boards bearing names of former pupils who gained county scholarships. The Crown public house closed in 1938 when its licence was transferred to the Flying Fish at Carbrooke.

It used to be the custom for the children to go round the houses singing on 14th February. On their way to each house they would chant 'Goodmorrow Valentine, Curl your locks as I do mine. Two in front and one behind, Good Mother Valentine'. They were given cakes, apples and sweets in appreciation of their songs. After dark, Valentine parcels were placed on doorsteps, with loud knocking to arouse the occupants. 'Snatch Valentine' created much excitement in trying to capture these before they were snatched away by a long string.

The Hall and Hall Farm were built in the mid 1800s. The Hall, designed on Italian lines, was intended for a shooting box. A large range of buildings at Hall Farm was constructed for a mill. The Tower Clock, a folly, stands in the park adjoining Hall Farm. The base of this structure is two cottages built in the form of a cross, surmounted by a tall clock tower with a domed cap.

The Crown is the only flint dwelling in the village, and was almost derelict for several years until it was restored as an attractive house. Several shops and the Methodist chapel have been converted to dwellings.

LODDON

Before the bypass was built in the mid 1970s, the main route from Norwich to Lowestoft took you straight through the small town of Loddon. If you have time to spare, it is well worth taking a detour to visit its many attractions.

On the bridge over the river Chet stands Loddon water mill, the remains of a grain and seed dressing business at its height at the beginning of the 20th century. Wherries carried all manner of loads, including grain, timber, wool, and coal, up and down the river until before the last war. The Mill now houses a reproduction furniture business and the adjoining Mill House a pine furniture and gift shop. The river Chet, connecting to the Yare at Hardley Cross, and thence to the Broads via Breydon Water, was straightened and dredged to accommodate the wherries and is now a thriving centre for holiday cruisers in the summer months. The area around the staithe is an attractive, quiet place to sit and watch the river.

Continuing up this old street one comes to the church of Holy Trinity facing the Church Plain. Built, it is believed, close to the site of a Saxon chapel of St Mary, Holy Trinity was completed in only three years in the early 1490s. Sir James Hobart, Attorney General to Henry VII, was the chief patron of the church and lived at nearby Hales Hall. The church has a beautiful stained glass window showing the coats of arms of the old wealthy families of the area. The church also houses what is alleged to be the original poor box from the old Saxon church, but, in fact, it probably dates from Tudor times. Above the church porch, approached via a steep, stone spiral staircase, is the Priests' Room Local History Display. Here the history of the village has been recorded, in pictures and words, for all to read and enjoy. The Church in Loddon has been an ecumenical ministry for over 20 years with St John's church in George Lane also playing a vital role.

At the further end of the High Street is the tiny Farthing Green where the town sign stands. Modelled by a local artist and cast in bronze it depicts Alfric de Modercope, a Saxon lord of the manor, who gave land on which Loddon is built to the Abbey of Bury St Edmunds. His hand rests upon a replica of the church poor box.

The old flint-faced building facing Church Plain was once the village school. Built in the 1850s, at public insistence, and with public money, it is now the branch library. Three modern schools have taken its place to provide for today's youngsters.

Domestic buildings in the town range from, what is probably the oldest, a 16th century farm house near Church Plain, through some fine 17th and 18th century town houses to award-winning council houses and, of course, a great deal of modern expansion. Somehow this modern growth does not detract from Loddon's village character, and the occupants, of course, contribute to its still thriving shopping centre.

❧ LONG STRATTON

Situated on the A140 Norwich to Ipswich road, Long Stratton is a lovely village that has grown so much in recent years that now it is almost a town. However, it still retains its village centre where the original old buildings remain, though most are now used as business premises.

The lovely church of St Mary is well worth a visit. Inside is the Sexton's

Wheel, which is depicted on the village sign on the Plain in the centre of the village. There are three other churches: pretty little St Michael's at the north end of the village, the Methodist church on Manor Road and the Congregational church to the south.

Near Flower Pot Lane shopping precinct is the Ice House which belonged to the old manor house. When the grounds were cleared to make way for shops and houses, the ice house was uncovered and left intact.

The village has three public houses, a restaurant, a baker, post office and many other shops. Public services provided include a bus service, a fire station, a public library and street lighting on all roads. There are also three schools and a leisure centre.

❧ LUDHAM

Ludham was mentioned in the Domesday Book. It was important enough for Elizabeth I to grant Bishop Redman the right to hold a fair after Trinity Sunday, and a market, which was held in the High Street.

Being surrounded by rivers, wherries plied their trades, bringing coal and possibly spirits and tobacco, as an Excise Officer lived at Staithe House. The wherries would return with reeds, malt, corn, flour and gravel to Yarmouth or Norwich.

Windmills abounded for grinding corn, and watermills for draining the marshes enabling the grazing of stock. Daniel England was a millwright and built many mills both locally and in the surrounding areas, employing up to 20 men. It was said that a millwright had to be a steeplejack, architect, carpenter, bricklayer and blacksmith. It was a dangerous job, working from heights and in water. All the transport was by horse and cart.

A century ago there were all types of craftsmen in the village, who made and plied their wares to make it self supporting. There were bakers, at least three blacksmiths, butchers, thatchers, a saddler, wheelwright, mole catcher, grocers, fish salesmen, inn keepers, boot and shoe makers, carters and dealers. There were paper makers, brick makers and a public nuisance officer. There was a master of the Board school and a mistress of a dame school. To add to the list there was a physician, and surgeon, millers and maltsters, grooms, labourers, and farmers. A horse leech kept the horses in good condition for pulling carriers' carts to Great Yarmouth and Norwich on Wednesdays and

Saturdays. There were also tailors, glovers and hairdressers. The smoke house for the curing of hams and fish and the slaughterhouses were in the centre of the village. The men often practised two trades in season. After the malting season was over, the men found employment in brickmaking and the farm labourers would go sea fishing or wild fowling and reed cutting on the Broads.

St Catherine's church is an imposing structure of stone and flint in Perpendicular style, consisting of chancel, nave and three aisles, north and south porches, and an embattled tower with clock.

The parish of Ludham consists of 2,993 acres. It is bounded on two thirds of its perimeter by rivers and marshland. The village itself is on high ground in a fairly compact cluster, but new building is causing this to spread onto former arable areas. There is little industry to keep the population of 1,500 in employment, but services include four boatyards, two garages, a builder and a thatcher, shops and two public houses.

Ludham also played its part during the Second World War with an airfield and training camp for soldiers (built within the village to camouflage its existence). During the summer many visitors admire the village, including the attractive village sign.

Each Christmas a link with the past is remembered by two charities left to parishioners who were in need. Gifts of land bring in rents which are administered by the Ludham Ancient Welfare Trust and the Emily Clark Trust is administered by the vicar and church trustees. These are in the form of dockets for coal or groceries.

🍁 MARTHAM

On approaching Martham from any direction the church of St Mary stands proud, on a small rise surrounded by ancient trees. A place of worship has been here since before Domesday records, but the present one dates from the 14th century. It is well worth a visit, as there are angels in the roof and carved pew ends. In the room behind the organ, part of a gravestone can be seen which relates the extraordinary circumstances of a man who apparently married his mother. Sometimes the church tower is open but you need good legs and lungs for the climb.

The population here has fluctuated from 400 recorded in Domesday to over 1,000 about the beginning of the 14th century, but the Black Death took its toll and it was not until the census in 1941 that over 1,000 was recorded again. However, since the railway's demise in 1963, freeing more land for building, the number of people has gradually grown to over 2,000 now. The bungalows built then attracted retiring couples from other areas.

Of the ponds on the green, two are visible and an odd third one shows up after heavy rain. The ducks and attendant gander dabble away. The two 'Duck' signs by the side of the road help to guard the little families wandering all around from early spring to late autumn. Tourists come in coaches, decant, feed the ducks and go on their way. In the winter, when duck numbers increase, villagers take care of their feeding, and break the ice on the nearest pond so that the ducks have a place to swim.

Shopping in the village is a pleasure with almost all needs being provided for. Yarmouth is nine miles away to the east and Norwich 18 miles to the west. Even on a dull day there are clusters of folk talking and that is the friendly side of Martham.

There are numerous paths to walk, the river Thurne being about only one mile away. Martham Broad is a restful beautiful place, where rare dragonflies and maybe the swallowtail butterfly might be seen. The marsh flowers are quite local to the Broads generally, some such as the six foot marsh sow thistle are roundly cursed but there are many insignificant treasures to admire. Winter gives a bonus of golden reed contrasting with blue sky and water, while in the village proper the thatched cottages stand cosily around the green.

🍁 MATLASKE

The only new building in this small village, which is clustered round the entrance to Barningham Hall, is the rectory. The nearby church of St Peter has a round tower, medieval windows and a 15th century font. Sir Charles and Lady Stella Mott-Radclyffe live at the Hall, which was once the residence of the Paston family. The interior of the Hall was rebuilt by Humphrey Paston, and he laid out the grounds. The grounds are open to the public at times during the summer, and teas are served.

The partly ruined church of Barningham Winter stands in the grounds of the Hall. Only the chancel still stands, and this is entered through the ruins of the tower and nave. Inside the church is bright and well tended, and there is a brass to John de Wynter, whose family owned the Hall some 500 years ago.

The road to Squallham and Wolterton leaves the village opposite the entrance gates to Barningham Hall. The village shop is at the corner of this road. Here the villagers can buy groceries etc, and for a few hours each week it takes on the duties of post office.

Some distance from the village on the road leading to Little Barningham and Saxthorpe and Corpusty, the old Board school still stands. This has been closed for many years and is now divided into private dwellings. In the other direction, towards Aldborough, there is a small enclave of council houses lying just beyond the church, with the new rectory on the other side of the road.

🍁 MILEHAM

Mileham is situated on what was in the 11th century the main east Norfolk route to King's Lynn. The first evidence of habitation is mid-Saxon, though pieces of Roman pottery have been found and a Roman silver dish, now in the British Museum, was ploughed up in 1839. The village is at the head of two streams, the Nar which flows to the west and the Black Water to the east.

The church of St John the Baptist at the east end of the village has original stained glass dated 1340. The ruins of a motte and bailey castle are on farmland in the centre of the village. Robert Coke bought the manor of Burghwood in the mid 16th century. Sir Edward Coke was born here in 1552 and baptised in Mileham church – the entry is in the register. He later became Chief Justice and Attorney General to Queen Elizabeth I. The Coke family of Holkham Hall have historic connections with Burwood Hall, Mileham (also Tittleshall and Godwick). Thomas William, 'Coke of Norfolk', built the present farmhouse in 1793 and was a pioneer of farming with 20 acre fields and four-crop rotation.

Village life revolved round the many and various farms and 'the Hall', Mileham Hall (demolished some 50 years ago). Electricity was brought to the village in 1947 and that meant that water could now be extracted and pumped into homes for the first time from the local bore. It also meant that when the power failed, as it often did, the water ceased to flow too. All is changed now and very reliable.

This is still very much a farming community and surrounded by farms which include two dairy farms, one with a Guernsey herd and one with a Friesian herd. There are also several businesses with agricultural connections.

The blacksmith, shoemaker, sweet shop, bakery, three pubs, village pound

144

and the coal house have all gone. The base of the village sign is made from flints of the coal house and stands on the site. The sign depicts the castle and the 10th century Viking sword, now in Norwich Castle Museum, found in 1945 when the moat of the former Burghwood Manor was cleared.

The post office and general store is at the centre of the village, a lifeline to those with no means of transport as there is no public transport for many miles. The local coach company's weekly trips to Dereham, Fakenham and Norwich are a vital link for those without cars.

There is a well established nursery, first opened in 1964, and opposite it the local playing field, land bequeathed to the village many years ago. The primary school built in the 19th century and extended some years ago is one of the focal points of the village. The other is the village hall which has been rebuilt and was reopened in 1996.

Over the last few years in particular the village has grown. A small estate of bungalows has been built on the site of one small cottage and an area of waste land, two big houses have been built on the once formal garden of Mileham Hall, infilling has occurred all along the length of the village street, and various barns and farm buildings have been converted into homes. The rectory has been sold. The population is approximately 550.

🍁 MORNINGTHORPE

Morningthorpe is a very small village in south Norfolk which was mentioned in the Domesday survey as having two manors, one Boyland, the other Thorpe. Thorpe was overlorded by the abbots of St Edmunds until the Dissolution of the Monasteries, when after changing hands several times it was bought by Sir Ralph Shelton. He subsequently sold it to the owner of Boyland Manor, John Gurney. In the mid 1600s Nicholas Gurney was High Sheriff of Suffolk and Charles Gurney High Sheriff of Norfolk.

The church, St John the Baptist's, has a round Saxon tower housing three bells, which appears to be unchanged since it was built. The church was restored in 1889 at a cost of £1,150. This restoration left the interior with few remaining traces of its earlier appearance. The rood screen has gone, but the rood-loft stairs still remain. There is still some medieval stained glass in the top lights. The piscina in the chancel is probably 15th century. There is a quiet charm and beauty about this church, and also the village it serves.

145

🍁 Mulbarton

The common is the principal landmark of Mulbarton; an area of open land set within a triangle of roads. Today, the common is a recreation area for the rapidly increasing number of people in the village. A move to enclose the common aroused great opposition in 1865 and development on the perimeter has been resisted with partial success. In earlier times, the common must have been vital to the community; a place to graze cattle and keep them from the surrounding open fields.

The name Mulbarton is 'Moklebartunatuna' in the Domesday Book and probably means 'an outlying dairy farm'. The old heart of the village is at the north end of the common, nearest to Norwich. The parish church of St Mary Magdalene with its huge flint tower and the nearby red brick tithe barn are a splendid sight at night when they are floodlit. There is evidence that a Saxon church existed at the time of Edward the Confessor and served as the parish church until the present building was founded by Thomas St Omer, lord of the manor, in the 13th century. It is said that he built the church as a penance for hanging a man from East Carleton, who was later proved innocent.

Thomas St Omer is commemorated on the parish sign at the north end of the common. The other gentleman depicted on the sign is Sir Edwin Rich who was a benefactor of the village, and whose charity is still administered today.

The manor house is near the church. Called the Old Hall it is a 16th century building, but even older houses have stood on the moated site. Nearby, too, are the pond, the pub and the Mill House where a windmill stood until the 1930s.

The fields south of the common have become modern housing estates, and an application for 400 more houses on the Cuckoofield Lane site has been submitted. A well-equipped children's play area has been installed on the common, and farmland has been developed to provide a village hall, a Scout hut and cricket and football pitches to cater for the needs of this expanding village.

🍁 Mundesley

Mundesley is a village on the north Norfolk coast whose population doubles in the summer with the arrival of many holidaymakers. All enjoy the long stretches of sandy beach and the village is proud to fly the yellow and blue flags denoting excellence of sand and water quality.

Ancient occupation is evident from the discovery of Roman coins and several Saxon burial urns in the cliffs and surrounding fields. For centuries the main occupation of the villagers was fishing or farming but in 1898 the railway arrived and Mundesley was 'on the map'. Hotels were built and extensions put onto small houses to accommodate the visitors. There had, of course, been many visitors before the railway, a famous one being William Cowper the poet, who stayed in what is now known as Cowper House during 1795 and 1796. Also, whilst attending Paston School in North Walsham, Horatio Nelson is reputed to have visited frequently, arriving on his pony at the New Inn, now the Royal Hotel. Unfortunately the railway is no more, and it was closed in 1964. A housing estate now stands on the site of the station and its forecourt.

All Saints' church stands on the cliff-top and records show that a church has been on this spot since the 11th century. Over the years it was allowed to fall into disrepair but restoration was eventually put in hand in the early 1900s and completed in 1914. Inside is a war memorial to those who fell in the two World Wars.

There used to be a thriving water mill in the village where local farmers brought their corn to be ground. Sadly the mill itself burnt down in 1956 but the mill house still stands adjacent to the pond with its unusual overshot water wheel.

Mundesley has a flourishing Infant and Junior school in modern premises. The characteristic old Victorian school is now used as the village library, entering through the door marked 'Boys'. Another building that has had a change of use is the coastguard station. This now houses a voluntarily manned Coast Watch on the top floor, the remainder being converted into 'The Smallest Museum in the World', illustrating the village's past and maritime history.

The nine-hole golf course is well used by both residents and visitors and a driving-range has now been opened nearby.

In the past ten years there has been much housing development both in and around the village. The population has doubled but Mundesley has retained its heart and identity as a busy and attractive seaside community.

🍁 MUNDFORD

Mundford lies along the southern bank of the river Wissey as it meanders through the quiet beauty of Breckland. The village, with instant access to the A134 and A1065 main roads, is eight miles north of the ancient settlement of Thetford, four miles from Brandon and near the prehistoric flint mines of Grimes Graves in Weeting, the neighbouring parish. Evidence of Mundford's origin has been plentiful, including a Saxon quern unearthed during excavations on the site of the primary school, a Saxon mass burial and remains of a Saxon dwelling to the west of the village.

Two of the oldest buildings in the village are West Hall, a Tudor manor house which has been in continuous domestic occupation, and Rosemary Cottage. The latter was once the Cherry Tree Inn and it is said that Charles II stayed here during his flight from the Roundheads before he escaped to exile on the Continent. Also in the village was the Pear Tree Inn, now thatched cottages, in which drovers stayed while their cattle were shut up for the night in a small pound opposite Nelson Cottage.

For centuries the world passed Mundford by, until the last 30 years or so when it has expanded from a small village of some 300 people to its present population of nearly 2,000. Mundford's growth went hand in hand with the expansion of Thetford which became an overspill town, and it is to Thetford that many people in Mundford look for their employment. In former times, farm work and forestry, in the thousands of acres of Forestry Commission pinewoods which border the village, were the main occupation for the menfolk. Nearby Lynford Hall, with its huge estate of which Mundford then formed part, saw many of the women employed in service.

Today Mundford is a village which others in the area look to as their centre, a village with well above average shopping facilities, and catering for a wide spectrum of social functions in a well-appointed village centre. A feature of the village is the parish church of St Leonard, founded in the 13th century with a fine, ornately carved screen attributed to Comper. Its spire catches the eye from all approaches to the village.

Parts of Mundford, particularly the old flint cottages with their thatched roofs, are in the conservation area near the village green. Here stands the village sign, and the Methodist chapel looks across the green to the old coaching inn, the Crown. The green, a focal point in the older part of the

148

village, and the acknowledged starting point for many rallies and processions, is surrounded by substantial, dignified houses and a former inn, the King's Head.

The local farms are mainly given over to the growing of sugar beet and barley and the rearing of poultry and pigs. Formerly Mundford had three commons, the quaintly named Day Common, Night Common and Asses' Common.

Residents are fortunate in that there are many pleasant walks including two clearly signposted public footpaths and plenty of paths through the forest rides which the sandy nature of the soil makes readily accessible all year round. The roadside edges of the forest are fringed with deciduous trees, mainly beech, which soften the dark green of the pines. Entering the forest walks, one may see squirrels foraging for beech mast or sweet chestnuts, hear the harsh cry of the jay and see, deep in the pines, a deer running through the bracken.

🍁 NARBOROUGH

Narborough is an ancient parish with a varied and interesting history. Traces of Bronze Age, Iron Age and Roman occupation point to the fact that people were working the Narborough soil for centuries before William the Conqueror's Domesday Book listed 'Nereburh', its 41 working men and their taxable assets. The river, winding across the northern part of the parish, must have been an important factor in attracting early settlement.

For the next 600 years village life was dominated by two families – the de Narburghs, who took their name from the village, and then the Spelmans, powerful manorial lords who owned practically the whole parish.

In the old part of the village, the Ship Inn stands as a reminder of the three overlapping ages of Narborough's transport history. The railway ran close by, barges laden with coal and grain from King's Lynn unloaded at the nearby staithe, and the Lynn to Narborough turnpike road ended there. The coming of the railway in 1846 was fiercely resisted by local landowners, but many people were saddened by its closure in 1968, predicting perhaps an even more hazardous trunk road through the village.

In the First World War, Narborough could boast one of the largest aerodromes in Britain, home to hundreds of officers and men of the Royal Flying Corps. A single aerodrome building, out of over a hundred, remains.

After the Second World War, Narborough was a small self-contained community of some 350 souls, with most of the workforce employed at the maltings and on the farms. Much of the old village was demolished in the 1950s, marking the end of the old way of life. Historically valuable buildings, such as the old tithe barn and the 18th century almshouses, disappeared. Outstanding buildings, such as All Saints church, Narborough Hall, the old corn mill, and a few other fine old houses provide a link with the past, while the relatively new housing estates to the south of the old village provide homes for most of the 1,200 or so inhabitants.

In the last few years Narborough has gained a new school and a new community centre, while recent projects include the establishment of an amenity area by the crossroads, renovation of the churchyard wall and a village sign. The long-awaited bypass has arrived, making Narborough a safer and more pleasant place to live.

❧ NEATISHEAD

Neatishead is a small sprawling village to the east of Norwich. About 500 people live here, and this number has not varied much in the last hundred years. There have been no large-scale building schemes, possibly because of the absence of mains sewerage. Several old cottages have fallen down, or been demolished to make room for new houses and bungalows.

A village school has existed here since 1846, started by the Preston family from nearby Beeston and Barton Halls. In 1863 the school was enlarged to accommodate 140 children. In 1990 the village celebrated the official opening by the Bishop of Norwich of a new primary school built on the field behind the Victorian school.

The Victory Hall, where most entertainments in the village are held, is so named as it was bought as a war memorial for the village after the First World War. Before that it had been a clubroom for members to meet, chat and read a selection of the daily newspapers of the time. The Clubroom Committee would hire out the room for special functions.

Neatishead used to be quite prosperous in the days of horse traffic and working horses. No fewer than four blacksmiths were busy at the beginning of the 20th century, three carpenters, an undertaker, a harness-maker and a horse collar maker (using sedge from the marshes). Corn was ground and animal feeding stuffs supplied from the mill. Many of these trades were still active up to the Second World War. Indeed the mill is still there, but not the same miller. His trade today is combined with haulage work. There are few villagers now who keep chickens and a pig in a sty at the bottom of the garden. For a time in the mid 1920s a rubber vulcanising business was carried on, but it did not survive long.

The parish church of St Peter is active and in 1990 celebrated the bicentenary of its last major overhaul. Now the latest refurbishment has been completed and the church is resplendent with reconditioned pews and new flooring.

❧ NEWTON FLOTMAN

To the traveller who speeds through Newton Flotman it may seem to be just another Norfolk village, but if one has time to look there is much to see. Newton Flotman is six miles south of Norwich on the A140 Norwich to Ipswich road. The river Tas runs along its boundary into Saxlingham Thorpe and Tasburgh, forming the Tas valley. Its double name originates from being a new town when the Tas was much wider and needed a ferry or 'flote-man'.Today it has over 1,200 inhabitants and is still growing.

The church of St Mary dates from about 1300; the new rectory was built in 1986. The village school is a C of E voluntary-controlled primary with 100 pupils. The purpose-built doctor's surgery and the post office and village store are in the centre of the village. The Village Centre and the playing field are at the top of the village and there will be improved access when a link road is provided by the planned housing development on Flordon Road. In 1997 the garage on the A140 became a specialist motor cycle shop and in 1998 the 'Old School' became a dance/drama studio – both making use of their prime sites on the main road.

In 1990 the village sign was erected by the Parish Council on King's Green, which was given to the village by Mrs Joy King in memory of her late father and husband. In 1996 the Alan King Playing Field was also given by Mrs King as a permanent memorial. The village sign depicts a Saxon ship, the 16th century bridge (now bypassed) and the 14th century church. It is embedded in a mill stone to emphasise the village's connection with Duffield's mill across the river at Saxlingham Thorpe.

151

Visitors are recommended to turn off the A140 onto the old road and see the medieval bridge over the river Tas which flows up to Rainthorpe Hall, a beautiful Elizabethan house often used as a background for films.

🍁 NORTH & SOUTH CREAKE

North and South Creake are villages in north Norfolk, linked by the river Burn; each was mentioned in the Domesday survey. The villages, mainly agricultural, have developed differently; North Creake as a linear village whilst South Creake was grouped around the nucleus of its church.

As seen today, North Creake's St Mary's church is the outcome of rebuilding in the 1450s by the Calthorps. In West Street is a fine three-storied tower mill, reputedly the smallest corn mill in Norfolk, built about 1820. Now minus sails, it was in use as a corn mill until the end of the 19th century. The *Gentleman's Magazine* of 1779 reported the discovery of two Iron Age urns containing 1,409 coins. The lord of the manor is Earl Spencer of Althorp.

On the road to Burnham Market, a sign points to Creake Abbey. This house of Augustinian canons was used by pilgrims on their way to the shrine at Walsingham. It was a priory until 1231, when King Henry II raised it to the status of an abbey. As it was a small house, this caused jealousy among the canons of the much larger Walsingham Priory, that was never to become an abbey. The site of the ruins is one of the most peaceful in the county. At a point in the village called 'Little Wells', until recently stood the base of the market cross. Unfortunately, it was removed and dumped accidentally.

Within living memory South Creake had two activities that were unusual in a small village. The first was at Bluestone Farm, named after a glacial erratic, ie a blue boulder. Traditional methods of cultivating a mixed farm had been used until the early 1930s. Then came the great experiment of turning Bluestone into the first fully mechanised farm in the country, the beginning of a process that was to reduce so drastically the number of workers required for a given acreage. The same innovators produced what they claimed to be the first British breakfast cereal, marketed as *Farmers' Glory*. The second activity was the conversion of a disused brewery into a razor blade factory, employing a good deal of local labour.

North Creake Stores

The village sign on the green at South Creake has on one side the church of St Mary and a ploughman at work, indicating that each had a part in the life of the village. The other side depicts a splendid battle scene, said by legend to have taken place at a nearby hill fort, where blood flowed down the hill, and known as Bloodgate to this day.

Until the 1930s, each village was virtually self sufficient, but each now has only a shop, post office and a pub. Many houses are now owned by holidaymakers, or by retired people.

NORTH ELMHAM

The parish of North Elmham is bounded on all sides by water. The village, situated about five miles from Dereham on the B1110 Dereham-Holt road, has grown considerably over the years. It has a fine church, the remains of a Saxon cathedral, a house called Nelson House where a relative of Lord Nelson lived,

153

and the vineyard which produces Elmham Park wine.

The cathedral dates from the 7th century and was established by the Anglo-Saxon bishops. The Danish invasion brought about its decline, but in the early 10th century it was revived and became the centre of a diocese covering East Anglia. Later the centre of the diocese was transferred to Thetford, and thence to Norwich. Bishop Despenser converted Elmham cathedral into a defended manor house, a 'weekend retreat' for the clergy and their friends. Now in the care of the Department of the Environment, the ruins and grounds are well maintained and draw many visitors all the year round.

Just across the road from the church and the ruins, in Elmham Park, archaeological excavations were carried out between 1967 and 1972. These revealed the remains of Anglo-Saxon timber houses, and an extensive burial ground. Finds here, and from nearby Spong Hill, are now exhibited in Norwich Castle Museum.

Medieval St Mary's church has some interesting carved pew ends and a peal of eight bells, often rung by visiting campanologists. The church looks at its best when filled with flowers, decorated for Christmas or Harvest Festival, or for our own Flower Festival.

At the end of Eastgate Street is the station, long closed to passenger traffic. The Railway Preservation Society has plans for reopening the line between here and Wymondham. The old trackway is a popular walk with local people, and the next station up the line, County School, is being restored as a tourist attraction.

The old North Elmham station has become a centre for light industry – not popular with surrounding residents, but needed by the village. Yet there has always been noise and activity here. United Dairies once had a big depot on the site, sending milk as far as London every day. The small community at County School, although not in Elmham parish, have connections with the village through 'the school'. This was a home for Barnardo boys. They were encouraged to join the Navy and kept fit by walking to Elmham church on Sunday.

A public footpath runs through Elmham Park, giving fine views of the lake, a different colour every day, and skirting a wood where aconites and snowdrops herald the end of winter. There is a dovecote and a venison house to see, and the parish pound is visible from the Heath Road section.

Although many village people work in the surrounding towns, Elmham is still in the centre of an agricultural area. Farmland surrounds it and there is seasonal work at fruit-picking time and in the vineyard. It is an active village with many clubs for all ages. Come and visit us some time: the cathedral grounds are ideal for a picnic on a fine day.

🍁 NORTH & SOUTH LOPHAM

The neighbouring parishes of North and South Lopham lie one above the other on the southern border of Norfolk, about six miles west of Diss.

The Lophams are well known for their 'wonders' but no one can agree how many there are. Firstly there was a self-grown stile, formed by a tree growing in a strange shape. The second was the Oxfoot Stone, a flattish slab of sandstone measuring three feet by two feet which has an impression of the hoofprint of an ox. It lies at Oxfoot Stone Farm in South Lopham. And another 'wonder' often included on the list is the Lopham ford, a point in South Lopham where the river Ouse and river Waveney begin.

Each village has its own church, St Nicholas' in North Lopham and St Andrew's in South Lopham, most unusual with its tower in the middle of the church. There is also a post office/general stores and a pub in each, the White Horse and the King's Head. The school in North Lopham serves both villages.

The Fen at South Lopham is a conservation area, famous for its Great Raft Spider. It attracts many visitors each year.

🍁 NORTHREPPS

Northrepps is a pleasant village situated nearly three miles from Cromer. The village is approached from all directions by winding country lanes and abounds in flora and fauna.

The community is made up of many different types of houses, including some thatched. Northrepps Hall was the home of Sir Thomas Fowell-Buxton, who worked so hard to achieve the abolition of slavery with his friend William Wilberforce. In the early part of the 19th century experiments on the famous 'breeches buoy' were carried out under the direction of Miss Anna Gurney, who by her enthusiasm in the pursuit of saving lives at sea won the respect of the local seamen. When Trinity House placed a lightship at Happisburgh following her recommendation, the seamen named it 'The Gurney Light'. Miss

The Parson's Pleasure at Northrepps

Gurney lived at nearby Northrepps Cottage, which is now a restaurant set in beautiful countryside.

The fine church, dating from before 1066, was built to its present standard during the 12th to 15th centuries, and is dedicated to St Mary the Virgin. A beautiful rood screen donated by John Playford was removed at the time of the Reformation, stored in a nearby barn and restored to the church in 1911, but owing to its damaged condition it was not placed in its original position.

The village pub is named the Foundry Arms, which takes its name from a foundry that used to be situated nearby, where in 1830 the Gallas plough was first developed. This was widely used until 1920. The plough appears on the church weathervane which was donated by a local craftsman, Mr John Golden, to commemorate the coronation of Queen Elizabeth II in 1953. A former wheelwright at the foundry, 'Old Summers', was the ring-leader of the local smugglers. They once tied the chief Preventive officer to a post whilst they disposed of their contraband. Everyone in the village turned a blind eye when questioned. An ally of the smugglers was Mrs Sally Bean, who lived in a cottage on Shucks Hill, still standing today. The cottage had a 20 mile view of the countryside on the south side which enabled her to give warnings when the Preventive officers were about.

In 1977 a village sign was erected to commemorate the Queen's Silver Jubilee, with no fewer than eleven symbols depicting aspects of village history: the church tower, two shields, St Mary the Virgin and St Benet's Abbey, a cittern, a barrel and post, fetters, a breeches buoy, a car radiator, a Gallas plough, a bridge and a poppy.

The radiator is that of the Rolls-Royce Silver Ghost. Henry Royce stayed in the village while he was developing his famous car. The shield of St Benet's Abbey reminds us of William Rugg, born in Northrepps. He was the last Abbot before the dissolution of the monasteries in 1536 and was Bishop of Norwich from 1536 to 1550. The cittern, a lute-like instrument, reminds us of John Playford, born in 1623, who wrote *A Booke of Newe Lessons for Cittern and Glitten*. The bridge depicted is one of only two remaining of the original 17. The poppy blooms on the edge of our cornfields and lanes; we are on the fringe of Poppyland.

The village school, built in 1879, still flourishes with between 60 and 80 pupils. The population today is 815. In July 1996 a fine new village hall was opened with facilities for the disabled and parking for 50 cars. The village includes large farms both arable and stock, and the Cherryridge turkey farm and processing plant.

This must be the only village in north Norfolk to have an airport, used by private light aircraft and enthusiasts of paragliding, microlight flying and model aircraft.

❧ NORTHWOLD

Travelling along the A134, 18 miles from King's Lynn, and with yet another twelve miles to go before reaching Thetford, Northwold can be seen half a mile away nestling among the trees. It is a long village for it has been contained between the turnpike road to the south and a loop of the Wissey to the north.

The church of St Andrew is still at the centre of the village, and possibly so fine because Hugh of Northwold was Bishop of Ely (1229–54) when the present building was begun and because the money from several charities has been bequeathed for its upkeep – the first in 1479. It contains a unique feature on the north wall, next to the altar; it is the largest Easter sepulchre in the country and dates from about 1480. A wall-hanging near the door gives an explanation of its original use in pre-Reformation ritual. It is now some nine feet by eleven feet, but was originally larger as the chalk from which it is made is not the most durable material.

There are several chalk cottages to admire, some with cinder galletting; whether for strength or decoration is unknown but a good example can be seen opposite the junction of the street and the present Methwold Road. Knapped flint cottages can be seen at the western end and at the last property to the east in the hamlet of Little London. The Manor Farm House has the date 1635 on the gable end and it and Old Farm, almost rebuilt and now renamed, are probably the oldest dwellings still occupied. Opposite Hall Lane is Sycamore House, a three storied dwelling unusual for Northwold. This Georgian-style house is built in front of a much older property, both of which, at one time, belonged to the owner of the village tanyard – no doubt a thriving business in times past.

Walk along Hall Lane to see the school, village hall and almshouses; the dedication stone (date 1874) can be seen from the village hall car park. These three establishments all owe their existence to Caroline Amelia Norman, childless widow of one-time rector Richard Charles Manners Norman. Caroline was the daughter of John Julius Augerstein, a Russian Jew, who lived at Weeting Hall some six miles away. It was the Augerstein collection of pictures that was the foundation of the National Gallery.

Hovell's Lane borders the sports field, home to thriving clubs for cricket, bowls and football. The field contains the site of Hovell's Manor, a one-time moated dwelling now only visible from aerial photographs. Northwold has not been blessed with village green nor pond but it has the greater advantage that the main road never went through the centre of the village nor is the present main street straight enough for traffic to attain much speed. Life is best suited to the pace of walkers and cyclists. At present there is no industry and probably no more than a score of men are employed in agriculture in the village, while practically all other employment must be found outside and some of the cottages are second homes; yet it does not give the appearance of a dormitory village.

☙ NORTON SUBCOURSE

Norton Subcourse is situated in the south-east of Norfolk, bounded by the river Yare, Loddon and the neighbouring village of Thurlton. Besides the village itself, which lies on the edge of the marshes, there are many scattered farms and dwellings in the area.

Norton is the last village before a chain ferry which crosses the Yare to Reedham and is very popular with tourists.

It is said that in pre-Conquest times there was a priests' settlement on the marshes. A track led from the settlement to a tower which was used by the priests as a fortress. In case of invasion they would transfer themselves and their valuables to the fortress. Using ropes they would climb up to a doorway halfway up the tower, then pull the ropes up after them. The tower is now part of the church and the doorway is still there. The church was built in the 13th century and has a dual dedication: the nave to St Mary and the chancel to St Margaret. Set in the north wall is the tomb of Sir John de Norwich who founded the church. There is a 13th century stone font, some original stained glass, and a list of vicars from 1277.

The old Methodist chapel is now a community centre and is used two days a week as a day centre for the elderly, by the youth club and choir. There is a village shop and a garage and the mobile library calls once a month. Moving out of the village towards the ferry there are two drainage pumps which formerly used wind power to pump water from the surrounding marshes. The last building before the ferry is the Cockatrice Inn which was once a house of ill repute, due to smuggling, but is now a private house.

Due to a deliberate policy of non-expansion, Norton Subcourse has remained a small working village which continues to provide a gentle focus for this area on the edge of Britain's newest National Park.

☙ OLD BUCKENHAM

Old Buckenham is 17 miles south-west of Norwich, with a large green at its heart. The green, which is one of the largest in the country, is watched over by the Green Rights Holders, whose rights were granted in medieval times.

When the Domesday Book was compiled, this village was known simply

159

Old Buckenham Windmill

as Bucham or Buccheham. There was a castle, which was abandoned in 1146. The Norman lord of Buckenham, William d'Albini, then built a new fortress some two miles away to the east. A new village clustered near this later castle and it came to be known as 'New Buckenham' whilst the former village was referred to as 'Old Buckenham'. The earthen ramparts of both the old and the new castles can still be seen, the first alongside Abbey Road, the second on the road approaching New Buckenham.

There are two shops and two pubs in the village. The main centre for recreation is the village hall, which was opened in 1979. The smaller Memorial Room adjoining the village hall was built in 1983 with money provided by the 453rd Bomb Group, who were stationed in the village during the Second World War.

All Saints' church is unusual because it has a thatched roof and an octagonal tower from the foundations upwards. There are royal links within the church, there being a carved stone face of Henry I's widow, Queen Adelicia. This lady married William d'Albini in 1138, three years after the King's death. She was reputed to have been one of the most beautiful women in the kingdom and she was 35 when she married William. According to the chronicles she bore him seven children and died in 1151.

On the north chancel wall is a memorial to Lionel Robinson, a wealthy Australian businessman who lived at Old Buckenham Hall from 1906 until his death in 1922. One of his most celebrated achievements was when he arranged for the Australian touring team of 1921 to play a representative England XI on the cricket ground he had lovingly created at Old Buckenham Hall from turf brought over specially from Australia. Although England declared at 256 (Hobbs 85 retired hurt), rain stopped play and the match ended in a draw. The cricket ground remains today.

The church also houses a bier which is thought to be one of the oldest in the country. It is made of oak, has collapsible handles and would have been used by all the parishioners for their burials. The date 1655 is carved on the side.

Old Buckenham Windmill was built in 1818, with the largest diameter tower in England and five pairs of stones. It was in operation until 1926 producing flour and feed. It is owned by the Norfolk Windmills Trust, the cap and sails being restored in 1996 after years of decay. It is open to the public on the second Sunday of each month and on Bank Holidays during the summer.

🍁 OLD HUNSTANTON

Tucked away at the very north-west corner of the county, Old Hunstanton has as neighbours the North Sea to the north and the Wash to the west. The name Hunstanton (sometimes, but not invariably, pronounced 'Hunston') has variously been held to mean 'Hunstan's town', or 'Honey Stone Town' after the brown carrstone quarried nearby and used for building purposes. Formerly called Hunstanton, the village is nowadays known as Old Hunstanton to distinguish it from the town of (New) Hunstanton, the well-known holiday resort a mile away. The town, originally the southern part of the parish, grew up in Victorian times with the coming of the railway. The main effect in the village of this upheaval was the construction of a championship golf-links behind the dunes of the beach to the east.

Village history goes back to the time of St Edmund (who was shipwrecked here in AD 855), but the foundations of the bridge carrying the A149 coastal road over the river Hun to the east of the village are said by some to be Roman, and shards of Roman pottery have been found. The Domesday Book states, as might be expected, that the occupations of the inhabitants were fishing and agriculture, something which is largely true today.

Hunstanton (village and town) is one of the few places in Britain where the foreshore is privately owned. The Le Strange family, squires and lords of the manor for more than 800 years, not only own the beach (and, according to a quaintly-worded charter, everything in the sea as far as a man riding a horse can throw a javelin from the low-tide mark), but they also hold the title of Lord High Admiral of the Wash. In the 1930s the famous German long-distance swimmer, Fraulein Mercedes Gleitze swam the Wash from Lincolnshire to Norfolk. As she came ashore at Old Hunstanton, the then squire stepped forward and claimed her as his legal property!

The ruins of a chapel, said to have been built by St Edmund as thanksgiving for his survival from shipwreck, stand on the clifftop near the early 19th century lighthouse. The light was extinguished at the outbreak of the First World War and never rekindled. The lighthouse is now a private dwelling. In the War the village was the home of a very hush-hush government listening-post. Hippesley Hut, actually a bungalow, housed a unit which monitored groups of German zeppelins, sending the intelligence by telegraph to London; although it was so secret that even now little is known of its activities.

The first lifeboat started service in 1867, and we still have one (after a gap from 1931 to 1979). In 1920, Old Hunstanton was selected by the RNLI for tractor trials to replace the horses which up to then dragged all British lifeboats to the water. The present lifeboat, *Spirit of America*, was provided from a British-American appeal.

Of course, a parish bordering on the sea cannot have avoided being involved in smuggling in the 18th and 19th centuries; and in the churchyard can be seen the tombstone of a Light Dragoon who was shot in 1784 by smugglers while assisting the local customs officer. That the killers were never brought to justice, in a small community where everybody must have known everybody else's business, suggests that the authorities may have secretly considered that the payment of customs duties was a more barbaric practice than murder. One of the lanes in the village is still called Smugglers' Lane.

The large church of St Mary the Virgin is 14th century. It contains several tombs of the Le Strange family. The fact that the font is Norman suggests that there must have been an earlier church on the site.

The only thing in the village that might perhaps be classed as an industrial plant is the waterworks. 'Grandfather's Bath', the spring which feeds the Hall moat, rises in the Hall Park and is the source of the river Hun. Together with other springs it produces a sufficient quantity of good drinkable, but hard, water for us to be able not only to use it ourselves, but to export it to the rest of north-west Norfolk.

In September 1977, the Queen's Jubilee year, Old Hunstanton WI presented a new village sign depicting the legend of the Le Strange family and the family crest together with the WI crest. In the brick and flint plinth on which the sign stands, a box was buried containing one of each denomination of the year's coins with a list of the prices of tea, coffee, bread, cigarettes and a farmworker's wages. The sign was blessed by the vicar of St Mary's church.

❧ ORMESBY ST MARGARET

Ormesby St Margaret is a large village on the edge of Broadland and a mile or so inland from the coast. Ormesby was one of the many villages in this area settled by the Vikings. These 10th century residents of Ormesby are shown on the village sign, erected in 1971 to celebrate the 50th anniversary of Ormesby WI.

The woodland of the Lacon estate enhances the centre of the village, making a backdrop for the village green and memorial green. Some of the village's oldest and most interesting buildings face the green. This unusually large green of about two acres was given to the village by the Lacons, after the re-routing of a village road so it no longer passed Ormesby Hall. The green is commonland and until the First World War a regular market was held.

The church of St Margaret stands on high ground and can be seen from the centre of the village. This 15th century church has a Norman doorway arch and a fine embattled west tower, with one bell. The church contains brasses and memorials of the Clere family, including Sir Robert Clere of 1529 and Lady Alice Clere of 1538, aunt of Queen Ann Boleyn. In the churchyard there is an impressive family vault belonging to the Lacon family. In earlier times Ormesby boasted five churches when the village was spread over a greater area and made up of a series of hamlets.

'The school on the green' was built in 1875 and was Ormesby's only school until 1970 when a middle school was built. It closed in July 1989 with the opening of a new first school in the village. The school was under the trusteeship of the churchwardens and has not been sold, but made into a community centre.

One of the roads leading from the centre of the village has the unusual name of Wapping. Follow this road round and you will find yourself in a hidden area of the village. The cottages in Wapping were built in the 1840s on land that had previously been gardens or allotments. A bricklayer from East London, called Richmond, built the cottages over a period of years. He is reputed to have walked from London to Norfolk and worked on Ormesby's Wapping in the summer months and returned to London in the winter. He was a thrifty chap and used seconds and kiln bottom bricks from Ormesby's brickworks and got the fishermen and beachcombers at California to save him useful pieces of driftwood, timbers and oars, which were used for the interior woodwork of the cottages. This led to the cottages being quaint and irregular in size but adding to their charm. When in London, Richmond worked on the new tenements that were being built in East London at that time, and some of the cottages bear the names of the buildings he worked on, eg, Paradise Place and Prospect Place.

Practically all reminders of the Midland and Great Northern railway have disappeared, although the station house and two crossing houses remain.

Nothing much remains of the old self-contained agricultural village, with its rural trades and market gardening. The village has grown considerably since the Second World War. Ormesby is a friendly and beautiful place in which to live and despite its size still remains a village, offering all its inhabitants all that is best in village life.

🍁 OVERSTRAND

Overstrand is a pleasant seaside village in north Norfolk. It was originally a fishing village and the buildings on the cliffs where the fishermen lived and worked formed a community known as Beckhythe. Fishing is still carried on and many of the family names of those who man the crab boats today may be found in old records.

Sadly the village has lost some of its character but there remain several flint cottages and also many impressive buildings to remind us of the era, from the turn of the century to the First World War, when Overstrand was known as the village of millionaires. The popularity of the area for holiday visitors started with the coming of the railway to north Norfolk, and an article in a London newspaper in the late 19th century by Clement Scott extolling the virtues of the peaceful area he called 'Poppyland'. He coined this name because of the many wild red poppies growing in the grass and wheatfields, along the hedgerows and on the cliffs in the area from Cromer, eastwards as far as Sidestrand (the neighbouring village about two miles east of Overstrand). The interest in Poppyland, aroused by poems and books by Scott, encouraged many notable artists and literary figures of the time to visit Overstrand. Victorian and Edwardian hotels, flats and private houses still stand as a reminder of those days.

At the turn of the century no less than six millionaires had houses in Overstrand. On the cliff the young Edwin Lutyens was the architect for a conversion of two villas into a grand residence for Lord and Lady Battersea. This was called 'The Pleasaunce', and had extensive and attractive grounds and gardens designed by Gertrude Jekyll. Next to the church stands Overstrand Hall, also by Lutyens, for Lord and Lady Hillingdon. A large house, now divided, was originally 'Pear Tree Cottage' owned by Lord Randolph Churchill, father of Sir Winston Churchill, who stayed in the village on more than one occasion, and is said to have mobilised the Navy for the First World War, as First Lord of the Admiralty, when staying here.

165

St Martin's church was built in 1914, incorporating the ruins of a medieval church. In the years between, a new church, Christ Church, had been built alongside the ruins, but when this proved too small the old church was restored and rebuilt. It contains several tombs and memorial plaques to members of the Buxton and Gurney families, including that of Sir Thomas Fowell Buxton, a colleague of Sir William Wilberforce in the abolition of the slave trade.

Also in the church is a memorial to Anna Gurney and Sarah Buxton, cousins, who lived in nearby Northrepps Cottage and founded the Belfry School. The name derives from the fact that the school was conducted in the church belfry until the school building, chiefly of local flintstones, was built in 1830 about 700 yards along the road.

The school, all these years later, still serves the village and is an important part of village life. Overstrand is a thriving community of over 1,000 inhabitants. There are six shops and many busy clubs and societies which meet and help one another, catering for many varied needs and interests.

PENSTHORPE

Pensthorpe was once a small village south-east of Fakenham. Anglo-Saxon cemeteries of the 4th and 5th centuries found in the area have provided many clues to the past. Pensthorpe village is no more, but it is the home today of one of the largest collections of waterfowl in the world.

Gravel extracted along the river Wensum produced huge lakes, which with thought and ingenuity have been landscaped to produce an ideal habitat for wildlife and waterfowl, as well as meadow and waterside walks. Pensthorpe can be found, well signposted, off the A1067 Fakenham to Norwich road.

PENTNEY

Pentney is an attractive village off the A47 between King's Lynn and Swaffham. The church of St Mary Magdalene is a long building, the oldest part of which is Norman. It is mainly noteworthy for the discovery of six Saxon brooches, dating from the early 9th century, in the churchyard in 1977. These were declared treasure trove and valued at £135,000. Mr King, who found them while he was digging a grave, donated £25,000 to the church so that the roof could be repaired.

There is the stump of a market cross to the south-west of the church. From here there is a fine view across the lakes formed by gravel pit workings. Birds in increasing numbers are to be found on the sand banks, many of them geese.

Pentney Abbey was an Augustinian priory founded in the 12th century. Only the gateway remains, a two storey building with battlements, built of flint.

The old Narborough and Pentney railway station has now been converted to a house. Over the old crossing is the Pentney Leisure Centre. Pentney Park caravan site attracts many visitors in the summer months, and nearby Bradmoor Lakes are a pleasant area for a stroll or a picnic.

PLUMSTEAD

Plumstead is a small village lying between Little Barningham and Baconsthorpe, on the road leading to Holt. It is a mixture of old brick and flint cottages, two farm houses, a group of council houses and some new houses and bungalows. The old pub, the Cherry Tree, is now a private dwelling and houses have been built on its bowling green. The group of council houses provides the link between the Cherry Tree and the 'Cherries' on its bowling green and the older houses in the village.

At the far end of the village a well restored house bears the title 'The Old Post Office', with a Penny Black painted on the wall. From this end of the village the road runs east for a good half mile to the Board school at Matlaske.

Plumstead church of St Michael has been well restored. The chancel dates from about 1300 and there is some 15th century stained glass in the windows. Until quite recently the churchwarden lived in a very small cottage next to the church, leaving it twice each day to unlock the church and looking after the cleaning of the interior and tidying the churchyard.

PORINGLAND

Poringland was once the two villages of East and West Poringland. The main village, once known as East Poringland, is situated approximately five miles

167

from Norwich on the Bungay road. This village has grown in recent years with quite an assortment of different dwellings, most noticeable along The Street, where tiny old cottages nestle alongside more modern properties.

At the heart of the village is All Saints' church with its round Norman tower, and along the mile long street there are a wide range of businesses to cater for all the needs of a growing population. The village hall is an ancient corrugated iron-clad building but it provides shelter for many local groups. To the rear of the hall are Poringland primary and nursery school alongside the Memorial playing field and pavilion, home to Poringland Wanderers football teams, a bowls club and a children's corner.

Poringland village sign, located by the village green and pond, was donated by Poringland WI in 1970 to commemorate their 50th anniversary and depicts the oak tree painted by John Crome. The original tree may or may not still be alive in someone's back garden.

Poringland is no longer a peaceful village as heavy traffic thunders through the main street throughout the day, but there are quiet public footpaths still to be found on the outskirts of the village. One can walk past the Roman Catholic church via fields and bridleways to Brooke or past the Free church and the newly planted Poringland Wood across fields to Stoke Holy Cross.

All that remains of West Poringland lies half a mile from the main village along the Shotesham road. It consists of a few cottages, a farm and a barn grouped around a green and pond. Only the site of St Michael's church marked on maps reminds us that this was once a village in its own right.

🍁 RANWORTH

The broad on which Ranworth is situated is in fact Malthouse Broad, to the staithe of which barley used to be brought in wherries for malting. The Maltsters public house is a reminder of those days. Ranworth Broad lies behind The Old House and can be seen from the floating information centre of the Norfolk Naturalists Trust.

In 1827 a wherry at Ranworth was used for a totally different purpose: that of 'cooping' a number of Norwich voters to prevent them voting in the aldermanic elections. Captured and imprisoned on a wherry moored in the middle of the broad, they were not released until it was too late for them to get back and vote.

168

The magnificent church of St Helen, which dates back to 1370, overlooks both broads. It is famous for its 15th century rood screen still resplendent in its original paint, uncovered and cleaned by experts but not added to in any way. Of equal interest is the wonderful Antiphoner, written and illuminated 500 years ago by the monks of Langley Abbey, with the finely painted miniatures as fresh and bright as the day they were painted.

REEDHAM

The village of Reedham, about twelve miles south-east of Norwich, lies on the banks of the river Yare, with a road running along the riverside and another road above on the higher ground aptly called 'The Hills'. The river has a very fast running tide with a rise and fall of approximately three feet, and it flows from Norwich to Great Yarmouth, where it enters the North Sea. It can be crossed at Reedham by a chain ferry which carries three cars at a time and operates all the year round. In summer, of course, it is very busy and a wait of an hour is often experienced at the height of the season as eager holidaymakers queue up to make the crossing.

The river is also crossed at Reedham by a railway swing bridge, an iron bridge which was built in 1846 and carries trains running from Norwich via Reedham station to Lowestoft. The swing bridge is now electrically operated and will swing open to let yachts pass through. There are also large sea-going vessels which pass through, like the cargo oil boat *Blackheath*, a common sight in winter as she labours upriver taking fuel to the sugar beet factory at Cantley. It's a tight squeeze through the bridge but skilful steering triumphs.

The early 1900s saw paraffin street lights in the village, put there after a customer from the Lord Nelson, an attractive Tudor building and a public house, fell in the river and was drowned. With the coming of electricity to the village the street lamps disappeared into private gardens and no street lighting has been introduced since but the Lord Nelson does have a spotlight to save history repeating itself outside the pub!

Trading wherries were once seen passing through Reedham up to Norwich with their goods, calling at the Brickmakers Arms on the waterfront. Today, the Brickmakers Arms has become the Briar Cottage Tea Rooms, selling delicious cream teas. The Ship Inn provides other refreshments and moorings. Today, there are three boatyards in the village, Pearson Marine and Sanderson's serving the hire fleets of the holiday industry and Sea Coral who build and furnish luxurious fibre glass boats for private use.

Pettitt's Feathercraft and Bird and Wild Life Park is a big tourist attraction in Reedham, and is continually expanding. It all started in 1921 when Victor Pettitt started in business with a few poultry in a disused railway carriage on a smallholding in Reedham. In 1948 he had on his stand at the Norfolk Show the first quick-frozen poultry in the country. It is quite common to see peacocks strutting down the lane as they wander out from the wild life park and sweep majestically amongst the gravestones in the churchyard.

There has been a church dedicated to St John the Baptist on the existing site since Saxon times. In 1981 the thatched roof of the church caught fire, caused by a cigarette from a workman as work was in progress on the tower. The church was completely gutted and has since been rebuilt, though not with a thatched roof. Loss of plaster on the north wall exposed the wall structure in an interesting herringbone pattern of wrought blocks of freestone interlaid with bricks, undoubtedly of Roman origin and thought to be once part of a Roman lighthouse. The Department of the Environment was very interested in this and contributed a generous amount of money towards the restoration of the church on condition the bricks were left exposed and the church left open in the daylight hours.

It must be good healthy air around Reedham for there are at least three centenarians buried in the churchyard. One Richard Pottle lived to be 108 and has a road named after him, Pottles Lane.

One unusual leisure activity in the village is a tug of war team called 'The Vikings', taking their name from the early visitors who came to Reedham in bygone days. They have built their own hall as their social centre and in 1988 became champions of East Anglia in a great pull.

🍁 REEPHAM

Leaving the north-west section of the Norwich outer ring road, the Reepham road eventually leads into Reepham, but it will be almost ten miles of pleasant undulating country before the towers of the twin churches can be seen above the treetops.

Once there were three, the parish boundaries meeting in the one churchyard, but All Saints', Hackford was destroyed by fire in 1543. Its ruined tower was taken down in 1790 and all that remains today is a small part of the wall. St Mary's, dating mainly from the 14th century, now serves the three parishes of Reepham, Whitwell and Hackford. The chancel of St Michael's, Whitwell is connected to St Mary's by a choir vestry and remains consecrated, though the main part of the church is in use as a meeting hall. The bells in the tower of St Michael's are still rung by local and visiting ringers.

Reepham is a 'town' from the days when a busy cattle market was held in what is now the car park in Station Road. It is a shopping and business centre for the surrounding rural areas and a good variety of shops can supply most needs. The spacious Market Square is closely lined with a variety of Georgian buildings. Market day is Wednesday, and the WI Market is held in the Bircham Institute. The Market Square is the focal point of life in Reepham (population about 2,000) and has for generations been the venue for outdoor gatherings.

Many smaller buildings of historical interest lie in the picturesque narrow street beyond the churchyard and market place. Quiet now, this was once a busy thoroughfare, the names and facades of some of the houses still showing their use as farms, ale houses, shops and a bakery. Almost the whole of the older part of the village is designated as a conservation area, the aim being to avoid unsympathetic development so that the rural aspect of Reepham is preserved.

Once there were two railway stations, at Reepham and Whitwell, but today the old track provides a pleasant country walk in a half circle around the town with attractive views of Reepham in its wooded setting. There are many field paths within minutes of the market place and an ever changing landscape as the farming year progresses.

🍁 REYMERSTON

Reymerston is a peaceful village three miles from Hingham and six miles from Dereham, with a population of about 144. Most of the land is farmed by about eight farmers. It is heavy land, and lots of primroses and mistletoe grow in the village. There is a gravel pit on the road to Hingham.

The church of St Peter was built in the 1300s and has several interesting features, including a Belgian communion rail which may date from about 1700 and some 16th century stained glass. It is now in the Barford group of parishes. There is one shop in Reymerston (which has been in the same family for over

70 years), but no pub, no school, no chapel and no village green. The village hall, built in 1956, helps to keep the community together. A few new bungalows have been built and two barn conversions have created an art gallery and a flower shop. A golf course with a restaurant has been opened. Perhaps Reymerston's most famous resident is Wing Commander Wallis of Reymerston Hall, who invented the giro plane.

🍁 ROCKLAND ST MARY

The early settlement of Rokelunda (so named because of its rooks, which are a feature of the present day village sign) became the village of Rockland St Mary, lying between the river Yare and the Norwich to Loddon road.

In years gone by, but within living memory, the village had its own brickyard, a blacksmith, two foundries, a slaughterhouse, a baker and butcher and a number of market gardens and farms providing employment for the villagers. Produce and bricks were shipped by wherry from the staithe, leading off Rockland Broad, or by cart. The railway never came.

Rockland Staithe and the New Inn, Rockland St Mary

172

The staithe is now a popular overnight mooring for pleasure craft and the Broad, which links the staithe to the main river, is much used by anglers and wildfowlers. On its banks is a hide provided by the RSPB and a footpath running from the village grazing marshes to the river.

Nowadays many of the 350 houses are occupied by those who work in Norwich or who have moved from other parts of the country on retirement. The village still has a shop and post office, a hairdresser and a public house which was built to serve the needs of the workers in the brickyard, which closed at the beginning of the Second World War.

The forge and many other small businesses have gone but the village school, built in 1840, survives next to the Margaret Mack Village Hall, which was named after a former President of the WI who sadly died at an early age.

There is a second hall, known as the Parish Room, which was established as a reading room on land gifted by the Hotblack family. They were local landowners to whom memorials are to be found in the village church, which occupies a site to the west of the village on which it has stood for some 700 years.

🍁 ROCKLANDS

Rocklands, with a population of about 700 people, lies on the edge of Breckland, an area of heath, conifer forest and flint. Despite its name, it is not a 'land of rocks' but an area of undulating countryside.

Originally there were three parishes, each surrounding an ancient flint church: Rockland St Peter's, All Saints and St Andrew's. Nowadays all that remains of St Andrew's is a ruined tower, inhabited by pigeons, which stands stark against the skyline. Nearby, All Saints' church is of Saxon origin and contains a rare Saxon sepulchral slab which now rests in the chancel. In the churchyard is the school room building which was built in 1851 by the rector to provide a place of education for the parish children. St Peter's church, on the opposite side of the village, is of slightly later origin and has a round tower with an upper octagonal belfry. Inside are an ancient rood screen and pews which were removed from Tottington church, now enveloped in the nearby Ministry of Defence Battle Area which was created during the 1939–45 war.

At one time Rocklands had seven public houses but nowadays it only has one – the White Hart behind which the Bowling Club hold their matches.

173

There is a playing field and children's play area with a pavilion beside the football and cricket club pitches. Each Monday there is a Thrift Shop where anything from second-hand clothes to garden produce is sold for playing field funds. Not far away is the village hall which is again supported by fund-raising from such events as the Annual Horticultural and Craft Show and hire of the hall for functions. It is also home to the village playgroup. The village shop and post office provide a great service to the parishioners. Local children attend the village school which numbers between 60 and 70 pupils aged from four to eleven years old. They are able to extend their school activities by using the playing field and village hall as well as studying nature and the changing seasons along the nearby country lanes.

🍁 ROLLESBY

This village, eight miles north-west of Great Yarmouth, lies near the 200 acre Rollesby Broad, which is linked to Ormesby and Filby Broads. The first evidence of settlement was by the Beaker Folk circa 2000 BC, who came to Eastern England from Central Europe. They received the name from their distinctive bell-shaped beakers. Rollesby derives its name from the Danish Rolf or Rollo, a common name among sea kings.

St George's church is built on high ground at the west end of the village. The base of the tower is Saxon, but the rest was started by the Normans in the 11th century. The remainder of the church is 13th and early 14th century, when work was interrupted by the Black Death.

Rollesby's most famous son was Thomas Godwin or Goodwin DD, born 1600. Educated at Cambridge, he became an eminent divine and author of several religious works. He was the first Minister of the City Temple in London. He became chaplain to the Council of State under Cromwell and was believed to have been connected with Old World Cottage. This bore a plaque 'T. G. and M. G. 1583', and is sited opposite the church.

The original Rollesby Hall was Jacobean, built in 1618 by Leonard Mapes. In 1824 it passed to the Ensor family who greatly extended it. This has now been demolished and a new Hall built on the site.

The House of Industry (workhouse) for the East and West Flegg Hundreds was erected here in 1776, at a cost of £2,300, on 22 acres for 400 people. It was the shape of the letter H to segregate the sexes. The workhouse was

Rollesby church

administered by a governor, matron and chaplain under the control of 48 guardians. The Petty Sessions for the two Hundreds were held at the workhouse until 1939 when it was commandeered by the military. It is now a guest house called The Old Court House.

In 1840 the National school was built to accommodate 90 children, and enlarged in 1892 to hold 100. The school closed in 1924 and the current one is now on the main road. The old school was burned down during the war and the village hall is now on the site.

Although not a tourist village, Rollesby Broad is an ideal spot for fishing and sailing as this group is isolated from the rest of the Norfolk Broads. No motorised pleasurecraft are allowed on the broad as it is used as a reservoir. Now as always Rollesby remains primarily an agricultural village.

🍁 ROUGHTON

Roughton is about three miles inland from Cromer. A Neolithic barrow has been traced by crop markings from the air, and four tumuli on the heath have revealed beads and an urn.

The church of St Mary is mainly 14th century, but the round Saxon tower is notable for the inner doorway about twelve feet from the ground, and for the herringbone decoration near the base of the exterior. After the Black Death, the village was moved from the east of the church to the north-west and it has grown up there over the years.

In a cottage built in 1500, religious murals have been found on the upstairs walls, but there is no evidence as to who lived there. There is nothing to confirm that it was the residence of the priests.

There have been various charities for the poor of the parish, and in the 19th century a Free school was founded which is still open. It is one of those under threat of closure.

A turnpike road was built in 1611, parallel to the present Norwich Road. Where the two join was probably the original post office. There were a number of coaches from Norwich to Cromer which stopped at Roughton, one of these being the 'Lobster Coach' owned by Thomas Cook.

In the Domesday Book, two mills are recorded as having existed. The present mill was built in 1614. It was burned to the ground in 1906, and was rebuilt in 1977 as a home for the First Rural Scout Group.

A forge was in use 150 years ago, having three or four flues so it was quite large. The present forge is now converted into a house and a craft centre.

In 1933, the mathematician Albert Einstein, famous for his Theory of Relativity, escaped from Germany and lived in a hut on the Gunton side of the village.

Roughton is a flourishing village with about 750 inhabitants. There is a supermarket, post office and service station, a fruit orchard, a riding school and a bowls club which was opened in 1950, and various activities take place in the village hall.

RUNTON

Runton is fairly unusual as it is open village divided into two halves – East and West – though this single identity has tended to become lost over the last few years.

West Runton is a Site of Special Scientific Interest. It lies on a freshwater bed which is part of a complex series of marine and freshwater deposits known as the Cromer Forest Bed dating from over half a million years ago. A wealth of fossil mammal remains have been found here, most famously in 1990 the remains of a huge elephant. This spectacular find is of international significance. Two full scale excavations were undertaken and the precious remains are to be found in the Norwich and Cromer museums.

Situated on the vulnerable North Norfolk coast, between Cromer and Sheringham, Runton has suffered losses through erosion. Efforts have recently been made at West Runton to protect the coastline.

The parish church of the Holy Trinity is situated in West Runton and dates from pre-Norman times. In the early years there was an unhealthy rivalry between Runton parish and Beeston Priory but in the 16th and 17th centuries the benefices appear to have been combined. The fabric of Holy Trinity became very dilapidated. It was not until the 19th century that restoration work was put in hand – and it goes without saying that this continues to this day. The church is in the familiar flint and brick work which so characterises this area.

Methodism came first to East Runton, in 1845, and the remains of the original chapel are incorporated into the enlarged building of 1897. It was not until 1951 that a chapel was built in West Runton, in memory of Willie Long, a fisherman and evangelist of some note.

177

It was the purchase of the estate of the Rev Paul Johnson by Sir Thomas Buxton in the early 19th century which was to have a significant impact on Runton. He set up model farms, made coverts and plantations and fenced in the dole lands. He brought much needed employment to the village and there appears to have been little opposition to his activities even though he often ignored the rights of others. His family was to build the school in East Runton in 1852 on land adjoining the Lower Common and enlarge it in 1858. Although closed in the 1950s the school buildings are still in use, party as a Anglican church and partly as a private dwelling.

Runton was further influenced by the building of the railway. This increased the holiday trade from the turn of the 20th century, with Runton acting as an overflow accommodation area for Cromer and Sheringham. Many of the terraced houses in East Runton were built specifically for the holiday trade. Now this holiday trade is a significant source of employment and is a major influence on the village and its surroundings. Camping was popular between the two World Wars and since the end of the 1939–45 war caravan sites have been developed, mostly along the cliff. These are viewed with mixed feelings by the villagers especially since a successful challenge to the old tradition by which the caravans were removed in the winter months. This tradition was founded on the belief that these sites were on 'Half Year' land which had to be free for grazing of animals between October and April each year. It is the holiday trade which has encouraged the several high class restaurants to be found in the village, including the 'Mirabelle' which enjoys a nationwide reputation. Similarly, the expansion of the riding stables at West Runton to become a Shire Horse Centre, also with a national reputation, owes much to the holiday trade and it is a source of pride that such a small village should boast conservation work of such importance.

Fishing remains an important activity – with the crab and lobster trade for which this coast is so famous – as does farming. Both are valuable links with the past, for other industries have now disappeared including the brick works, gas works and herring smoking.

If the area is rightly famous as one of outstanding natural beauty, so also is it famous for its local families – the Abbs, the Greens, the Brownsells and the Leakes, to name but a few. Many holiday families who have for successive generations made their annual trip here have happy recollections of the fathers, mothers, grandfathers and grandmothers of the present generation of Runton families. But the village has also become a favourite place for retirement especially for those with long-standing links forged by happy holidays at Runton. The old and new villagers have blended in well, sharing perhaps a common love for this an ordinary English village but with its own attractive nature.

🍁 SAHAM TONEY

Saham Toney has a long history of human habitation. The site of Pages Place, still a farmhouse, was a thriving farmstead when the Domesday Book was compiled in 1086. A small Romano-British market town prospered in the southern half of the village for at least 400 years, and supported a larger population with better communications than at any time until the reign of Queen Victoria. Situated on the edge of Breckland, in its centre is a large privately owned mere, as old as the last Ice Age, where it has been said, were once lake dwellings.

The village has a large flintstone church dating from the 13th century which has had many alterations over the years but is still an imposing building. It once boasted three windmills, a small brick kiln; a lime kiln; two blacksmiths; four chapels; seven public houses and several general shops. Now only one chapel, one public house and one post office/general store remain even though the village has doubled in housing over the last 40 years.

As the age of the motor car has taken over from the horse, a breaker's yard and a car repair service has replaced the blacksmiths' forges. A small unit produces hand-made wooden toys. One business started by a local man was built up into a fleet of coaches and is now owned by a larger company, but still based in the village ferrying school children and local inhabitants to larger towns and on outings.

There were once a few eccentrics scattered among the mainly sober, pious citizens. One gentleman insisted on being buried on his own land, still called the 'burying ground', and one clergyman built a 'folly' of a ruin in the rectory grounds – the road beside was called 'the Ruin Hill', while yet another cleric excommunicated a gentleman of the parish for omitting to pay his tithes, which led to questions being asked in the House of Commons. Another inhabitant, repenting of his bibulous ways, turned teetotal and poured all his beer and wine in the river Wissey, which enraged his fellows so much that he was driven from the parish, whereby he committed suicide and was buried at 'Crossways', possibly at Threxton.

179

Parkers School at Saham Toney

In one thing Saham Toney has indeed been fortunate, and that is in the number of enlightened benefactors who have added considerably to the amenities of the village, particularly in the field of education. Edward Goffe, who died in 1612, built and endowed a school. It is now a fine private house. He built four almshouses for single people, also now a private house. Rev Parker, in the 19th century, built the present Parker's School, which has been incorporated into some larger modern buildings with all the facilities required by more than 100 school children. He built a smaller school at the north end of the village on Saham Hills, now a private house. He must have been a man of compassion, showing consideration for the little legs of four and five year olds, tramping up hill and down dale in all weathers. He also built Saham College, a school for boys with accommodation for boarders, a very fine building which is now two private dwellings.

More recently Florrie Carver's bequest provided the church with an area for making refreshments and a toilet. In 1989 Mr Neville Wells Cole MBE left the village eleven acres of land, half of which was sold for housing. The proceeds of the sale funded a new village community centre which was completed in 1997.

🍁 SANDRINGHAM & WEST NEWTON

The villages are very privileged and proud of being part of Her Majesty's Sandringham estate. The two villages are like twins – they have individual identities but definitely belong to the same family.

The houses are built mainly of brick and carrstone, a local sandstone of attractive brown colour. The people are mostly employees and pensioners of the estate. Due to mechanised farming there are more pensioners than young families, but despite this there is still a flourishing school in the village.

Both villages have a church and the West Newton church keeps close contact with the school, where they take part in festivities such as Harvest Festival and Christmas. Sandringham church is famous for its silver altar and many memorials to the Royal Family, whereas West Newton church is a typical parish church.

Behind West Newton church stands the village hall built in 1911 by Mrs Farrer, the American wife of Rev Farrer, the rector. During the 1930s Queen Mary had the 'Little Room' built on the side of the hall to be used as a work room for such as quilt making. This room is now known as the WI Committee Room. Both Her Majesty and Queen Elizabeth The Queen Mother continue to show interest in the WI as they attend the January meeting as members.

West Newton no longer has a village shop, but has retained its post office. There is no public house, but a club was instituted by King Edward VII for the villagers and this is the meeting place for the Seniors Club.

Two ancient roads cross the estate, the Icknield Way and the Peddars Way. Situated in a field near West Newton Farm there was a Roman villa, excavated in 1949. It has been extensively plundered for building material. In the nearby ruins of Appleton church, Roman tiles have been found built into the fabric of the tower. Further excavation produced evidence of a hypocaust and of extensive iron smelting on the site.

West Newton was added to the Sandringham estate in the 16th century when the family owning the land was named Cobbe. They lived at Sandringham for around 200 years. At the time of the Civil War Colonel William Cobbe raised a band of local militia and marched to defend King's Lynn against the Roundheads. For this action his lands were sequestrated during the Commonwealth and when Charles II was restored the lands were returned to him for his loyalty to the Royalist cause.

181

As the years progressed the estate belonged to the Hoste family, then the Hoste Henlys and then the Hon Spencer Cowper, stepson of Lord Palmerston. In 1862 it was bought for the Prince of Wales, later Edward VII. There followed a programme of rebuilding and renovating. New cottages were built, also larger houses such as Park House, now the Leonard Cheshire Hotel for the disabled.

🍁 Saxlingham Nethergate & Saxlingham Thorpe

The Saxlinghams lie seven miles south of Norwich beside the busy A140, where two little valleys join and lead down to the river Tas through pleasant water meadows full of marsh marigolds and beside the wooded Smockmill Common.

Saxlingham Nethergate was one of the first areas in Norfolk to be designated a conservation area, because of its outstandingly attractive landscape and village. Along the village street reed-thatched houses are grouped appealingly round the pleasantly designed war memorial, which won a Royal Academy award for its architecture. Further on the small Church Green provides another picturesque focal point, with the simple grey flint church of St Mary the Virgin at one end, flanked by the 17th century Old Hall and the late 18th century Old Rectory designed by Sir John Soane.

By contrast, the present Saxlingham Thorpe straggles along one side of the A140 with only the large modern mill buildings on the other side, though these are on a site mentioned in Domesday. New houses have replaced old cottages, shops and a blacksmith's forge. On the main road only the old toll house remains but there are a few old buildings, including the old Baptist chapel and the prestigious 18th century Lodge, along the two by-roads leading to Saxlingham Nethergate. Intriguingly, Saxlingham Thorpe church, now a ruin, stands a mile away, alone in fields.

The Nethergate church incorporates some Saxon-Norman features. It has clearly been extended and the roof has been raised. Most of the building now visible is 14th century. It is most celebrated for its wealth of medieval stained glass, much of it being the earliest in Norfolk. There are many well carved gravestones with very interesting inscriptions.

182

Some of the stained glass came from the ruined Thorpe church of St Mary Magdalene, the earliest phase of which can be dated at about 1050–1100. Pottery finds in nearby fields show that the village grew up round the church but began to move away by the 14th century. It went westward towards the main road, but first to the present hamlet of Foxhole, where most buildings are timber-framed. There was some migration to Saxlingham Green, which was called Eastgate Green until 1871 and always was part of Saxlingham Nethergate.

The green still appears an idyllically rural scene, with its surrounding cottages and small farmhouses, many of which have been sold and modernised recently. During the work all were discovered to be timber-framed and to belong to the period of the 'Great Rebuilding' of late Elizabethan and early Stuart times. Fieldwalking has proved that the green once extended as far as Hill House and the charming 16th century eyebrow-windowed Hill Cottage, which has now been completely refurbished. Saxlingham Hall, on the green itself, and now a nursing home, was the 17th century Home Farmhouse, with an added Queen Anne brick front, and was modernised and extended by Edward Steward in 1850. The Steward family became lords of the manor and patrons of the living in 1824 and have been closely associated with the village ever since.

Modern farming practice has radically altered the character of Saxlingham village life. Instead of many small tenant farmers, with large numbers of farm workers running mixed and dairy farms, there are now a few large arable farms which have had most hedges removed and which are run by few workers, though one farmer still has a flock of sheep and local children are encouraged to watch lambing and shearing. Unwanted farmhouses and cottages have often been sold to people who work outside the village and this fact, together with the great increase in car-ownership, has closed most of the small shops, workshops and pubs. Saxlingham Nethergate still has its village stores and post office and Saxlingham Thorpe still has its pub – the West End.

🍁 SCOLE

Scole is one of the most southerly villages in Norfolk, on the river Waveney border with Suffolk. It is positioned in an area said to be one of the best examples of pre-Roman field boundaries. This can be seen in the way the Roman road, now the A140 trunk road, cuts across original square fields. Until 1665 the river Waveney was crossed by the paved Roman ford, then a wooden bridge was built to expedite the crossing for stage coaches and other travellers from Norwich south to Ipswich and Colchester.

Scole is approximately 20 miles from Norwich, Ipswich, Thetford and Bury St Edmunds and was a natural choice for a staging post. It was near the crossroads that, in 1655, the White Hart Inn (now the Scole Inn) was built, a magnificent Dutch-gabled, three-storey brick building. The inn also became the area post office with 40 horse-drawn coaches a day. Now long gone are both the great round bed for 30 sociable travellers and the huge carved wooden sign that spanned the turnpike road. In the parish register is a proud entry among the births and deaths that in 1671 King Charles II breakfasted at the White Hart Inn. During the 1780s the highwayman John Belcher had his headquarters at the inn and rode his horse up the Jacobean oak staircase to hide in a bedroom when pursued by the law. The gate put at the top of the stairs to stop him can still be seen.

All the employment as ostlers, postboys, blacksmiths and wheelwrights rapidly declined with the coming of the railway through Diss, which led to the removal of the main post office to that market town. The importance of the village diminished but there was a flax factory by the river, and village trades such as bootmaking, basketmaking, building, blacksmith, brewing and farming still gave employment along with the three large mansions and four public houses.

St Andrew's church was on the 7th January 1963 deliberately set on fire and almost totally gutted. The church was reconsecrated by the then Bishop of Thetford on 17th September 1964.

Almost facing the south porch of the church is a unique headstone commemorating the re-interment of four early Christians who were originally buried in the village about 1,600 years earlier. Surface finds and small-scale archaeological excavations on either side of the main Ipswich to Norwich road, where it crosses the river Waveney, have produced much evidence of Roman occupation of the site. In an area to the north of the river, where the new development of Robinson Road and Clements Close now stands, the bones were discovered in 1983. From the fact that they had been buried well away from the known pagan cemetery, their position in the ground, and that there were no grave goods, it is fairly certain that the bodies had been given

Christian burial. After professional examination the bones were re-interred in the present churchyard on 9th February 1988.

Shortly before the Second World War, council houses were built to the north of the ruined tower mill. More were added after the war when the village had its own doctor, cycle shop, post office, antique shop, garage and general store. In 1964 the first of four housing estates was built to the south of the Diss to Bungay road, in the river valley.

After more than 30 years campaigning, the bypass on the Norwich to Ipswich road (the A140 trunk road) was officially opened in 1995 and with the east/west bypass on the Bury St Edmunds to Yarmouth road opening the same year much of the traffic that had been progressively choking and fragmenting the village became a distant rumble in the background. The comparative lack of vehicles passing through Scole meant the village shop, which had closed in the early 1990s, reopened and with a new hall built onto the village school a sense of community has developed again.

❧ SEA PALLING

Sea Palling is situated 18 miles north-east of Norwich on the B1159. It lies on the coast roughly midway between Cromer and Great Yarmouth, and close to the Broads. There is a good sandy beach, pollution free, which borders on an area of outstanding natural beauty. From the village there is access to several miles of beach and dunes which abound in wildlife and flowers. Seals are often seen off the beach and many species of birds may be seen, especially during migration.

The population of Sea Palling is at present about 450. Fluctuating over the years, it is interesting to note that in 1876 it stood at 485, dropping in 1921 to 346. This decline seems to have continued and in 1983 the population was approximately 340, several houses having been demolished over the years. However, this trend has been reversed, and now with new houses being built in the village it looks set to return to its former level.

The church of St Margaret is Saxon with 14th century additions. In 1779 there was a great fire which destroyed several houses, barns and a granary, and a few days later a further separate fire took a farmhouse and outbuildings. Although there are signs of the church having been affected by the fire it luckily survived. In the church are boards commemorating the lifeboats, which tell of the gallant rescues by the men of Palling. Originally run by the beach companies, the Sea Palling lifeboat station was taken over in 1858 by the RNLI and maintained by them until it closed in 1931. During this time the Palling lifeboats played a very important part in saving many lives from the ships that perished on the Haisbro sands. There is now an inflatable boat manned by the Palling Volunteer Rescue Service.

Several old cottages still exist in the village and Palling Mill still stands in good repair though without cap or sails. Not far from the church stands Moss Fen Lodge, which was built in 1979 from reclaimed materials as a faithful copy of a 16th century house. Much to the delight of the owner it was registered as a grade II listed building by the Department of the Environment.

Probably the most devastating event to befall the village in living memory was the great east coast flood of 1953 when the sea broke through the dunes and inundated the northern end of the village. Many of the old flint cottages were swept away and seven people lost their lives. After the flood great efforts were put into building new sea defences and the Environment Agency has recently constructed a series of offshore reefs to protect the beach in future. Another event which shook the village in more ways than one was the destruction of the original village hall in 1940. It was blown up whilst being used by the military as a store for detonators. Sadly several soldiers were killed and there was some local damage. The explosion was heard for several miles around. The hall was replaced in 1956 by the present village hall which is now much used as the centre of activities in the village.

In the past, fishing and farming were the main occupations of the village folk, with repair of the marrams for the Sea Breach Commissioners another source of income. Four men were employed permanently on this work, supplemented by local fishermen during the period when they were unable to go to sea. Many cottages took in paying guests during the summer season to boost the family finances.

Today, through mechanisation the number employed on the land has dropped dramatically, and fishing as a full time occupation is virtually non-existent. A few people are still employed in shops, but more commute to Norwich or Great Yarmouth or are self employed, working from home. The holiday accommodation is now mostly at the caravan sites in the village, though bed and breakfast is still available.

🍁 SEDGEFORD

Sedgeford grew as a typical example of medieval ribbon development. It hugs the B1454 on either side, beginning with a fairly steep (for Norfolk) hill coming two miles from Norfolk Lavender corner on the A149. The road winds its way past the war memorial and on to Docking, with branches off to Snettisham, Ringstead and Fring.

Numerous new houses have filled in between older properties, bringing country-loving young families to live alongside those who have lived here for generations, such as the Wagg, Frost, Raines, Parsons and Clelland families. There are a few holiday homes but not a disproportionate number.

An archaeological dig at the 'boneyard', a few hundred yards from the village centre, is likely to continue for up to 15 years. The young archaeologists are also surveying the church and bringing to light many interesting facts. A small triangle of grass near the church and a thickly overgrown hedge towards the Snettisham road from the church are all that remain of the medieval green and pound.

There is an active playgroup and drama group. Cricket and football teams use the playing field and an indoor tennis club is flourishing half a mile out of the village near the old Sedgeford station, now a private house. The permanent way is an access road to fields with a wealth of wild flowers growing undisturbed, including the hoary mullein indigenous only to Sedgeford and Heacham. It is possible to identify over 24 different flowers and plants 'along the line'.

Old farmhouses surrounding the village are all privately owned dwellings now, with the small acreages previously attached to them integrated into three large farms. Sheep have made a comeback in the last few years. In 1970 there were about six, now each farm has a huge flock, illustrating the diversification farmers have been compelled to make.

🍁 SEETHING

Situated in south Norfolk, Seething retains the charm of a traditional Norfolk village with several buildings still having thatched roofs, although many have been lost through fires and modernisation over the years. Seething is mentioned in the Domesday Book as Sithinga, a township with two churches, and the thatched church of St Margaret and St Remigius stands in a triangular plot of 'Poor Lands' in the heart of the village.

The round tower is early Norman and in the 1870s was said to have 'commandeered a view extending on a clear day from Norwich Cathedral on one side and Yarmouth Monument on the other'. One of the chief architectural treasures is the beautiful seven sacrament font, dated 1485. It was sent to Norwich to be 'cleaned' in 1862 when the painting and gilding were removed. In the 1930s wall paintings were uncovered dating from the 14th century.

In Seething Park, owned in the 1700s by Thomas Kett Esq, a battle is believed to have been fought and, after skeletons were disturbed when digging foundations for farm buildings, Thomas Kett had a monument erected in the garden of Seething Hall about 1720.

An attractive focal point in the village is the mere, with 17th century Pond Farm and clay lump farm buildings on the roadside. Now where Suffolk Punch horses used to drink, local small children feed the ducks and a road sign warns 'Wild Fowl'. The manor house nearby was the home for several generations of the Crickmore family, and several graves are in Seething churchyard. Further on are two 17th century thatched houses.

In 1947 a large playing field was given to Seething and Mundham by T. S. Fisher Ball in memory of his mother. Here stands the village hall, the second on this site. There are two shops, a butcher's run by R. J. Balls following generations of his family in this trade and still maintaining a traditional delivery round, and a post office and general stores run by F. H. Freestone whose family ran the post office in 1912. Although shopping habits have changed both shops play an indispensable part in the life of village people.

Seething lost houses in 1941 when the airfield was built and this was home, during 1943–1945, to Americans from the 448th Bomb Group. Four hundred and fifty men were killed flying from here and memorials are in Seething churchyard and the airfield, now owned by Waveney Flying Group. In 1987 the restored Second World War control tower was dedicated, with many veterans coming from America, and it is open to the public the first Sunday of the month, May to October.

❧ SHELTON

Little owls call, Canada geese fly into the moats, foxes emerge from their earths, wild flowers grow on the verges, and wild roses, blackberries and old man's beard tumble over the hedges in the small hamlet of Shelton, population about 75, tucked away in south Norfolk.

If Shelton is peaceful now, it had some rousing days in the past. The Shelton family lived here for some 500 years, and Sir Ralph Shelton (died 1497) built the church of St Mary and the Hall. The church still stands, large and bright inside, the east end filled with medieval glass from the chapel of the old Hall. The lovely rich colours from the windows fill the church, even when the sun is not shining. All that remains of the old Hall, built on an acre of ground surrounded by a wide moat, are parts of the curtain wall and the remains of some towers, though some ancient brick in the still-standing Great Barn is said to have come from the old Hall. The present Hall, 300 years old in parts, is built on the site of the old one. A nearby meadow called the Dark Park contains numerous moats and mounds, and is said to be the place where the first inhabitants lived. Deer grazed in the park around the Hall, and the tithe on the land was a deer and two hinds.

Sir Ralph's son, John, married an aunt of Anne Boleyn. She became governess to Princess Mary and Sir John was steward to the household of Princess Elizabeth. When events became unruly at Court, the Tudor princesses were sent down to the peace of Shelton!

Sixty or so years ago the whole village was involved with farming. Then it was possible to meet someone who had never left the village but many people today work outside the village. But how pleased they are to return in the evening to the peace and solitude of Shelton.

❧ SHIPDHAM

The A1075 snakes its way up the hill from Dereham ready for one headlong dash through Shipdham – the scourge of the modern-world heavy traffic. Perhaps Long Shipdham would have been a better name for a village over a mile long with a population of some 2,500. Even as late as the early 1920s the village had no proper road surfaces.

189

It boasted at one time some 20 public or beer houses. A worker getting paid on a Saturday could be both drunk and broke before he reached home. There was little need in those days to go outside the village, as there were shops to cater for all needs – even the cyclists' touring club had a tea room near the green, at which on certain evenings the local branch of the spiritualists would meet in a back room, only to be the target of the local lads who would tap on the window at the right moment and scare everyone inside.

Shipdham even boasted its own fire service with a horse-drawn pump, and on one very hot summer's day the thatch on the King's Head public house caught fire. The fire chief was informed but had to make sure for himself in case it was a false alarm. He then had to cycle back and catch the horse. By the time they arrived, the place was well alight. The first thing to be saved was the beer from the cellar. One fireman was so drunk that he fell down the ladder and broke an arm and a leg.

Modern-day Shipdham is as different as chalk and cheese. Most people work outside the village – at Dereham, Watton or Norwich. There are still some shops, but only two public houses now. It has a very modern doctors' surgery – and too, with the changing needs of the village, a garden centre and a farm shop. There is a fine new school, which is also used by the village as a community centre at evenings and weekends.

Shipdham has strong links with America as during the Second World War the 44th Bomb Group was stationed at Shipdham airfield. Many of these airmen made lasting ties – some by marriage, some by coming back for visits. There are three memorials to their gallant war effort and on 14th May 1943 they took part in the raids on the Rumanian oilfields at Ploesti when 52 aircraft were lost out of 179. In the parish church of All Saints, the Stars and Stripes hangs next to our own Royal British Legion flag. Many young men from Shipdham gave their lives in both World Wars and are remembered each Armistice Day service in the lovely old parish church with its fine cupola and spire.

🍁 SHOTESHAM

Shotesham lies mainly on the north side of the valley of Shotesham Beck, a tributary of the river Tas, and is seven miles south of Norwich. It is a widespread village, originally two parishes, All Saints' and St Mary's. Both churches are still in use, along with a busy Methodist chapel.

Within the village boundaries there are two ancient woods. The long, narrow, fenced common, with the beck running through it, is grazed by horses and cattle on summer lettings and then rested in the winter. The planting of copses on the edge will enhance the area and replace individual trees gradually being lost through age and weather.

Shotesham has a variety of architecture, including among many listed buildings Shotesham Park, which was designed by Sir John Soane. There are also thatched houses, a Georgian coach house and pub, and a variety of old farmhouses and cottages. There are two small groups of council houses, many of which have been bought by their former tenants. There is, however, very little contemporary housing, the trend being to convert old agricultural buildings to form groups of houses and bungalows. As in many villages, facilities once thought vital have disappeared, lost, because of the increase in personal transport, to Norwich. The village school was closed, while the post office and store was closed and absorbed into the house of which it was a part.

A strong link between history and the present is represented by the Greenwich almshouses and at their centre the Trinity Hall. The almshouses were built by the Mercers' Company of London to commemorate the birth of Henry Howard, Earl of Northampton. His mother was travelling in Norfolk in the 16th century when the imminent birth forced her to stop in Shotesham, where she and her infant son were well cared for. The eight houses were originally to be let to elderly men in the parish, but now accommodate both sexes, and the end two are large enough for married couples. All the houses are rent free and residents receive pocket-money. Trinity Hall is available to any village organisation without charge and enables many village activities to thrive.

🍁 SNETTISHAM

Snettisham is one of the coastal villages along the north-west Norfolk coast, bordering on the shores of the Wash, though the village centre is over a mile from the sea shore. Bordering the marram grass and stony beach is a large community of holiday chalets and caravans, with a supporting cast of shops and clubs, and also the well known RSPB bird sanctuary.

The village centre still retains a market place, with a selection of shops and houses. These are mainly built in the local carrstone, still quarried on the village outskirts. These golden brown houses are known as 'gingerbread houses' in these parts. Dominating the village square is the Elizabethan Old Hall, for many years the home of the Strickland family, now a Sue Ryder Home. Approaching the village from King's Lynn, a sharp left turn leads you down to the beach. The first part is called Station Road. The line through to Hunstanton from King's Lynn lasted a little longer than most as this was the railway that served Sandringham House, with a very grand and beautiful halt at Wolferton.

In the past, as is the case in other rural areas, Snettisham had many more shops. However there are still two general stores, two hairdressers, a chemist, newsagent, and post office, among others. One of Snettisham's landmarks is St Mary's church, renowned for its situation on high ground east of the village. There is also a Methodist chapel and Salvation Army citadel.

Over the past 20 years a good deal of building has taken place, which has attracted many retired residents. Snettisham also has a designated industrial area, already occupied with several garages and auction rooms. One of the local farms is now a tourist attraction, and there is also a builders' merchant and three public houses.

With the opening of the bypass the village has been bisected, with the commonland and coast cut off from the village, making the crossing of the road very hazardous for children and elderly and disabled residents. Still, one compensation is that the road from King's Lynn is still one of the prettiest drives, whatever the season, to be found in Norfolk.

❧ SOUTH WALSHAM

In the 12th century South Walsham was actually two distinct parishes, each with its own church standing within one churchyard. This situation was created when the whole area was owned by two powerful landlords.

One church was dedicated to St Lawrence and the other to St Mary. Through the varying periods of history the churches stood side by side for seven centuries. Then in 1827 fire destroyed most of St Lawrence's. It has been completely restored thanks to many grants received from English Heritage, Historic Churches Trust, Broadland District Council etc and is now the venue for art exhibitions, concerts and recitals. St Mary's church possesses many items of interest including a mid 15th century rood screen and a fine 18th century organ.

Today the road which runs from Norwich through South Walsham and on to Acle is the B1140. A Norwich to Yarmouth bus service is available. The village possesses a well stocked grocer's and a post office/general shop. It also has a well known antiques shop and a boatyard for boating enthusiasts. A brand new village hall was opened by the Lord Lieutenant in 1991.

In the vicinity of the church, the B1140 goes over a narrow stream. It is difficult to imagine that less than a century ago this was navigable by wherries. In the 19th century wherries carried cargoes of barley to the malthouses at Ranworth. Other wide waterways leading to South Walsham Broad were used to bring up coal and take away corn.

Today, South Walsham is an area of delight for local residents and for those enjoying Broadland holidays. There are more new houses but changes have not been too drastic and are continually monitored. It is still principally a farming area, with fine old farmhouses and crops alternating between sugar beet, potatoes and corn. The village green is situated alongside the road running through the village. The village sign was presented by the Women's Institute in 1975. It depicts the two church towers, a windmill, a Viking and his ship. Alongside the green stands the picturesque 18th century public house, the Ship. Opposite Forge Cottage was once the home and shop of the village blacksmith and farrier. From this central spot walkers can easily reach Malthouse and Ranworth Broads. A little farther along, South Walsham Broad is also accessible by walking half way down School Road, then across the field by the Bier Way footpath and so on through Kingfisher Lane, flanked by picturesque thatched cottages, to the water's edge. The Bier Way footpath was used until recently to convey the biers of the dead from the Low Town end of the village to the local churches.

Going back to the village green area, one can see the imposing wrought iron gates leading to South Walsham Hall. A beautiful avenue of conifers and rhododendrons leads down to the main frontage. The present building was probably built during the 16th century and is now a hotel and country club. During the war the Hall was used as billets for the Army. Afterwards, like their predecessors at the Hall, Henry Lord Fairhaven and his family entered fully into the life of South Walsham. On his death in 1973, the Hall and its immediate grounds as they exist today were sold separately. However, the

Brass casting of the Walsham Witch

extensive woodland garden was retained by the Fairhaven Trust and is open to the public during the summer months. Its entrance and car park is in School Road and visitors come from miles around to enjoy seeing many rare shrubs and plants in the beauty of an especially tranquil broadland setting.

Speaking briefly about curious legends, older locals often talk about the Walsham Witches. It is thought that such talk could date back to Cromwell's time when an old woman could be accused of witchcraft. During the early part of the 20th century, a South Walsham wood carver made a mould from a drawing of a witch sitting astride a broom, with an owl on her shoulder and a crescent moon before her face. Brass castings were produced and sold locally. Ornaments, corkscrew handles, candleholders etc were subsequently purchased depicting the Walsham Witch.

The most recent jointly created walk by Anglian Water and the Broads Authority is a seven-mile circular river Bure walk from South Walsham to Upton. Most of the footpath is along the water's edge and is of particular interest to boating and wild life enthusiasts. Wind pumps and the ruins of the main gate of St Benet's Abbey, the monastery founded in 1020, are also visible along the way. Part of the return walk is through natural woodland, with bluebells, primroses etc growing in abundance. The original dwelling of the chamberlain of St Benet's Abbey still exists. This is now Chamery Hall Farm and, apart from the churches, is probably the oldest remaining building in South Walsham. Its link with ancient history is not forgotten.

🍁 SOUTH WOOTTON

The village of South Wootton, to the north-east of King's Lynn, is no longer distinct from the town, whose growth has blotted out any recognisable divide. In contrast to neighbouring Castle Rising it has little claim to fame, but with North Wootton it has shared a measure of Rising's history through the lordship of the manor and the Howard family.

For centuries the village was almost entirely confined to a small area bounded on the east by a common, known as the green. The green had three ponds; today only the largest remains, but it is significant in being fed by a spring which was probably the source of the water supply which was piped from South Wootton to the Augustinian monastery in King's Lynn in the 16th century. It is recorded that in the Saxon era there were many salt works in South Wootton and nearby areas bordering the Wash.

Between the site of the village and the sea lie some two to three miles of farmland and marshland. Reclamation of the marshes and work to improve drainage and prevent flooding have been long established practices. Exceptional tides and flooding have been very significant in the 20th century. The farmland produces good yields of cereals and root crops both on the marshland and the drier sandy soils to the east of the village, and the marshlands also support cattle. Some of the farmlands can be traced back to the 14th century. Up to the 1950s villagers were able to take advantage of grazing rights on the green, which was conveniently barred by gates during the winter season. Market gardening, especially of cucumbers and tomatoes in large glasshouses, was a prominent feature in the earlier part of this century.

On the north-east of the village, bordering Castle Rising, lies an area of woodland known as Wootton Woods, which used to be a popular playground for children from King's Lynn, with its silvery sandy outcrops.

The recorded population of South Wootton in the 19th century had been about 150, and it was only after the First World War that this number noticeably increased. In 1930 it passed the 400 mark, and reached 2,000 by

1970. During this period the town reached out, and the boundary between town and village was lost as development proceeded on both sides of the then one road from town.

Inevitably the identity of South Wootton has suffered. Very few of today's inhabitants in the area of the parish can claim to have been born in South Wootton. While it remained a true village, South Wootton listed among its residents various artisans, such as the blacksmith, shoemaker and tailoress, along with the coalman, the horse-breaker, pig dealer and dog breeder, but that scene has gone. Now it is to the nearby town that the daily worker goes, or indeed to larger towns 50 or even 100 miles distant.

South Wootton is not without amenities – the Swan Inn, post office and grocery store remain well established at the centre on the road once known as Town Street, opposite the large pond on the green, the home of a host of ducks. (The green, now trimly levelled grassland, belatedly has come to be known as the common!) A first school and a junior school are each housed in modern premises. The church of St Mary, dating from Anglo-Saxon times and with a particularly fine Norman font, has just been restored and reroofed after a serious fire. There is also a Methodist chapel.

The eastern arm of the parish, stretching to Knight's Hill, has recently provided a new and different focal point in the village with the establishment of a Co-op supermarket with filling station and car park at the entrance to a new housing development bordering on Reffley Wood and Sandy Lane.

Gone are the days when one could walk down the middle of lanes that are now busy thoroughfares, and wooden seats graced the triangle of grass where now a congested crossing of roads is controlled by traffic lights. Village or suburb – that is the present dilemma of South Wootton.

🍁 SOUTHERY

A village on the edge of Norfolk with a population of approximately 1,200. The Great Ouse flows to the west side, with the Little Ouse to the south meeting at Brandon Creek on the Norfolk/Cambridgeshire border. The A10 road ran through the village until a bypass in the 1980s took the traffic away from the village to the west side.

The flat fertile fenland, which is below sea level, surrounds the village on the east, south and west with heavier soil on the slightly higher ground to the north. From many points in the village Ely Cathedral can be seen on the horizon. It has always been an agricultural area but with transport and modern farming methods life has changed dramatically from the days of the horse and cart.

Many years ago in severe winters the rivers would freeze over with ice strong enough for skating. Skating contests on the Great Ouse were the highlight of the winter, Southery having some very good skaters. When a quick thaw came in the severe winters there was a fear of the fens flooding due to the rivers being unable to cope with the sudden influx of water. Older people in the village can remember several floods, with many a tale of houses and the like being swept away. The cutting of a new river in the surrounding area and the widening of the Great Ouse has taken away this fear.

Many of the older properties have been demolished and most sites now have modern bungalows and houses built in their place. They had fascinating names such as Bugs Row, Forresters Row, Puttys Yard and Chapel Row (Chain Row on the deeds). A few of these houses did not have a fixed staircase, a purpose-built ladder with wide steps was used instead. A few years ago the 'Lighthouse' was demolished. It was a tall house at the end of a row known as Avenue Row and there was a recess in the gable end, bricked like a window, where the lantern used to be. The two largest houses in the village, the Manor and Hill House have also been demolished.

Ruins of the former St Mary the Virgin church stand majestically overlooking the village, with the present church standing nearby with a spire that can be seen as you approach the village from any direction. A plaque in the present St Mary's lists the names of rectors from 1300. A short distance from St Mary's is the Baptist church and at the west end of the village (formerly Townsend) is the Methodist church. The primary school with approximately 100 children on the roll is situated in the centre of the village. As Southery is situated six miles from the nearest railway station, buses are the only public transport, reaching out to Downham Market, Ely and King's Lynn. Due to modern farming methods not so many people are employed on the farms and people now travel out of the village to work.

197

🍁 SOUTHREPPS

Southrepps is situated in the north-east corner of Norfolk just two or three miles from the coast. It is a pleasant place in which to live in spite of the bitter north winds that sometimes blow from off the sea in the early spring. The area is rural, mainly given over to agriculture, and looks out onto open fields and in summer the most glorious sunsets.

It is a friendly village, peopled by those who were born here and many others who are newcomers. There are several organisations, a bowls club and a football team. The new village hall that has been built in recent years by the people of the village was a result of their own efforts and shows the strong community spirit that exists.

The village is split in two by a large tract of farmland. Upper Street has the post office with its grocery department, and another little general store. The church of St James stands out prominently and can be seen from afar as one approaches the village, and the Vernon Arms offers its hospitality to those seeking the village pub.

In the other part of the village at Lower Street stands the Methodist chapel, and a little further on is the school, built some hundred or so years ago. It still serves the locality for primary children. Lower Street too has its own small shop to serve its residents.

Still further one comes to the Suffield Arms, which serves refreshment to weary travellers, opposite to which is the local railway station of Gunton on the Norwich to Sheringham line. However, its use to the village is threatened for the future as only a few trains are scheduled to stop there while the others pass straight through. The bus service is sparse so most people rely on their own transport.

Southrepps has many pleasant walks along quiet green lanes around the outskirts of the village and along one of these in the Northrepps direction, there is to be found an old Quaker cemetery with one or two ancient tombstones still standing. It seems that at one time there was a strong Quaker element in these parts.

🍁 STANHOE

Stanhoe is a small village surrounded by farmland. In the past this was sheep country and flocks in their hundreds roamed the heaths and pastures between the villages. After enclosure, arable farming gradually took over and barley and then stock raising became dominant. Today, the fields around Stanhoe have more diverse animals and crops than ever before. Stanhoe also has its rare breed animals with a small herd of Dexter cattle.

With such agricultural activity it is a surprise to find that the number of full time farm workers living in the village is no more than twelve compared to the 110 of a century ago. Largely because of this fall the village's population has dropped since its peak of 517 in the 1850s and today is little over 200.

One of the main changes in Stanhoe in recent years has been the rapid growth in second homes and by 1997 more than half the housing stock of the village was occupied for little more than a few weekends and holidays a year. This means a decreasing full time population and the running down of local facilities. Two of our three shops have closed, and now one shop serves as post office, general store and also as the place to put up notices, book the village hall, buy local raffle tickets and just keep up to date with what is going on. If it ever closes the village will miss it more than most people realise. In spite of its small size, Stanhoe still has one pub, the Crown (the second, the Norfolk Hero closed within living memory), a good village hall, enlarged from the old Victorian reading room with money raised during the Jubilee celebrations, and a fine playing field. The lease for this was signed in 1995 and it replaces the old playing field which was originally part of what the old squire of the village called his 'South Lawn' and which was in regular use for cricket and football matches until it was mostly ploughed up in the late 1950s.

All Saints' church is a large but generally rather plain church, not the sort that people come miles to see, but nevertheless it has interesting features and at over 750 years old is the one feature of the village which has remained relatively unchanged throughout the centuries. Keeping it in good repair is a constant headache and Stanhoe was one of the first villages in the area to have a Village Gardens Open Sunday as a fund raising event and also stages an annual concert.

In many local villages the Methodist church has closed within the last few years, but Stanhoe's chapel is still going strong and also holds an annual fete.

The Hospital Sunday parade and service which began in 1919 was an annual event until the early 1990s when it ceased, the last village in the county to abandon this event.

To outsiders the small stretch of water opposite the post office is what typifies Stanhoe. This was originally known as Eastmere, then as the name 'mere' lost its meaning, Eastmere Pit. From that it was shortened to The Pit and as such remained until recent times with the arrival of non-Norfolk speakers to whom the word pit meant a hole full of rubbish. It then became The Pond and as such it is likely to remain. Until the last epidemic of Dutch elm disease it was shaded by a row of trees, but then other native species were planted and the ring of trees and shrubs is thickening. It is a fine stretch of water, a popular place for tourists to stop, feed the ducks and admire the view.

STIBBARD

Stibbard lies about half a mile from any main road. It can be approached by any of four roads coming from Ryburgh, Guist, Wood Norton and Fulmodeston; these are country roads with green verges where primroses grow in springtime, dog roses in the summer and blackberries in the autumn. These roads will bring you into the heart of Stibbard where, within a very small distance, you can find the medieval church, the school, the village sign, one of Norfolk's prettier Methodist chapels, the post office and the village hall.

There were 453 souls in Stibbard in 1845 and the population remained fairly constant through the Victorian period. Numbers fell during the early years of the 20th century, but the village is growing a little now not, fortunately, by estates, but by new houses here and there. At one time there was a baker's, a blacksmith's forge (on the Guist road), several brick kilns and two village stores selling everything from working boots to pills for the back-ache. The baker's had gone by 1929; the forge lasted a bit longer, much loved by the children for its warmth and cheerfulness. Two stores survived until the 1950s, but now there is just the post office open for three mornings a week. There were once two pubs, the King's Arms in the centre of the village (now a private house), and a beer house at the Ordnance Arms. This last is now fully licensed and adds an exotic touch to Guist Bottom by sporting a Thai restaurant. It has come a long way since the days when old Jessie Bunn served beer in a stone jug from the cellar and went to bed by candlelight.

Stibbard WI was founded in 1926 and reached its golden jubilee in 1976. Having at that time the metal sculptress Ros Newman living in Tyler's Barn, she was commissioned to make a village sign. The result was a unique monument, much admired by visitors and known to all locally as 'Fred'. He is a ploughman pushing a Norfolk plough, the man himself being welded out of a variety of agricultural implements and a soldier's tin helmet. Three years after the sign was erected a piece of meadow in the centre of the village was drained and converted into a children's playing field with goal posts and swings, a breathing space for the young in this intensively cultivated county.

Stibbard has many incomers, but also a solid core of families with long association with the village. All these families can no doubt remember when Stibbard had a silver band and a cricket team which, for away matches, could command a coach-load full of supporters. Enthusiasm was perhaps greater than skill, for it is recorded that on one occasion they played Foulsham with the following result: Stibbard first innings – 11 all out, Foulsham first innings – 15 all out, Stibbard second innings – 13 all out. Foulsham then went on to win the match!

🍁 SWAINSTHORPE

The milestone indicates that Swainsthorpe, a small, pleasant village, is exactly five miles from Norwich on the A140 Norwich to Ipswich road. Turn off this major road into Church Road and see one of the most splendid village entrance views in Norfolk. The road leads up a small hill with the church standing sentinel at the top.

This is St Peter's church, one of the round tower churches of Norfolk. It is probably pre-Norman with some evidence of Saxon work. On the door frame can be seen Elizabethan heads and a mass mark sundial that helped parishioners to attend services on time. Inside can be found a Norman font and many accomplished memorials of eminent ex-residents of the parish. There is a brass plaque on the wall dated 1628 to commemorate Capt Havers who served under Queen Elizabeth I. A 'devil's' door, blocked up in Puritan times, can clearly be seen on the north side which led to the original village green.

Crossing the railway line and leaving the village, on the right-hand side, can be seen an interesting building, called The Vale. Now converted into flats this was formerly an old people's hospital, and originally the Swainsthorpe Workhouse, built in the 19th century by the Henstead Union in conjunction with the Humbleyard Hundred. The site of the Humbleyard meeting place can still be seen near the bend where the road meanders towards Swardeston.

Returning to the main road, the Dun Cow public house has stood beside the A140 for more than 300 years. Its name is associated with local folklore concerning *Dun*ston village, *Dun*ston Hall and the terribly ghostly cow of *Dun*ston Hill. The old pub sign, now sadly missing, used to say:

'Come in friend, you are sure to find
The Dun Cow's milk is to your mind.'

🍁 SWANTON MORLEY

The population of Swanton Morley is 2,130. There is a church in the village, and until a few years ago a Methodist church which has now been turned into a house. Many years ago there was a papermill, and one of the three public houses is called the Papermakers' Arms. The others are the Angel and Darby's. There is also a windmill. The sails were found to be unsafe and taken off in 1910, but the mill is still in good shape and is used for storage.

There is also a baker, a butcher, a general shop which is also a newsagent's, a post office, a garage and filling station, a small garden centre and a nursing home. During the Second World War the RAF were here, but this has now been taken over by the Army, as the Robertson Barracks.

The new village hall is used by every age group from mothers and toddlers to the Friendship Club for over-60s. There is a big play area where football is played, two bowls clubs and a cricket club.

🍁 TACOLNESTON

The best approach to Tacolneston (pronounced 'Tackolston') is from Norwich on the B1113. There is a medieval church with pine trees, ancient tombstones, and a moat on a sharp bend opposite the 17th century Old Hall with its mellow brickwork. This conservation area continues down the hill to the manor with its three-tiered porches, the green with thatched cottages, the Pelican pub

Tombstone dated 173½ in Tacolneston churchyard

(c1686), and the old trees surrounding Tacolneston Hall, which dates from the reign of Queen Anne.

Past the Victorian first school the road continues on with a mixture of old and modern buildings, a fish and chip shop, and small housing developments at either end of the village. There is another manor house where an open frontage of trees and fields is preserved to maintain the true character of the village. Set back on the right are the village hall and recreation ground with a new play area, netball/tennis court and cricket/football pitch. At its most southern point Tacolneston adjoins Forncett End, whose pub and two shops are much used by village residents.

The village has a well-balanced population of over 700, many of whom commute to work in Norwich. Although 'outsiders' have moved into the village, there are many old families still resident, including farmers of several generations. The local school is a focal point of village life, as is the church, which is part of the Wreningham group of seven parishes.

Mention Tacolneston and people say, 'Ah yes, the TV mast,' which at a maximum height of 650 ft is a local landmark. A second, smaller mast came into operation in 1998. The BBC station transmits all five TV channels and

BBC radio. In addition, other firms rent radio telephone facilities and it houses East Anglia's transmitter maintenance team.

'God has had a profound influence on my life and work,' says Kenneth McKee, Tacolneston resident, a pioneer of hip replacement surgery. His first three total hip replacements were carried out at the Norfolk and Norwich Hospital in 1951. Since then thousands of people have been indebted to him for the new lease of life that this operation has given them.

TAVERHAM

Taverham is a pleasant village on the north bank of the river Wensum. It is about six miles from the centre of Norwich in a north-westerly direction. The first recorded mention of Taverham relates to the time of Edward the Confessor.

The village boasts a fine church, probably dating from Saxon times, although the first mention of it is in the Domesday Book. It is basically Norman with building added in Decorated style in about 1350. It is a simple and unpretentious building, dedicated to St Edmund, King and Martyr, well kept and well attended. The village also has a patron saint, St Walstan, who was a Taverham man.

Taverham Hall was rebuilt in 1859 after a fire destroyed the previous building. It is a fine building in Elizabethan style. After the estate was broken up in 1920, it became a school.

A rather unusual mill existed at Taverham until 1899. The paper mill made very superior paper, used for bibles, legal documents, bank notes and even *The Times* newspaper. The remains of the sluices can still be seen.

The village had many nurseries until recently. The houses were rather scattered in the village until the 1960s and 1970s when it became a desirable dormitory village for Norwich. In 1951 there were about 700 people living in Taverham, in 1990 there were over 6,000, not counting Thorpe Marriot.

Now there is a village hall with fine sports facilities and a library. Local efforts by the villagers have made this possible and are still helping to maintain the hall.

Coupled with the nearness of the countryside, the river, Ringland and Deighton Hills, it is a pleasant and agreeable place in which to live.

❧ TERRINGTON ST CLEMENT

Terrington St Clement, about six miles west of King's Lynn, is reputed to be the second largest village in England. It was in existence in Saxon times, as remains of a Saxon building were found in the church during 19th century restoration, and there is a record of a gift by Godric in AD 970 of the lands of 'Turringtonea' to the Abbey of Ramsey.

At that time it was probably a small settlement on raised ground amid desolate marshes. Those marshes have gradually been reclaimed over the past 300 years and are now one of the most fertile parts of the country. Here are grown cereals of every kind, sugar beet, potatoes, and a variety of fruit and flowers. One tourist attraction is the African Violet Centre.

Years ago everyone worked on the land but, with the modernisation of farming, many people now go daily to town to work. However, a modern link with the ancient industry of agriculture is the Experimental Husbandry Farm operated in the village by the Agriculture Development Advisory Service. Here research is conducted into the effects of soil and climate on different varieties of crops. It is also the leading station in the country for pig production.

One industry which has completely disappeared is the making of salt, which was a valuable commercial commodity in the Middle Ages. Evidence still remains of the mounds of waste left from the evaporation of water over heat to extract the salt, and traces of the old fires were found when foundations were dug for a housing development now called The Saltings. This industry ceased in the 16th century.

There were once three windmills in Terrington. Two have completely disappeared; the bottom three storeys of the third are now a feature of a well known Terrington garden.

The smithy has been run by the same family for generations. They no longer shoe horses but repair modern machinery and produce beautiful wrought-iron work as well as metal fabrication for the building industry.

In the centre of the village is the parish church of St Clement, known as 'The Cathedral of the Marshlands'. It was built between 1342 and 1400. The tower, which is 87 ft high, is separated from the main building, and from it there are magnificent views from the cliffs of Hunstanton to the east to Boston Stump to the west.

The village offers many shops and amenities including doctors' surgeries, chemist, sub post office, garages etc. The High School takes pupils from surrounding villages as well as from Terrington. A regular bus service runs through the village on its route from Spalding to King's Lynn. For many years there has been a retained fire service here.

In 1977 the Women's Institute presented the village with a sign. The design incorporates sheep and strawberries, both of which have contributed to the economy of the village. The coat of arms is of the Hammond family and the motto means Prepared and Faithful.

In 1989 the Peter Scott Wash Coast Path was opened. Starting at the East Lighthouse at Sutton Bridge, one can walk ten miles along the bank on the foreshore of Terrington Marshes to West Lynn. The foreshore is a haven for birds, and samphire (a marsh plant rich in minerals) grows in abundance. This is collected, boiled or pickled and eaten, and is a great delicacy.

❧ THARSTON

Although the earliest known reference to Tharston occurs in the Domesday Book it is clear that the parish, with its well-defined boundaries, was in existence long before 1086. The present ecclesiastical parish covers much the same area as it did when William the Conqueror commissioned his survey, and it is likely that the main settlement, recorded as being one and a half leagues long and half a league wide, was in the area which is known as 'The Street'. Much of the boundary between Hapton and Tharston is defined by a branch of the river Tas, referred to in old Tharston and Forncett documents as the Nelland river. Although now shallow and insignificant for most of the year, there is no doubt that boats came up the river as far as Tasburgh and Hempnall in the 14th century.

A particularly noticeable feature of the Tharston landscape is the predominance of 'hollow ways', or lanes which run in deep cuttings between high banks. These lanes often mark the ancient boundaries between the enclosed land belonging to the manor or the rectory and the open fields and lands held in common by the villagers and smaller farmers.

Highfields is usually referred to locally as 'Plump', and this informal name is of great interest. The Norfolk Militia was organised by recruiting soldiers from the villages in the various Hundreds, and local churchwardens' accounts refer to the provision of guns, swords, bandoliers and corselets, and to the sending of men from the villages to train with the militia in the 'town armour'. An old meaning of the word 'Plump' referred to a company or troop of soldiers (especially spearmen or pikemen), and it is very likely that the local place-name is a survival from the days of the gatherings of the local militia.

The most potent influence on the topography of the village was Major General Sir Robert John Harvey, who was lord of the manor of Tharston at the time of the enclosure of the parish in 1804, and who held the estate until it passed to his son at the time of his death in 1860. General Harvey was knighted in 1817 for his services in the Peninsular War and set about the reorganisation and reconstruction of properties on his extensive estates with military zeal. It is possible to follow his military career, through the various battles and engagements in which he was involved, in the names given to his properties in Stoke Holy Cross, Forncett and Tharston.

There is no documentary evidence for the foundation of the first church at Tharston, but the Domesday Book (1086) records a church endowed with 40 acres of glebe land. The earliest surviving fabric at Tharston church is the chancel, which is probably late 13th century and would have been built at the expense of the prior of Pentney. The atmosphere of the interior of the church today is very much that of the 19th century restoration.

The hill-top site of the church must have been a place of importance for many centuries, and there are wide views across the Tas valley to the north and east. It is unusual for the principal entrance to a church to be on the north side, but here, as at Tasburgh, this has been dictated by the position of the village street. Near the north gate is the old village school, closed in 1951, which was built on part of the glebe land in the 1870s.

🍁 THOMPSON

Thompson is home to about 350 people. Since 1942, when the army mapped out the Stanford Training Area (locally called the 'Battle Area'), its most direct access to Thetford has been cut off and it has been geographically on the road to nowhere. The present main road to Thetford takes a large curve around the Battle Area, with the three roads which now take you only to Thompson leading off it. As a result the village gets little heavy traffic, although it does get many visitors. The village's western boundary is part of the ancient road of Peddars Way, which also marks the limit of the Battle Area.

The village is in two distinct parts. Approached from Thetford the first 'half' of the village is grouped near St Martin's church, parts of which date from the 14th century. It was extensively restored in the 17th century. Having become dilapidated and threatened with closure restoration was needed again in 1913 and was organised by Rev Charles Kent, rector of Merton, and Prince Frederick Duleep Singh. New houses here have flint walls to echo those of the church. Close by are old thatched cottages and a large old house called College Farm. Features are the hump-backed bridge over the stream, cottage gardens, and the pretty little tree-lined lane of Butters Hall and Thompson Common.

College Farm is so named because in 1350 the then lords of the manor, the de Shardelowe brothers, gave their manor to the church, creating a collegiate church. The six brethren, of whom one was elected Master, lived together in the house or college given for this purpose and ran the affairs of the manor and church until its dissolution in 1541. The house eventually became a farmhouse. Restoration revealed many interesting features of medieval architecture. Examples of its ecclesiastical origins can still be seen, although it is now a private house.

Leaving the church behind, the road passes through open fields to the main part of the village. The first buildings are farmhouses, farm buildings and the school with its sensitively designed new extensions. Further on is the crossroads with the small green containing the bus shelter and the village sign which depicts travellers on Peddars Way – a pilgrim, a goose girl and a Roman soldier – as well as the arms of the de Shardelowes. To the left is the village hall and to the right, towards Griston, is the famous thatched inn, the Chequers.

There has been some new house building in recent years, mainly as in-fill between older properties, of which many have been restored. The village possesses timber-framed thatched houses as well as some built of bricks made at the brick works which once existed here. The majority of the houses face open land, an attractive feature.

Within the parish a number of natural and not quite so natural features can be enjoyed. Of these perhaps the loveliest is Thompson Common with its collection of pingos – circular ponds created during the Ice Age. Fed by underground springs, the top layer would melt slightly each Ice Age summer and the silt held in the ice formed a deposit around the base of the lens-shaped domes. After the Ice Age the water was held as round ponds within the silt banks. The common is owned and cared for by the Norfolk Wildlife Trust and contains an abundance of rare plants and wildlife. It forms part of an eight mile Pingo Trail walk.

Not quite so natural is Thompson Water, reached via Peddars Way. A man-made lake dug out of an old peat fen at the behest of a past Lord Walsingham in approximately 1854 to improve the sporting facilities of the Merton estate, it is now owned by the Norfolk Wildlife Trust. It provides a haven for bird life, fishing facilities and marked nature trails which link with other parish footpaths. It is fed by the stream which winds around our village, past the church and through areas of marsh, meadow and woodland with parts of the Pingo Trail following its banks.

🍁 THREE HOLES

Three Holes is a very small village, situated on the A1101 between Ely and Wisbech. It is approximately eight miles from Wisbech, eight from March and eight from Downham Market and lies just within the Norfolk boundary. The original name for Three Holes was Wadingstow, at least from the early 13th century. This was the point of the Old Croft river where Upwell Town ended.

In 1609, an order was made by a Session of Sewers at Ely for a new bridge at Wadingstow, to include 'three arches, each eight foot broad with three sufficient doors to shut in times of necessity and want of water for the navigation through the town of Well [now Upwell]'. This is clearly the origin of the 'Three Holes bridge' which gave its name to Three Holes. People have suggested that it was named after The Three Eaux (waters) but until the construction of the Middle Level rivers through Three Holes, there was only one Eau and the name Three Holes is much older than the Middle Level, which was cut through in the 1840s.

Indeed, the old Methodist chapel, which was closed in 1982, was originally the hostel for the accommodation of the navvies who built the Middle Level. The chapel was later bought by Mr Walter Cawthorn and consecrated as a Primitive Methodist chapel in 1850. It became a Methodist chapel in 1932.

The Middle Level rivers are still used for fishing but to a lesser degree. Twenty five years ago, the quality of fishing deteriorated. Exact causes were unknown. In the last few years, the quality has improved dramatically. Bream, roach, pike and eels are caught. Up until a few years ago, bus loads of Yorkshire fishermen would arrive in the village on Sunday mornings.

Once the rivers seemed to be frozen every winter and skaters came from a wide area. A fire was lit in a barrel on the ice at one time. Obviously all was well! When the season was in full swing the local cry was, 'If she cracks, she bears, if she bends, she breaks!'

A local inhabitant hired out rowing boats in the summer and the boats were moored by the Three Holes bridge. Now there are only a few visiting long boats and pleasure craft which have navigated the waters from March.

First swimming lessons for local children, in fact their only swimming lessons, were in the Middle Level at 'the bathing place' and a favourite high-board was the top of the bridge. The only snag was that they had to have a bath after the swim to get rid of the mud! But it was all fun.

The main occupation used to be soft fruit farming, market gardening and orchard farming, although there are still some larger arable farms. There is a children's playing field beside the village hall, a pub called the Red Hart, two garages, one of which is an MOT testing station and sells newspapers and groceries, and an excellent corner shop which is also the post office.

🍁 THURGARTON

A cluster of about a dozen small houses, farm cottages, council houses and three former farmhouses stand near a minor road junction. The outbuildings of one farmhouse are still used for agricultural purposes. The village general store, long closed, was housed in one of a pair of semi-detached cottages, and the village pub, the Old Bull, was in the central larger cottage with courtyard which is now a private house and upholstery workshop. A Victorian post box is near the crossroads.

Other houses are scattered over the surrounding area. Some distance away from the village and each other stand Thurgarton Old Hall (1733) and Thurgarton Hall, both working farms. The latter stands close to the church, All Saints', a thatched building, recently restored and now in the care of the Redundant Churches Fund. Inside there are wall paintings and inscriptions, and a series of splendidly carved bench ends. There is also evidence that at least one sermon failed to hold the attention of a boy with a knife who was dreaming of a sailing ship and carved a picture of it into the bench he was sitting on.

At the crossroads by the church there is a flint and brick cottage, but the former rectory is some distance away nearer to Aldborough: it is now privately owned and called The Grange. The previous rectory, Thurgarton Lodge, is still further away, and in the past decade has seen use as an antiques business, later a workshop for machine knitting, but is now a private house. Nearby, an octagonal house, recently converted from a farm, was originally part of the Hanworth Hall estate.

Manor Farm, dating from 1638 and recently restored and modernised, has outbuildings converted for use as a successful furniture-making business. Nearby is a smallholding where pigs, chickens and guinea fowl are reared.

🍁 THURLTON

The village of Thurlton is situated in the south-east of the county, just a few miles from the Suffolk border, between Hales and Haddiscoe. It is approximately 14 miles from Norwich and eleven miles from Great Yarmouth. Thurlton is an Anglo-Saxon name and evidence has been found of this early settlement.

The partly thatched church of All Saints dates from Norman times with alterations in the 15th century when the tower was built. This tower houses the bells, which were cast in 1632 and are believed to be the earliest complete set of five bells all cast at the same time. They were given by Thomas Denny who was a churchwarden and whose name appears on two of the bells. Inside the church is a 15th century oak screen with fine carved detail which includes the Thurlton Dragon, and a wall painting which is possibly medieval. In the churchyard is the tombstone of a Norfolk wherryman who was drowned in 1809 and whose ghost is said to wander the marshes on misty nights following the Jack o' Lanterns.

There has probably been a White Hart Inn where the Hales road meets the Haddiscoe road since the time of Richard II, but the present early 18th century building has been a private house since 1973. Villagers still talk of the circuses (including an elephant) that took place on the meadow behind the inn.

In the centre of the village stands the lower part of an old corn mill known as Great Goliath. This is featured on the village sign along with the church and a tractor which symbolises modern farming. The design for the sign was

211

The Old White Hart, Thurlton

chosen from a competition organised by the WI, made up by the village blacksmith and painted locally.

The Thurlton, Norton & Thorpe Village Hall was built in 1970 and is of an unusual hexagonal design. There is also a bowls club with a county standard bowling green. At one time there were three pubs in the village but now there is only one – the Queen's Head. The post office and stores is still well supported as is the mobile library and the school is flourishing. New houses continue to be built on any infill sites and absorbed into this modern, working village with an ancient past.

🍁 THURTON

Thurton village is seven miles from Norwich on the A146 road to Beccles and Lowestoft. The village has been growing slowly over the years but recently has been expanding much faster. The church, St Ethelbert's, is an ancient, thatched-roof church with a fine Norman arched door. The registers date from 1560. There is some very fine stained glass in the windows, which were restored in 1988. Some of this is reputed to have come from Rouen Cathedral at the time of the French Revolution and to have been donated by the Beauchamp family who lived at Langley Hall.

Many of the properties in the village were owned by the Beauchamp family. The public elementary school, as it was known then, was erected in 1868 mainly at the cost of Sir T. W. B. Proctor-Beauchamp and enlarged in 1895 for 100 children. The Fuel Allotments are let and the money, originally, was used to buy fuel for the widows of the village. As there is now insufficient money to buy fuel, money is given to the widows of the village instead.

Mrs Todd moved to the village as a girl of seven in 1904 when her parents took over the George and Dragon public house. This is a very old building over 400 years old and has some very old oak beams, but has changed much over the years. There was a farm with the public house and the landlord had to be a farmer as well. She lived at the George and Dragon for 54 years altogether and remembered very different times from those of today. The pubs were open from 6 am to 10 pm. In those days workers locally at the forge would go to the pub for a drink before going to work at 7 am. Rent day at the pub was an event. Near to Michaelmas Day the tenants of properties of the Langley estate living in Thurton and Carleton would come to the pub to pay their rents and the estate clerk and secretary would be there all day and had to be supplied with refreshments and heating if the weather was cold.

When Mrs Todd was a small girl the road through the village was not made up as it is today and the traffic consisted of only horses and carts and wagonettes which carried people to Norwich. Herds of cattle and sheep were driven from Norwich market by drovers to Haddiscoe marshes. Sometimes these would be bedded down for the night at the George and Dragon. The drovers would find refreshment at the pub but slept with the cattle. Their collie dogs were of great help in controlling the herds and preventing them from going onto other people's property.

Opposite the George was a forge and carpenter's shop owned by Mr Ellis. This was quite a large concern and there were three forges with three blacksmiths at work all day shoeing horses and making implements and parts for machinery. The carpenter's shop made wagons and tumbrils and wheels for these and gates etc for the local farms. The wagons were painted and were displayed at the Royal Norfolk Show where the firm had a stand. Mr White was the wheelwright and carpenter and also made coffins. This was a major source of employment as approximately 20 men worked here. The business later passed to Mr John Keeler and then to Mr Arnall Capps and to his two sons Peter and John.

🍁 THWAITE ST MARY

Situated approximately two and a half miles from the Norfolk/Suffolk border and the market town of Bungay, Thwaite St Mary is a tiny hamlet comprising some 20 houses and a small thatched church. The name Thwaite (the 'h' is silent) derives from the old Norse word meaning 'clearing' and over the centuries the spelling has varied – Tweyt and Thwayt appearing on old maps.

Buildings of interest in the village include Thwaite Hall, a large Queen Anne house with an estate stretching towards Mundham and Loddon Ingloss. The Old Messuage (or manor house) is said to be the oldest house in the village, dating from the Tudor period. Thwaite Lodge was formerly an inn, and the Old Rectory was built in the early 1800s, in the grounds of which were the coach house and the old Church schoolhouse (in use until 1924), both having now been converted to private dwellings. The rectory itself ceased to be Church property about 1936/37. During the 19th century the village boasted a blacksmith's and a shop, the latter building unfortunately no longer in existence.

The church dates from the late Norman period, the splendid original unporched doorway remaining in the south wall. The nave roof is thatched and the chancel, dating from 1737 but remodelled in the Victorian age, is tiled brick. On the east jamb of the doorway can be seen what may be an original consecration cross and there is a very well-defined mass dial on the west jamb.

During the Second World War, the close proximity of Seething airfield where the 448th Bomb Group of the American air force was stationed, resulted in Toad Lane being upgraded to a metalled surface, it previously being an un-made-up lane. Thwaite generally escaped war damage, apart from the east window of the church being blown out as a result of a bomb falling behind Thwaite Hall. Fortunately the roundels were salvaged and are incorporated into the replacement window.

Thwaite village sign, carved locally in elm on an oak post, features the church's Norman doorway and was erected in 1977 as a Silver Jubilee venture.

The village was, and to a certain extent, still is, a farming community, although in recent times with the conversion of old buildings into dwellings, there has been a modest influx of 'new' people. It is, however, a very friendly village.

🍁 TOFT MONKS

Toft Monks, which lies six miles south-east of Loddon, is mainly an agricultural area growing cereals, sugar beet, rape, beans and peas. There is also a chicken unit. The vistas are wide, punctuated by one or two small belts of trees and a few coppices. The village proper lies either side of the A143 between Gillingham and Haddiscoe. A garage, post office and the Toft Lion public house can be found here. About one mile to the north-west is Bulls Green, which is largely woodland with an area of grassland and a pond. Maypole Green, approximately one mile to the east, is an area of meadowland with a pond and some scrub.

The dwellings and barns of Toft Monks are on the whole vernacular and reflect its history. There is a Tudor-style house and a timber-framed house south of the A143 which are both moated. A further two timber-framed farmhouses can be found on Bulls Green and two Georgian houses to the north of the A143. Farmhouses and cottages built before the Second World War of Norfolk red brick with pantiled roofs can be found in most parts of the parish. In 1848 a Methodist chapel was built at Maypole Green, but has since become redundant and is now a residence.

The population of Toft Monks has changed from an agricultural community to a dormitory village, many of its inhabitants now commuting to towns between Norwich and Lowestoft. The population fell from 397 in 1881 to 283 in 1981. Due to housing development and the conversion of old buildings, today the population is over 310.

The village of Toft existed at the time of the Norman Conquest. By 1200 a small monastic community of two to three monks had been founded in what then became Monks Toft. The church was founded in the late 12th century and dedicated to St Margaret. In 1462 the church and some land, including the village greens, were ceded by Edward IV to King's College, Cambridge. Oak from Toft Monks' Great Wood was used to make the doors to King's. King's College have disposed of the land they held in the village and the greens have been vested in the parish council by the Commons Commissioner.

St Margaret's church is surrounded by fields and built of flints. Although it

215

was built between 1180 and 1220, there are many later additions and alterations. The most prominent feature of the church is the embattled tower which has two windows flanking it, thought to be Norman. A copy of an etching of St Margaret's by John Sell Cotman dated 1814 hangs in the church.

❧ TOPCROFT

Six miles north-west of Bungay, Topcroft has a population of about 220. The church is situated on one of the highest points in south Norfolk, indeed the top of the tower has been used by the Ordnance Survey as a chief observation point.

The round tower of St Margaret's, Saxon in origin, has been much repaired, in fact the whole building is a conglomeration of styles from Saxon to 15th century with several later restorations. As a parish Topcroft has suffered the usual vicissitudes of history. For instance, John Tennison, the rector who died in 1671 and was buried in the chancel, had earlier been ejected by the Parliamentarians after the Civil War, yet his son became Archbishop of Canterbury. In contrast, when the local United Reformed chapel fell into disuse a few years ago it was sold to the Russian Orthodox church. Every spring those walking through the Anglican churchyard are delighted by the myriad of wild flowers growing there, the colour and scent really lift the heart. Nowadays the greater part of the population lives nearly a mile away in a small valley.

There is also an extensive area covering several acres of arable land where there are indications of much older habitation. The discovery of some broken tiles, oyster shells and a few tesserae turned up by the plough suggests that a Roman villa once dominated the village, possibly about AD 200.

The fine houses in the modern village include the 16th century Street Farm, Topcroft Lodge, which has a Georgian facade added to the original 16th century building when the enclosures brought increased prosperity to the smaller farmers, and the moated Topcroft Hall, which was modernised in Victorian times. Of more interest is the fact that in the 15th century the latter was the home of Margery Brews, who found her way into history by marrying into the Paston family, writers of the famous Letters. Before 1400 it was almost unheard of to write a private, personal letter; even in the 15th century they were a rarity and in spite of increasing literacy would usually be dictated to a clerk. The Paston Letters, written in a consecutive series describing what happened to a particular family during the turbulent Wars of the Roses, are of absorbing interest, not least to historians.

🍁 TROWSE

Trowse, more correctly Trowse with Newton, is a place facing many changes in the 1990s. The name is said to have derived from the Anglo-Saxon word for tree house, because houses had to be built on stilts to avoid flooding.

The flint church, dedicated to St Andrew, dates from the 13th century, but towards the end of the 19th century it was almost derelict. It now has a reredos with a beautiful carving of the Last Supper copied from an Italian masterpiece by a man named Minns. A new pulpit, erected in 1904 as a memorial to Queen Victoria, has in front of it three life-sized wooden figures of David and two angels dating from the 16th century, which came from Holland.

The church has now lost its resident vicar, and the vicarage standing opposite has been sold as a private residence. The churchyard burial ground is full and has been closed, but the Parish Council retains its burial ground along Whitlingham Lane and allows villagers to be buried in their own parish.

Trowse Newton Hall was built by the Prior of Norwich in 1306 as a country seat, but only fragments of wall in Whitlingham Lane mark its site. The most important mansion is Crown Point, which received its name through its first owner General John Money who was present at the taking of Crown Point in North America. It was rebuilt by Sir Robert Harvey in 1869, and was bought by J & J Colman in 1872.

To quote the grandfather of one of the oldest members of the WI (about 1920): 'Trowse was a very unsanitary and very dirty place 70 years ago. Nearly all the women wore pattens to help get through the mud and the dirt. It was said one old lady went upstairs to bed with hers on'. This was because the drovers operated from here. They were responsible for driving cattle from Norwich market to London. One such, Tom Denny, had a dog who went with him on the Sunday to Saturday journeys, but while Denny came home by coach, the dog set off on his own accord and was back in Trowse to greet his master's return.

The coming of the Colman family and factory made wonderful changes for Trowse – these were said to have been copied by Cadbury's when they built Bournville. New houses were built, a school, a chapel and a home for the elderly for the employees at Carrow works, and it became a thriving community.

Sadly, in 1955 the Colman family moved from Crown Point with its wonderful site looking across the river to Thorpe, County Hall and Norwich beyond. It became Whitlingham Hospital, but at present stands empty. It has a unique conservatory restored in the early 1980s.

The Trowse bypass was opened on 20th May 1992. The then chairman Mr Colin Steward and his parish council organised a street party to celebrate the closure of the main road through to Lowestoft and the Waveney valley, thus removing 20,000 vehicles per day from our village. The extraction of gravel along the river Wensum was used for the bypass, and created two Broads, the Little and Great Broads. These will provide water facilities, rowing, canoeing, sailing and fishing, and offer a nature reserve for aquatic species of plants, birds, insects etc. Many other developments are planned and Trowse and its villagers look forward to some years of steady change during the close of one century and the early years of the 21st century.

🍁 UPPER SHERINGHAM

Upper Sheringham village is just a mile inland from the north Norfolk seaside resort of Sheringham. One could easily pass through this quiet little village, nestling under the bracken and heather covered hills of Pretty Corner and the tree-clad hills of Sheringham Park, and admire the flint-walled cottages, ancient church, Red Lion Inn, unusual reservoir, village hall and village sign, yet never realise that barely 200 years ago this was a busy, thriving community, with shops, woodyard and work places, whilst Sheringham was mainly fishermen's cottages!

The size of the village has changed very little, but what was once a parish workhouse, then a school, and a carpenter's shop and cottages, has been discreetly changed to houses and a row of five cottages, all blending in well with the existing properties. The shops have gone, but a sub-post office cum village stores is a boon to villagers and passing tourists, with whom the inn with its excellent meals and fine whiskies is also popular.

The 'Ancient Borough of Sheringham' became the two distinct parishes of Upper and Lower Sheringham in 1901 (Lower Sheringham being the seaside resort). The 14th century All Saints' church, with its flint walls and buttresses and square tower, was the parish church of both parishes until 1953. It is now one of the six churches in the Weybourne group. The building replaces an earlier Saxon or Norman church, of which nothing remains, except, perhaps the font.

The church has many memorials to the Upcher family, the newest being a fine oak screen which partitions off the tower and so forms 'The Upcher Room' (1988). Abbot Upcher bought the Sheringham estate in 1811, and commissioned Humphry Repton to plan the park and Sheringham Hall, seat of the Upcher family until Mr H. T. S. Upcher's death in 1985. The estate is now National Trust property, and hundreds of people visit its glorious rhododendron woods, the temple and gazebo every year. The Hall, originally called 'The Bower', now has a private tenant. Repton's Keeper's Lodge, rebuilt in 1904 after a fire, still stands at the south entrance to the park on the A148 Cromer/Holt road.

Abbot Upcher gave the reservoir, which provided the village drinking water right up to the late 1950s. The inscription 'ANNO PACIS 1814' records the first peace of the Napoleonic Wars. (Final peace did not come until a year later, after the Battle of Waterloo.)

The 1977 Jubilee village sign, near the reservoir, shows mermaids, to remind us of the one on the bench-end just inside the north door of the church. Legend says that she came up from the sea but could not stay, as, not being human, she had no soul. The sign also depicts *The Augusta*, Sheringham's first lifeboat, given in 1838 by the Hon Mrs Charlotte Upcher, in memory of her 20 year old daughter Augusta, who was born in 1816 and died of consumption. Wood used to build this and its successor *The Henry Ramey Upcher*, also given by the Upcher family (1894), is said to have come from the Sheringham estate.

Fishing and agriculture were the main sources of employment in earlier days. Now most villagers commute to Holt, Cromer and Sheringham for various types of work. The local district council's depot, here since 1935, brings commuters in to the village. Two thriving farms survive, but employ only a few workers. A family-run carpenter's business, with a new workshop, is in the village centre.

Most of the little groups and rows of flint-walled cottages belong to the trustees of the Upcher estate. All are kept in excellent repair. The village has only a few council houses and several of these are now privately owned. They, with other owner-occupied properties, amount to about half the total of village dwellings. To date there are very few holiday homes. Planned conversion of

219

barns and a farmhouse may change this. The 23 residents of The Dales, an imposing house, now a NCC Home for the Elderly, bring the village population to around 300.

Upper Sheringham residents have a reputation for longevity. Some years ago a popular women's magazine ran a feature on this. Interest was widespread, especially with Americans. The fact that folk grew and ate their own vegetables, and drank the then good village water was thought important, as was the quality of the rich soil. There are still nonagenarians in the village and a considerable number of people in their seventies and eighties. The good clean air (sometimes too bracing, coming straight off the North Sea!), pleasant surroundings and lack of stress must surely prove good reasons for the long, active and contented lives of the folk in this delightful Norfolk village.

🍁 WACTON

Tucked away to the west of Long Stratton, twelve miles south of Norwich just off the A140, lies the quiet village of Wacton, 1,044 acres of flat or gently-sloping land with a slow-draining clay and chalk subsoil which creates an environment as unique as the Broads or Breckland.

The soil, wet and muddy in winter, slowly dries until in late summer the clods become like concrete and huge cracks appear. It has evolved its own particular wildlife, especially cowslips and orchids, as well as causing problems to farmers, whose ingenuity over the centuries has enabled most of the parish to be cultivated by installing a network of ponds, ditches, streams and underground drains, now home to a wide variety of waterside plants and animals.

The buildings, though modest in size, have great architectural interest and beauty, as well as the occasional rarity: a restored 12th century Wealden cottage; the Hall, a large 15th century house on the edge of the common; a cottage bearing a fire insurance plaque. The more modern buildings range from Victorian terraces through pre-war council houses to modern bungalows, with a sprinkling of individually-designed properties of some merit.

The church of All Saints with its round Saxon tower and disproportionately large 14th century nave dominates the village. The tall Decorated-style windows in clear glass give the nave a sense of height, space, light and airy accommodation which contrasts well with the darker grotto-like atmosphere of conventional churches of that period. During recent repairs to the windows a small, delicately-worked roundel depicting the Apostles was discovered and is now displayed in a showcase in the nave. The neat churchyard is being managed for the conservation of wildlife, especially some plants found nowhere else in the village.

At the other end of the village lies the common, which covered 273 acres in 1533 and even as late as 1840 covered a quarter of the parish. Following requisition of land by the Ministry of Agriculture in 1942 the area was reduced to 82 acres. The goings are still held by local families under the watchful eye of the Pinder and Common keeper.

Wacton is fortunate in having a large number of footpaths and bridleways which give views across open fields little changed since medieval times and allow the countryside to be seen at close range whilst remaining near to the modern facilities of Long Stratton.

The village has been the subject of a research project by the Norfolk Research Committee, helped by the Wacton Society, and many interesting facts and artefacts have been unearthed, including some Roman and Romano-British pottery.

❦ WALPOLE

The villages of Walpole St Peter and Walpole St Andrew are amalgamated under one parish council, and are now known simply as Walpole. It is very close to the border with Lincolnshire, in what used to be called Marshland. The soil is very productive and is intensively farmed.

Walpole Island was indeed an island in the marsh, which stretched from the coast to Wisbech. This is the area where King John's lost treasure is said to be located. Various parties have looked for it, without success. In the 1930s a group of Americans had as their base the house called 'Dovecote' opposite St Peter's church, and spent a lot of money restoring it to the condition it is in today. They paid farmers two shillings and sixpence an acre to look over their land, but found nothing. Then a research team from Nottingham University tried a different idea. They tried looking for the causeway, by which they believed the King's baggage train had crossed the marsh. By taking core samples they established that there was indeed a different type of soil under a field of gooseberries. Then they too departed, and

221

King John's treasure has still not been discovered!

A derelict house near the church, reputed to be 16th century, has been beautifully restored. It is now known as the Manor House and is an asset to the village instead of the eyesore it once was.

The church at Walpole St Peter is known as the 'Cathedral of the Fens' and is famous for its annual Flower Festival, which was started by a former rector in the early 1960s. The church was built in the 13th century and the altar end is raised up to go over an ancient footpath known as The Chase. This makes a passageway under the church, known locally as the 'bolthole'. This footpath links the village with Walpole St Andrew. A new estate has been built on one side of the path, with a new school and playing field on the other. So the two villages are now effectively one, with one magnificent church (St Andrew's being closed). Hopefully this now quite large community will grow from strength to strength.

🍁 WALPOLE HIGHWAY

Walpole Highway is one of the Walpoles, comprised of St Peter's, St Andrew's, Cross Keys and the Highway. There is no village green. As its name suggests, a highway, the A47, ran straight through the middle. The village sign depicting farming on one side and the sea wall on the other was made by Mr Carter from Swaffham.

The village school is run by a husband and wife team, for infants and juniors, about 40 children in all. Local amenities used to be very good: two petrol stations, one with a good transport cafe, a butcher's shop, a post office, a general store, and a fish and chip business which still used coal-fired fryers. The latter closed down when the owners retired, and the post office, general store and one of the petrol stations have now also closed.

There is a modern village hall which is much in demand for wedding receptions and parties. The former Methodist chapel on the main road is now a residence. St Edmund's church is disused and local churchgoers have to travel two miles to the mother church of Walpole St Peter. The Bell Inn was the last pub and is now also a residence.

🍁 THE WALSINGHAMS

A short detour from the Wells-Walsinghan road brings the visitor to the heart of an early settlement at a ford of the river Stiffkey. A tiny green, a Restoration oak, a monument to Sir Eustace Gurney and a manor house, Berry Hall, dating from 1520, complete with Saxon moat, form a beautiful centrepiece to Great Walsingham, or Old Walsingham as the older generation call it.

The foundations of a small and ancient church lie in a field nearby but to the south of them stands St Peter's, on a hill overlooking the valley. It was built in the early 14th century in the Decorated style of Gothic architecture, has foliage-type window carvings and the original clerestory windows, one of the few examples to be found in the country. There is the oldest set of three bells by one bellfounder cast around 1330 and the pew ends feature strange animals, apostles and angels, while tile poppy-heads sport oak and foliage carving. This wonderful set of pews still have the kerb beams which kept in the rushes provided to warm the feet of a long forgotten congregation. All that is lacking is the chancel, which fell when the church was still thatched. You can see the outline of the beams from outside. On your way down the path don't miss the scratch dial on a buttress. If you stick a twig in on a sunny day, you can mark the passage of time.

The Black Death of 1348 caused the village to move across the ford. A former Methodist chapel, built in 1895 and now a Russian Orthodox church, is one of the best knapped-flint buildings anywhere.

Little or New Walsingham is better known, having come full circle to being a great modern pilgrimage centre as it was from Saxon times to 1538. In 1061 a God-fearing lady of the manor, Richeldis de Faverche, was granted a vision of Mary, Mother of God, who charged her to build a replica of the house in Nazareth where she had been living when the angel Gabriel told her she was to have a son, to be called Jesus. The Virgin chose two possible building sites. Richeldis opted for an area beside two holy wells. Work began and the men toiled all day with little result. The next morning, it is said, the house stood complete on the other site. Miracles began to be associated with this little wooden building. In 1153 the Augustinian canons came to Walsingham and a huge priory (now called the Abbey) was built where the Holy House could be cared for and protected.

Little Walsingham was built all at one time to cater for the needs of the pilgrims who followed the Walsingham Way (the Milky Way) to the Shrine. Inns, hostelries and shops lined the streets which were set in a grid pattern. Every king from Richard I to Henry VIII came to do homage at a shrine which rivalled Canterbury and was famed across Europe.

Now only the gateway, the ruined refectory and the mighty east window remain to give an idea of former splendour. High walls surround beautiful grounds where snowdrops and daffodils carpet the woods in spring; a rare packhorse bridge crossing the Stiffkey remains; and in the High Street are the only Grade I listed lavatories in the country. Much of the Rutland limestone from the priory can be spotted in local buildings.

The High Street is entirely medieval although many of the beams and jetties have been covered by Georgian facades. A few houses are unaltered and the newly-restored Richeldis House, part of the Anglican Shrine complex, was found to be the only surviving medieval open arcaded shop. The Pump, a very well-known landmark is post 1530. Originally it had a lofty pinnacle which was broken off during the rowdy celebrations which marked the Relief of Mafeking in 1900. In its place there is a brazier in which a fire is lighted on state occasions. If you are considering crime there is a bridewell (prison) designed by John Howard. This time capsule is untouched since it closed in 1861. It was at one time equipped with a five-bay treadmill. The Shirehall Museum is a preserved Georgian court house and houses the Tourist Information Centre.

In 1781 John Wesley preached in the Friday Market, and the Methodist chapel, now beautifully renovated, is the oldest still operating in East Anglia.

In 1897 the Roman Catholic church again made this village a place of pilgrimage and in the 1930s the devotion to Our Lady of Walsingham was revived by Father Hope Patten, who began building the Anglican Shrine.

Pilgrims come in ever increasing numbers from March to November, changing the face of the village. The High Street is jammed to capacity and gift shops, souvenir shops, and tea-rooms have replaced the draper, fishmonger, and hardware shop. The Roman Catholic hospices are in the village but their Slipper Chapel and the Chapel of Reconciliation are in Houghton St Giles. 'Slipper' may have come from the idea that the pilgrims took off their shoes there in order to walk the last mile barefoot, but it is more likely that the word 'slyppe', meaning a passage in a monastery which leads into the church, gave it the name. Plenty of literature is available for the visitor to both Shrine and the Chapel of Reconciliation.

The spired parish church of St Mary, built by the canons, was gutted by fire in 1961, maybe the result of a wiring fault, maybe a cigarette end from a vagrant, no one knows. The effect was made worse by the fact that the beams had been recently treated to preserve them. The church has been very well restored. Look at England's finest seven sacrament font. It is so good that a plaster cast was made of it for the Great Exhibition of 1851 in the Crystal Palace. Drops of molten lead from the fire can be seen on it. The Sydney Tomb escaped damage. The porcupine which is the family crest has lost its spines through the ages but a fine pair the knight and his lady make as they lie side by side. John Hayward designed the east window, incorporating the pilgrim kings, Richeldis, the statue of Our Lady, the Holy House, Father Hope Patten, and the Virgin holding the rebuilt church. A number of exhibitions of art have been held in St Mary's and some very fine works have been given by displaying artists. Naomi Blake gave one of her statues, John Riches a painting entitled *Spring Carpet*, and a ceramic commissioned by Peter Palumbo and executed by Ruth Duckworth is placed in the south aisle.

So, whether you want medieval or contemporary, Walsingham can satisfy you.

❧ THE WARHAMS

Leaving Wells on the A149, in the direction of Stiffkey, the visitor may turn on to the B1105, and will come to a small road on the left leading into the long scatter of the Warhams. To the west is Warham St Mary, and to the east is Warham All Saints.

If it is surprising to find two churches of the same denomination so close to one another, it is more so to find that once there were three. In 1795, the living of St Mary Magdalene was consolidated with that of St Mary the Virgin. This was the territory of the Turners, the agriculturalists of the 18th century.

The work of Sir John Turner was praised by Arthur Young, who wrote that Sir John was using a crop rotation of wheat, clover, lucerne and turnips, years before his Norfolk neighbours, Townshend of Raynham and Coke of Norfolk. After the death of Sir John in 1785, his estate was bought by Holkham, and the old Turner mansion was demolished.

To the south is one of the best examples of Iron Age camps in England, a great earthwork in a bend of the river Stiffkey. Two high banks with a valley between enclose a circle of three acres. The site has been preserved unaltered, except for a section of outer bank. This was removed when the meandering river was canalised. Almost certainly this was one of the homes of the Iceni, until the tribe was destroyed by the Romans after their great Queen Boudicca rebelled.

🍁 WATERDEN

The tiny parish of Waterden is quite close to Fakenham, off the B1355 road to Burnham Market, but so remote that only the determined summer visitor to the area will find it. Awaiting discovery is a farmhouse with a few cottages, the former rectory, and the delightful 11th century All Saints'. This little church, with its ruined tower, can have had hardly any parishioners in its most prosperous time. At one time it was so overgrown that it was difficult to see. The efforts of the Waterden farmer and of the Norfolk Society have preserved it, and it is well worth a visit.

The original village was in the valley to the north of the church, with a manor house and large barn. The latter is all that remains, adjacent to the present farmhouse. In the early 19th century, T. W. Coke of Holkham and his tenant began here their successful experiments to replace the traditional Norfolk sheep, bred for their wool, with a breed that would produce good meat, as well as good wool.

🍁 WATTON

Watton is in the heart of East Anglia, 21 miles west of Norwich with the Broads, Breckland and the east coast near to hand. In the Domesday survey it was called Wadetuna, and a market charter was granted to John de Vaux for a Wednesday market in the reign of King John (1199–1216). The market is kept to this day.

St Mary's parish church dates from the 12th century and has a Norman tower topped by an octagonal belfry. There is also a Methodist church in the High Street and both have regular attendances. In 1988 the Watton Christian Community Centre opened, uniting the parish church and the Methodist church.

A clock tower stands in the High Street, dating from 1679 and erected after a fire destroyed much of the town in 1674. Also in the High Street is the town sign of the Babes in the Wood, taken from the legend of the Wayland Wood where the babes were found.

There are playing fields and a sports centre. The Queen's Hall was completed in 1956 and is in regular use for dances etc. This growing and active market centre now has a population of between 6,000 and 7,000 people.

WAXHAM

Waxham is a small coastal hamlet 15 miles north of Great Yarmouth. It is all that remains of a once important town, large enough to have been divided into Waxham Parva and Magna, and records of its existence for over a thousand years are known. Erosion by the sea has caused its demise. Only part of Waxham Magna remains. A sandy ledge accumulated by wind was the only defence until the 19th century when an organised programme of repair was instigated and marram grass planted to give the dunes stability. After the east coast floods of 1953, metal piling and a concrete wall on the seaward side has given more permanence to the defences.

The dunes are designated a site of special scientific interest and are a bird-watcher's paradise. The surrounding marshlands, swept by the biting north-east wind have been partially altered by drainage for food production. Small copses are reminders of forests claimed by the sea, the remains of which can be seen when rough seas scour the beach to reveal trees and stumps embedded in the clay.

The population has declined from 113 in 1876 to the present-day 50. Children attended the village school built on the boundary with Sea Palling, until it closed in 1985. Children are now bussed to Hickling and Stalham. Another shared service was the coastguard station built on the boundary to combat smuggling, which was rife. The two villages finally amalgamated in 1937 to form a single parish.

Drainage mills were once a feature of the landscape and one still stands at Lambridge Staithe, but 1938 was the last time the sails turned as water was pumped from the marshes. Lambridge Staithe is situated on the New Cut, an artificial waterway from Horsey Mere. Wherries took grain from local farms to Yarmouth and brought coal on the return journey to fuel the steam engines that drove the mill. At the beginning of the 20th century a workman painting the sails was given an unexpected ride when the mill keeper, one Eliza Knights, let the sails go after he had spilled paint on her!

Holidaymakers, once catered for by the local farms and villagers to supplement their income, are now accommodated at a caravan park and holiday cottages. Small farms have been incorporated into the larger ones and now only four farms remain. The old Norfolk turkey once reared here has disappeared and a specialist unit rears the more familiar ones.

Waxham Hall, an imposing building faced with knapped flint, is believed by many to be the original Hall built in the 12th century but other experts maintain the architecture points to it being a baronial hall of Tudor times. During the First World War it was used by the military and left derelict. With the Hall is the largest tithe barn in Norfolk, partially destroyed in the hurricane of 1987. A cobble and flint wall surrounds the property, twelve feet high on the seaward side, with pinnacles on the angles and a large gateway which formerly had access to the coast road now covered by the sand dunes.

The church of St John was allowed to become derelict but was later restored, although the chancel was beyond repair, and now consists of nave, tower and porch. The register dates from 1713.

❧ WEETING

The Saxon village of Weeting-cum-Bromehill lies on the B1106, between Brandon and Methwold, a Breckland village on the edge of the fens. It has many historic places including Grimes Graves, prehistoric flint mines dating from 2300 to 1700 BC, a 12th century boulder flint church, and an 11th century castle and icehouse, built by William de Warrenne, son-in-law to William the Conqueror.

In the village can be seen remains of an old estate and Hall. The Hall, of Italian style, was built by Lord Montrath in 1770, and sold to John J. Angerstein in 1806, an eminent Russian merchant who later became a celebrated stockbroker and underwriter at Lloyds. On his death, his valuable collection of ancient and modern paintings were bought for £57,000 to form the nucleus of the National Gallery. After various uses by the government, including housing unemployed trainees during the 1930s, during the Second World War the Hall was used as an Indian hospital, visited by King George VI.

Army barracks were built in the Hall grounds, these were later used by Polish personnel. The Hall was demolished in 1954. In the Hall grounds houses were built for American servicemen.

The village school was built in 1770. In 1903 the school had 53 pupils and was promised a new school. It was not built until 1960! Notes from the school log record that taps were often frozen all day in the winter. Impetigo, scabies, scarlet fever and whooping cough were the main illnesses. The school was threatened with closure in 1953 but by 1979 there were 140 pupils.

The village began to grow with ten new council houses in 1954. The site for the petrol station and public house was bought in 1955 at the end of large concrete roads, where tanks were maintained during the Second World War. Refuse was collected only every six weeks in 1952. The first electric street light was erected in 1948.

Weeting is the home of a steam engine rally, a three day event enjoyed by over 20,000 visitors every July. Weeting's industrial area is near the railway station. Bromehill is also near the station. Here a priory was built in 1220, and suppressed in 1525. A working windmill stood on Mill Farm.

Weeting is surrounded by forestry, having become a National Park in April 1990. Pines were first planted in 1922.

🍁 WELLS-NEXT-THE-SEA

Wells-next-the-Sea is a small seaside resort and port for fishing and pleasure boats on the north Norfolk Heritage Coast. Wells has a population of approximately 2,500 (which swells greatly during the summer season) with tourism, farming and fishing providing the main areas for employment. The name of Wells is derived from the fact that it used to tap the springs of fresh water held by the underlying chalk on which it is built and many houses relied on their own wells – often inside the house itself – for their water supplies.

The beach, a mile from the quay, can be reached by road, miniature railway or by a grass covered embankment, all of which run parallel to the main shipping channel. Pine woods, sand dunes and a boating lake make a pleasant approach to the beach itself. Here the volunteer lifeguards patrol during the season and the coastguards and lifeboats provide help for any eventualities. Sailing, sail-boarding and water skiing are very popular during the summer months, with walking and birdwatching providing all the year round interest.

In Staithe Street, quaint and narrow, you will find many shops selling local produce. An old granary at the bottom of the street has been converted into a community hall and theatre, administered by the Community Association and used for local events. Adjacent to this is the Tourist Information Office, open only during the summer months.

At the centre of the town is The Buttlands, a spacious green ringed by trees and Georgian houses, traditionally the heart of outdoor activities such as the carnival, bonfire and numerous fetes.

There is a much-loved cottage hospital, built by public subscription, whose continued existence is due to overwhelming public support. The nurses home, situated next door, has been converted into a day care centre for the frail and elderly, where a nucleus of trained staff are ably supported by teams of volunteers.

The parish church of St Nicholas, destroyed by fire in 1879, was rebuilt on the same site, the present interior modelled to a very great extent on the old. Roman Catholic, Methodist, United Reformed and Quaker churches where meetings for worship are held regularly are also to be found in the town.

Between 1850 and 1880 there were some 40 public houses in the town but today many of these have been converted into private houses. The Golden Fleece, however, situated on the quay, remains as a public house. In its large upper room, originally a wool exchange, there are fine plaster reliefs showing St Blaise blessing the sheep, and Jason and the Argonauts. Across the quay, at the southern end of the embankment leading to the beach, is the original lifeboat house built in 1869. In those days the lifeboat had either to be rowed down the mile-long channel to the open sea or, at low water, pulled there by horses which first had to be caught and harnessed. This building is now the Harbour-Master's office and Maritime Museum. A memorial is to be found close by erected to the memory of eleven crew members of the lifeboat *Eliza Adams*, who lost their lives in 1880 when the boat capsized and failed to right itself because the mast had become embedded in the sand. In 1998 a memorial tablet was placed nearby to mark the centenary of the drowning of eleven coastguards attempting to bring stores ashore.

In the floods of 1953 and 1978 the embankment was breached, marshes flooded and great damage done to the houses in Freeman Street, adjacent agricultural land and the pine trees behind the beach. To prevent such a disaster happening again, electrically operated flood barriers have been installed which can be moved across the road when extreme high tides threaten.

🍁 WEST BECKHAM

Situated some three miles south of Sheringham on the scenic north Norfolk coast is the village of West Beckham and its smaller sister, East Beckham. They possess no great mansions, have no famous sons, lack a village green, but withal they epitomise the inland coastal villages of the area. They retain their original flavour of walls built from blue flint gathered from the nearby beaches, with local red brick quoins and ashlars, topped off with the traditional red Norfolk pantiles. It is a scattered community of some 300 souls.

There is a widely held opinion that Norfolk is flat. However, in this area where the Cromer Ridge was pushed up by the great glaciers thousands of years ago, the converse is true. West Beckham attains an altitude of 300 ft above sea level and thus claims to be one of the highest parts of the county.

It was no doubt this factor which led in 1938 to the erection of two radio masts, followed by others up to 400 ft high, being the first towers in the radar chain that was to play such an important part in winning the Second World War. At that time we played host not only to the 'pylons' referred to by Lord Haw Haw as 'the beastly things at Beckham', but also to two camps for the RAF personnel who manned them, but little remains to show the part West Beckham played in the war. However, even today there is an important radio communications relay centre for the emergency services and British Telecom.

The area has always been in the first line of defence because Weybourne on the nearby coast is rumoured to have some of the deepest water off the English coast. Since Napoleonic times this has been a defensive position, and even now in the autumn, when the ploughs are in the fields, they turn over and expose the shingle which was laid down for the cavalry lines in the First World War.

In former times the parishes were well cared for spiritually, having three chapels and two churches, but today of the chapels one has been demolished, one is a store, whilst the other has been made into a dwelling.

The church has the twin dedication of St Helen's and All Saints', which derives from the fact that East Beckham church, which fell into ruins 200 years ago, and West Beckham church, which was pulled down in 1890, provided the materials for the new church consecrated in 1891 and built on a new site with a rectory. It has a rare character in that the internal church walls are of

231

unplastered blue flints and the whole is in a garden setting, with none of the headstones usually associated with a church. The churchyard is half a mile away, still encompassing the foundations of the original church, where burials still take place.

A few hundred yards further down the road brings you to the site of the Erpingham Union or workhouse which closed in the early 1950s and was later demolished as it became unsafe. An imposing building, built of flint and brick in 1851, its likeness is to be seen today at St Michael's Hospital, Aylsham, which was another workhouse now put to modern use. The 'casuals' would walk, or tramp, the rounds of the workhouses at Aylsham, Beckham, Thursford, Gressenhall and Gayton seeking casual employment in the fields; in winter they had to be in the workhouse before the six o'clock bell and in summer by eight o'clock. Lodging was in exchange for work in the two acre garden, the laundry, hauling coals etc and when they went on their way they were fortified with a lump of cheese and some bread.

West Beckham derives its name from the Danish 'beck' meaning brook or stream. It has the singularity of two rivers within 100 yards of each other in the same field; one flowing out to sea on the north coast at Cley-next-the-Sea, whilst the other is the Beck, feeding Scarrowbeck and so to the Bure and out to sea at Great Yarmouth on the east coast.

The former pub, closed in the 1950s, has become a dwelling, and a farmhouse made into a comfortable pub. Whilst the conversion work was being carried out, a single child's boot, dating from the 17th century, was found carefully secreted in the inglenook. Many years ago, when all the farm work was done by men and animals, sons were of vital importance in the farmer's household, and it was thought that if a boy's single boot were hidden in the house that boy wouldn't leave home.

There are painters and silversmiths here, as well as commuters to the local towns and even as far as Norwich, whilst other cottages are let to holidaymakers who come to enjoy what is without question the best, most unspoiled, most secret part of Norfolk. Where 'fresh fish' means straight from the sea, caught and cooked the same day, and where bread is still baked in the family bakery and has crust on it, and the cockles and samphire are there for the taking, and above all there are the glorious, inspirational East Anglian skyscapes.

❧ WEST RUDHAM

The long barrow on West Rudham common, said to date from the Neolithic or New Stone Age period, suggests that there was a settlement here some 4,000 years ago. There have been many finds of rough tools, worked flints etc in the local stone and gravel pits. It was not until the 9th or 10th century that Rudham (spelled Rudeham in Anglo-Saxon times) emerged as a village. It is thought that it takes its name from a local ruling chieftain named Rudda. Situated on the A148, between Fakenham and King's Lynn, West Rudham is the source of the river Wensum, which meanders through meadows and farmland to join up with the Yare at Norwich.

The village extends to some 2,918 acres and for many years most of the land and cottages belonged to the Raynham and Houghton estate, but of later years much of the land has been sold to individual farmers and most of the cottages are now privately owned.

West Rudham Hall farmhouse is probably the oldest house in the village and thought to date, in parts, from the Middle Ages. The old tithe barn at Grove Farm, built in the early 18th century, was burned down some 30 years ago, but some cottages of similar date remain.

The Duke's Head public house was built about 1563 and extended in 1663. Until early in the 20th century the manorial courts for West Rudham Northall or St Faith's and West Rudham Ferrers were held there.

The church, dedicated to St Peter, is a 13th century building of mixed architectural styles. Some medieval stained glass has survived in the north windows and the church has several very interesting features. The living was consolidated with that of St Mary's, East Rudham, in 1720. The church was closed in the 1960s and services are held at St Mary's, but in 1979 it was leased to the Norfolk Churches Trust. A programme of restoration work was carried out and well attended services are held in the church three or four times during the year.

By the middle of the 19th century the population had grown to 487 and there were then 102 houses. Although agriculture was the main source of employment, there were over 20 tradesmen and businesses in the village. With the exception of the public house, none of these trades and businesses has survived, although various tradesmen and craftsmen from the village work in the neighbourhood and nearby towns, and there is now a building firm in the

233

village. One of the farmhouses now provides bed and breakfast and holiday accommodation and the barns have been converted to dwellings, the farmland having been sold.

The population started to decline during the last quarter of the 19th century and now numbers approximately 200. Although there are still families living in the village whose ancestors were here at the beginning of the 19th century, and most probably before that, because of problems with employment and housing many of the younger generation have had to move away and a large proportion of the people are retired. While there have been many changes over the years no large-scale building development has taken place and new buildings have been confined to infilling, so the general landscape of the village remains very much as it was 200 years ago.

WEST WINCH

West Winch today is a village of about 4,000 inhabitants, two miles south of King's Lynn. It straddles the busy A10, but the largest residential area is between the A10 and West Winch common.

'Parish and village of detached houses on or near the Setch turn-pike, three miles south of Lynn, partly in the low meadowland and common on the east side of the river Nar. Lord Henry Cholmondeley is lord of the manor but a great part of the soil belongs to small freeholders and a number of copyholders'. West Winch is so described in the mid 19th century Norfolk directories.

The common was (and still is) two miles in length and 210 acres in extent. Common grazing rights are attached to certain properties in the village. The common was a natural playground for all the village children. Grazed by cattle and horses since time immemorial, it provided a wide and seemingly endless supply of wildflowers to be carried home to mother and displayed in jam jars on the kitchen windowsill; mushrooms and blackberries were gathered in their season.

Most of the properties on the commonside were remote from the lanes that gave access to them and in the first 40 years of the 20th century, ground conditions permitting, the postman and several of the tradesmen would make their deliveries from the common at the rear, among these were Mr Crake the baker who came from Lynn with a horse drawn van. Mr Stanforth the village-based coalman used a horse and cart, as did the Co-op grocery man who called twice weekly either to deliver goods or collect orders and cash. The butcher was more up-market and used a motor van. Early summer brought the call of 'Sampher! Lovely Green Sampher!!' from the 'Sampher Man' who travelled the district with a pony and trap. Another summer visitor was the Stop-Me-And-Buy-One icecream vendor who rang the bell on his trike to signal his arrival. Less frequently the Betterwear Brush man called. Tramps did not often stray far from the main road but were quite often seen brewing-up under the trees surrounding the double pits (ponds) situated in Long Lane that led up to the main road.

The population has increased during the past few years, due to a large number of people retiring here from the London area and Essex. It is not a 'pretty' village, but one full of life, from the well attended St Mary's church, to the youngsters in the Mothers and Toddlers group. All the societies and clubs in the district are fortunate to have the William Burt Centre, a community centre catering for the needs of all, and named after one of the original West Winch families.

The chief landmark in the village is the newly restored windmill, which was allowed to fall into disrepair but in the past few years has been restored to its original state, with its now complete set of sails proudly dominating the village.

🍁 WESTON LONGVILLE

Weston Longville is a widely scattered village of some 2,767 acres situated between the A47 Dereham road and the A1067 Fakenham road about ten miles from Norwich. The area in 1888 was mainly cropped with wheat, roots, barley and hay. In 1937 these were still the main crops but due to extensive changes in the agricultural scene during the last 50 years, sugar beet, oil seed rape, peas, beans, and lately daffodils, Christmas trees and asparagus have been grown.

The parish church of All Saints is an ancient building standing in the village centre. The rood screen, dating from the early 15th century, has been refurbished to restore the fine detail. There is an exceptional wall painting of the Tree of Jesse and one of John the Baptist, both of which have been restored as far as funds will allow. In recent years due to generous gifts, spot lighting and extra heating have been appreciated. The restored bell-tower and re-cast bells were also a gift which Norfolk bellringers enjoy.

In 1836 most of the land belonged to the lord of the manor at Weston House. Fifteen farmers were tenants and in 1888 eleven tenants are recorded plus a tailor, veterinary surgeon, iron founder, agricultural implement manufacturer, gamekeepers, gardeners and carpenters to Colonel Custance at Weston House. The farms and farm buildings remained as part of the Weston estate until the 1960s. Since then most of the farmhouses and buildings have been sold and Weston House has become the clubhouse for the 18-hole golf course. Recently the estate was purchased by Anglian Leisure who have retained the Dinosaur Park with the adventure playground.

Fortunately the village still has a post office/shop, the Parson Woodforde pub is well favoured and the equestrian centre flourishes. The village hall struggles to survive financially but is well used for meetings, the newest being The Daisy Club, which was started by a younger parishioner to enable older people to meet regularly as our village is widely spread.

The diarist Parson Woodforde, who was rector of Weston Longville between 1776 and 1803, is famous for his record of late 18th century life. His memorial tablet in the church reads: 'His parishioners held him in the highest esteem and veneration and as a tribute to his memory followed him to the grave. The poor feel a severe loss as they were the constant objects of his bounty.'

During the Second World War a large area of land was used for an airfield which became the base for the US Second Air Division 466 Bombardment Group. After the war the airfield was acquired by Bernard Matthews who built on it the largest turkey farm in Europe, creating employment for many villagers.

The US Second Air Division provided funds for the village sign which stands by the church wall. A Stars and Stripes flag (previously flown on the Capitol building) was dedicated and presented to the parish of Weston Longville, to commemorate the last reunion of the group in Norwich in 1990. The Division, who were also in other parts of Norfolk, gave and still fund the American Memorial Library in Norwich in memory of dead comrades. Although completely destroyed by fire in August 1994 it will hopefully reopen within the new Norwich Central Library. Meawhile it is temporarily housed with the library in Ber Street, Norwich.

🍁 WEYBOURNE

The village of Weybourne has been in existence for many centuries (it is still occasionally pronounced 'Webbern'). There was a priory here in the 12th century, itself on the site of an Anglo-Saxon edifice, and behind the ruins on the north side there are still some walls of the old priory. Next to the church is the Abbey Farm House which, it is said, was probably built in the 14th century. Slightly out of the village to the south is what was a small lake, used by the monks for fishing. From this site runs a small stream, through the fields, under gardens, beneath roads, which finally reaches the sea via another pond which used to be full of eels.

The village before the Second World War was very different from today, being almost completely self-sufficient with shops and craftsmen to cater for every need. Nowadays there is only one shop with its post office and the size of the village has grown, but with the number of cars also increasing, people are quite prepared to seek those other services in the larger towns around. In 1960 there were about 300 people living here – today there are around 550 and this has meant many new houses and estates have been added to the old village.

The windmill still stands at the east entrance into the village, but whereas it and two other mills, one a water mill, the other a post mill, once provided a living for their inhabitants, it is now somebody's home. There is a modern village hall, built next to the old one – a wooden structure given by a Mr Land who lived in the Hall and was a director of Shell Oil, before the First World War. He gave it originally to be used as a YMCA for the troops stationed at the Muckleburgh camp and afterwards he presented it to the village to become the village hall.

Mr Monement donated the land for the bowling green further up the village street. He was a descendant of the great William Bolding, a chief benefactor to the church and additionally a man of many talents – architect, archaeologist and artist. His collection of photographs of old Weybourne and its inhabitants are now to be found in the Muckleburgh Collection which is on the site of the old military camp. Mr Bolding owned half the village with its many farms, a brewery, cottages and two of the mills, while the other half of the village formed part of the estates of the Earl of Orford and this included another three farms.

It is an area much appreciated by holidaymakers and birdwatchers and there are two caravan/chalet sites – one in the village and the other on the hill behind it. The North Norfolk Railway, formerly a link between Melton Constable and Norwich, has been reclaimed by a private company and runs steam trains along the coast, particularly during the summer but also on special occasions during the rest of the year.

For those coming into the village from Holt for the first time, the view from the top of the hill must be one of the most beautiful in England, especially in summer with the sun shining, but whatever the season and whatever the weather, the variations of colour and design make it impossible to tire of seeing it.

WICKLEWOOD

Wicklewood lies on rising ground in the centre of the county three miles west of Wymondham. It is a scattered, sprawling parish, a loose amalgamation of streets and hamlets linked by isolated farms and cottages. It is not a pretty village in the conventional sense, but it is an interesting one. Its character, like the soil it rests on, is firm and gritty.

Almost 2,000 years ago a road passed through here, carrying soldiers and traders between the Roman town of Venta Icenorum (Caister-by-Norwich) and the Icknield Way. The mid 1st century was a troubled time hereabouts and it may have been during the disturbances of Boudicca's revolt that the lovely Roman wine set now known as the Crownthorpe Hoard was buried for safe keeping. The delicately wrought bronze pan, bowls and duck-handled cups were still packed inside the wine strainer when found in 1982 and are now displayed in Norwich Castle Museum.

Wicklewood, named 'Wicklurde' in the Domesday Book, must have been a place of some importance during the Middle Ages. Two churches, All Saints' and St Andrew's, stood in the churchyard, each with its own priest and congregation until Bishop Thomas of Norwich united them as a single parish in 1367. St Andrew's was even then 'decayed', and nothing of its structure now remains above ground. In 1440 King Henry VI granted a charter for the holding of a market and two fairs in Wicklewood – an honour which suggests a village of some local importance.

All Saints' church lies at the western edge of the village. It is not a large church by Norfolk standards, but has a lofty tower which, unusually, lies to the

238

Wicklewood windmill

south of the nave and also serves as a porch. The present building is 15th century Perpendicular in style, though the sturdy pillars of the porch door are survivals of an earlier building. Its one claim to architectural distinction is the unique external facing of the walls in alternate courses of flints and thin bricks.

In 1776, the overseers of the poor from 23 parishes of the Forehoe Hundred chose Wicklewood as the site for their new workhouse. It was, they said, central for the area, convenient for Wymondham and a healthy place besides. £11,000 was quickly borrowed in shares of £100 each. The 'House of Industry' constructed from the proceeds was, and is, a splendid Georgian building. Here up to 400 poor people, officially referred to as 'the family', were cared for humanely, even generously, by the master and staff. The petty indignities and meannesses that made workhouses so abhorrent to later generations were not applied at Wicklewood until the London-based Poor Law Commission took control in 1834. After serving 150 years as a workhouse, the building became a hospital, then, briefly, a school, and is now part of a high quality housing development. As one villager commented, 'people used to do anything to keep out of the place; now they're queuing to get in!'

Wicklewood's other landmark, apart from its pretty little school building, erected as a Board school in 1878, is its windmill. This fine four-sailed mill, once one of two in the village, was built about 1845 and was fully operational grinding corn for flour and animal feed until the Second World War. After generations in the Wade family, the mill was given to the Norfolk Windmills Trust in 1977, since when it has been restored to full working order. The mill is open to the public from time to time and tours and refreshments are provided by volunteers and WI members.

WICKMERE WITH WOLTERTON

Wickmere is a tiny hamlet with a population of some 100 people. At one time it could boast a shop, school, post office and a blacksmith's, but sadly these have closed one by one.

The church of St Andrew, built by the Normans some 850 years ago, still stands in lonely isolation overlooking the main part of the village across the fields. The massive oak door leading into the church was made by craftsmen some 500 years ago and still has the great iron boss and heavy oak lock. The lovely 15th century screen with St Andrew still recognisable on one of the panels has been restored and stands just behind the beautifully carved pulpit.

Wickmere has close links with the Walpole family – descendants of Sir Robert Walpole, the first Prime Minister of England. Sir Robert's younger brother Horatio built Wolterton Hall in 1741 and it was added to in 1830 by G. S. Repton. The gardens, overlooking the beautiful lake, were laid out by Charles Bridgeman and altered in 1830. Ruins of a church stand in the grounds showing where the village used to be; the last baptism recorded was in 1740.

Most of the cottages in Wickmere are constructed of traditional Norfolk bricks and flints and were probably built about 300 years ago. With the exception of a few council houses and one or two privately built cottages, Wickmere has changed little over the years and still manages to retain its rural character.

WIGGENHALL ST GERMANS

St Germans is a growing village with a population of approximately 2,000. The river Ouse runs right through the centre of the village, with the lovely old church just below the bank.

Almost all the village landmarks are by the river. 'The Old Vicarage' adjoins the churchyard, while a home for the handicapped, formerly an old inn, stands on the bank. Two thriving village stores, one with a post office are all close to the river, as is the school and the village hall. There is now one popular village pub. Formerly there were four, and two of them are now lovely private houses, having been renovated.

On another road, still backing onto the river bank, is an old abbey. It has been restored and is now in use as a tile and kitchen shop which is famous for miles around. A really lovely old row of cottages was demolished some years ago to make way for an engineering works, but this is now used as a salesroom for garden and farm implements. Many of the villagers were employed by local farmers and some still are. There are orchards close by and many fields of grain and sugar beet.

In 1953 St Germans suffered greatly from floods, when the river bank was breached in several places. Following this a new channel was cut, giving us yet another river which is used for water sports and brings lots of visitors. There is also the Middle Level, another waterway that runs through to Bedford, draining land from miles away. At the St Germans end there is a huge pumping station, controlling the water and eventually allowing it through to the Ouse and then out to sea. The station was built in the 1930s and has now been electrified.

🍁 WINTERTON-ON-SEA

The village was known simply as Winterton until the 1950s when the name was changed to avoid confusion with Winterton in Lincolnshire.

The huge village church is a superb example of 12th century building by the monks of St Benet's Abbey. It boasts the highest church tower in Norfolk, in conflict with Cromer and Wymondham, and on a clear day the spire of Norwich Cathedral can be seen from the top, a distance of 22 miles.

The lighthouse is a dominant feature of the skyline, and a reminder of the treacherous North Sea. The flashing beam helped and warned mariners until 1921 when it ceased to operate. It has since been converted into a private residence. Up to the early part of the 20th century many of the cottages were built with timbers from wrecks off Winterton Ness and a large number are still standing today. In 1869 two lifeboats were installed at Winterton-on-Sea and

241

records show that nearly 600 lives were saved by the brave crews before the boats were disbanded in 1924.

Until 1954 the village economy was mostly based on harvest from the sea, fishing from the beach or by joining the fleets at Great Yarmouth or Lowestoft. Regrettably, this has all vanished with the demise of the fish stocks in the North Sea and the change to today's lifestyle. The village is still thriving in its popularity as a holiday area for those wishing to get away from it all, or to spend a day on one of our country's most beautiful pale golden beaches which is backed by miles of sand dunes. Rhododendrons and heathers grow in profusion to the north which is designated a Nature Reserve, and is home to rare butterflies, moths, dragonflies and is also the habitat for the natterjack toad. Every year sections of the beach are cordoned off to protect nesting terns.

A well known son of the village was Sam Larner, who, at the age of 80 years, made his first long playing record entitled, 'Singin' the Fishin''. He then went to London, and amidst great acclaim for his talent and memory, performed to packed houses. He only enjoyed fame for a short while as he died three years later, having lived all his life in the village occupying a little flint cottage with his gentle, charming wife, Dorcas.

There were two pubs in the village until the early 1980s but now there is just the 300 year old Fisherman's Return. A few years ago, on Boxing Days especially, this pub would be packed from wall to wall and enemies would meet, throw their arms around each other, drink together, forgiving and forgetting, for one day at least! Carrying on the folk singing tradition the villagers gathered there would listen to the fishermen singing and reciting their favourite ditty or limerick and woebetide anyone who performed, or interrupted, another's party piece!

At the turn of the 20th century the population was just 110, but over the years the inhabitants have increased to the present 1,500. There is still a village school with 84 pupils on roll. A new classroom was opened on 12th December 1996 by Mr R. Green and Mrs A. George, the oldest residents in the village, both of whom had attended the school as children. A purpose built nursery for four year olds and a link building with disabled access was opened on 12th June 1998. There is a post office, a thriving general store selling fresh meat and a fried fish shop, as well as a local fisherman selling wet and smoked fish from his house, thus linking us with the past.

❧ WITTON & RIDLINGTON

Under boundary reorganisation these two villages became one civil parish. However, each has a different history.

The Witton village sign shows a post mill, the church and Highland cattle. The mill was on the extreme eastern boundary until about 1925. There had been a mill on the site since at least 1797. The round house is still there in the grounds of Mill Farm House. The church of St Margaret has a Saxon round tower and several Saxon windows, and formerly wall paintings were visible. One lord of the manor, Lord Wodehouse, repaired the top of the tower, giving £200 for the work in about 1825, and the repair can still be distinguished. And the Highland cattle, what are they doing on the village sign? In 1934 a young Scottish farmer came from his native land to Witton Old Hall to farm, bringing a herd of Highland cattle with him. Part of Witton Old Hall is of 16th century origin and must be one of the oldest buildings in Witton.

Witton Hall is a modern building. The original was built by John Norris in 1777, but he didn't live to see it finished. This building was taken down in 1927, although a sunken garden shows where the cellars used to be. The oldest thing in Witton is a prehistoric burial mound on the extreme western boundary. Formerly there was a school, built by Lady Wodehouse in 1834 and used until about 1946. There was also a Methodist church, built in 1865 and closed in the mid 1960s. Both are now private houses.

Ridlington's village sign shows an owl, the church and a plough. For years an owl had a nest in an elm tree and there are still quite a number around the village. The site has been registered with the Hawk Trust. The plough commemorates the Plough Inn, now a private house and last used as an inn in May 1952. It is known to have been in existence at least since 1789 and it is said that in the 1600s the landlord supplied Witton church with wine. The church of St Peter has the four evangelists for pinnacles. Thanks to a grant, the tower has been repaired and made safe, saving it from demolition. In the First World War the chancel end was extensively damaged by a bomb dropped from a Zeppelin.

In The Street is a very old house, Dairy Farm, which was built in 1683. From outside it can be seen where the roof was raised. In Old Lane (formerly Nash's Lane) there are some buildings known as Nash's Farm. According to the 1845 *White's Directory* a Samuel Nash lived there. It is believed he bought

243

and gave the land in about 1822 on which Bacton Baptist church now stands. Church Farm opposite the church was built in about 1860.

Both villages had shops until quite recently. Witton's shop at Witton Bridge, although actually in Ridlington, had been in existence since 1828 and probably before that, and was the post office almost from the time such places started. It closed in June 1988. Ridlington's shop had been open since the 1850s, but ceased to trade in the 1980s.

The village hall which serves both villages started as a reading room for the men of Witton in 1908, but the present building was erected in 1968. In 1991 an extension was built for a new kitchen and toilets. Twice we have come first in the 'Best-run Village Hall' competition.

WOODBASTWICK

Woodbastwick, a picturesque village situated about seven miles east of Norwich, stands in the centre of an outstanding conservation area in the heart of the Norfolk Broadlands. The river Bure which flows out to sea at Great Yarmouth borders several miles of the estate.

The village, owned by the Cator family since the early 1800s, has only five or six privately owned properties on the whole estate. The population has decreased to about 100 at the present day. The land is farmed in partnership by the two sons of the present squire and is known as ROTAC farms. It is mainly arable with some sheep and is the home of the famous British White cows which have been here since the herd was established in 1840.

The estate comprises a large area of marsh land which is part of the 1,019 acre Bure Marshes National Nature Reserve. Many of the marsh dykes have been dammed to hold back the murky river water and they now support thriving plants and animals native to Broadland. These same marshes some 50 years ago were reed beds and local inhabitants used to harvest the crop – cutting the reed in flat bottom boats called lighters along the dykes. This reed was used for thatching, much on the estate where many houses are thatched, as is the church of St Fabian and St Sebastian which stands in the centre of the village. Adjacent to the church is the village green with its round thatched pump house, a source of water for the villagers in years gone by, and two thatched almshouses with their inscription 'At Eventide It Shall Be Light'. Also the old vicarage, now a private dwelling, stands nearby at the top of the

244

Thatched pump house at Woodbastwick

private driveway to the Cator residence. In the 19th century this vicarage was the village pub. Reeds are no longer grown on the marshes and indeed, apart from certain conservation areas in the centre of the village, many houses are being tiled due to the acute world-wide shortage of thatching reeds.

The flint church, a fine example of Norfolk thatching, is certainly medieval, possibly 15th century, and is unusual in being dedicated to two saints. The interior is Victorian, having been restored in the 19th century, and all the windows are of stained glass.

The family home Woodbastwick Hall, built between 1884 and 1888, was demolished in the late 1970s. It was built after an earlier Hall burned down in 1883 and had 52 rooms and 365 windows. Remaining parts of the earlier Hall were for many years used as a house and a convalescent hospital. After the Second World War the hospital and part of the new Hall became an Agricultural Training College for a while before being again fully occupied by the Cator family. Since the demolition the family have lived in the 'Old Hall' nestling beside the river Bure and close to Decoy Broad which for many years has, by kind permission, been used by the Sea Scouts as a camping and training area.

The village school which catered for about 50 children in the 1930s, closed during the 1970s when the number of children on roll was reduced to six. The local post office also closed in the early 1980s and another village loss is the blacksmith's forge at which the local smith could be seen making nails and horseshoes and shoeing the horses.

However, it is change rather than loss that encompasses Woodbastwick now and it has become the base of a well established engineering works and more recently the home of Woodforde's Brewery. The school after its closure was used for many purposes. For a while it housed a printing works, then a guitar making firm acquired it. Later it was used by a cabinet maker and now the wheel has come full circle and the Victorian school rooms are in use as a private pre-prep and nursery school.

🍁 WOODRISING

Woodrising is now a hamlet of around 40 inhabitants, consisting of 16 houses (seven of them thatched with Norfolk reed), a church with a ruined tower, and nearly 1,400 acres of arable, meadow and woodland, drained by the Blackwater river – which, a few miles downstream (just below the site of the old Hardingham watermill), becomes the river Yare.

Woodrising seems to have had a steady population of around 100 to 150 from the 11th century to the end of the 19th century and has certainly been a single estate since the time of Edward the Confessor.

A later lord of the manor, John Weyland (d 1767), built the great vaulted barn at Church Farm. His younger brother Mark was a Governor of the Bank of England, and his grandson John was a Fellow of the Royal Society. The Weyland family were probably the builders of most of the existing buildings in the parish, and the lordship remained with the family until in 1937 it passed to the 4th Earl of Verulam.

One of the rectors of St Nicholas, Christopher Sutton, flourished as an author in the early 17th century, was knighted, became Canon of Westminster and is buried in Westminster Abbey. The church appears to be 14th century with 16th century additions. The tower collapsed sometime before 1742, though a letter to the Bishop of Norwich dated 1st July 1602 already reports that 'the steeple ys in very great decay'. The bell frame was later re-erected in the churchyard under a thatched roof and is hung with a bell cast in

Whitechapel in 1861. Besides the numerous memorials, the church is noteworthy as containing one of the few remaining church barrel organs in working order, built in 1826 and restored in 1958. Notes of this pipe organ are activated by pins on a rotating barrel – like a giant musical box. The three barrels (one original, another from 1865) provide for 30 different hymn tunes.

The present Woodrising Hall is at least the third building on the present site. The last Hall, of which only the coach houses and walled garden now remain, was replaced after army dilapidations of the Second World War. The moat surrounding a yet earlier Hall also survives, and there are also two other moated sites and evidence of a Roman or Romano-British villa within the parish.

The estate is a well-known pheasant shoot, and anglers are well served by nearby Scoulton Mere (part of Woodrising estate) and an artificial lake in Woodrising water meadows, which also contain a small camping site.

🍁 WOODTON

Ten miles south of Norwich, Woodton has a population of 500. 'England's Hero' as everybody knows was Horatio Nelson. The people of Woodton take pride in the fact that his mother, Catherine Suckling, was a Woodton girl. The Sucklings were an ancient family ('Socling' in Saxon times) who can be traced in Woodton from the mid-14th century onwards as the local squires. In 1701 Rev Maurice Suckling became rector and, in time, grandfather of the Admiral. It is believed that the boy spent holidays in the village where he used to climb what is now known as Nelson's tree.

In the church are a number of monuments connected with the Suckling family, on the walls and in the aisles. This 14th century, largely flint church has the round tower found almost exclusively in Norfolk and Suffolk. As so often in these parts it stands well out of the village. In 1984 the belfry reconstruction was completed and the peal of six bells rehung. All Saints' had its own rector until 1964 when the parish became one of the eight in the Hempnall group, a change which taken overall was very much for the good.

In the churchyard is the tombstone of Ned Baldry, the huntsman, 1705-59. Robert Suckling, the squire, gave him a job in his stables at the age of 13 as a parish apprentice so he was probably an orphan or an abandoned child supported by the parish. He loved the horses and hounds, said to be 'the finest

247

pack' in the district, and became chief huntsman to the squire. So good was he at his job that he took his pack as far afield as Ireland and to the Court of Louis XV at Versailles. On his gravestone are the lines:

Here lies a Huntsman who was stout and bold,
His judgment such as could not be controlled;
Few of his calling with him compare
For skill in hunting fox or fallow deer;
He shewed his art in England, Ireland, France,
And rests in this churchyard, being his Last Chance.

Not far from Mr Baldry, in the wood along Nobb's Lane there is, rather oddly, the grave of a horse, *April Shower*. A hunter, it broke its back in 1910 and had to be shot and now lies in a very superior railed grave.

Woodton Hall used to stand impressively behind the church but in 1839 Robert Suckling sold the whole estate to Robert Fellowes of Shotesham Hall. The two men fell out, there was a ferocious confrontation at the end of which Fellowes kicked Suckling down the steps. Quite deplorable of course, but even worse was that in his rage Fellowes then totally demolished the building. No Hall, no squire – perhaps this is why the feudal attitude has over the years waned to extinction.

Today it is a friendly community which has almost become a small dormitory village for Norwich. Husbands and wives spend their working hours in Norwich, Bungay and Loddon, no longer toiling on the land. Those born in Woodton accept the incomers, many of whom are retired folk, quite happily, welcoming their co-operation in the numerous village activities.

WORSTEAD

Worstead is a fairly scattered village of 900 souls, twelve miles from Norwich and six from the coast. Around the village square stand some fine old houses built in the 1600s. A fair was held here on Saturdays until 1666, when the threat of the plague closed it down. The primary school was built in 1845. There is also a post office, the New Inn built in 1825, a railway station, a food processing factory, a large church, and a Baptist church in one of the outlying hamlets called Meeting Hill. In 1986 a large village hall was built, opened by Her Majesty Queen Elizabeth the Queen Mother. All this is surrounded by rich farmland, sheep and dairy herds. People are employed on the farms or in the factory.

Over 30 years ago a three day village festival was started to restore the church. This has grown in size and popularity with the years and thousands flock to the Worstead Festival each year, making the village famous again.

Early in his reign, Edward III married a Flemish princess, and encouraged the immigration of Flemings. Many settled around Worstead, where the Norfolk sheep produced the long staple wool used for making the worsted cloth. The village became very prosperous. In 1379 the weavers built the magnificent church of St Mary, the existing church of St Andrew not being large enough. Today a new housing estate stands on the site and is named St Andrew's Close. Some 20 years ago a weaving guild was formed and spinning and weaving were carried on in the church, until 1995 when the guild transferred to the Baptist church at Meeting Hill, where it still flourishes to this day.

In about 1937 Sir Harold Harmsworth, the newspaper magnate, bought the Hall and demolished it, intending to rebuild. War came and this was never done, and today Worstead has no Hall.

Over the years changes have been made and new houses built, but gone is the butcher, the baker, the blacksmith, the tailor and, sadly, the village shop.

✺ WRENINGHAM

Wreningham, situated about eight miles from Norwich and three from Wymondham, was originally three parishes, Wreningham All Saints, Wreningham St Mary and Wreningham Nelonde. The village sign depicts the joining of the three villages into one.

All Saints' church is built of flint with limestone dressing, and the east and north walls of the chancel are rendered. The base of the tower appears to be Early English of about 1250–1300, but the upper stages were rebuilt in 1852 after they had collapsed. The nave is in the Perpendicular style of about 1450. On the north side of the nave is a transept built in 1852 to provide the necessary 150 free seats to qualify for a grant, as recorded on the cast iron panel in the vestry. The south porch was rebuilt in flint in 1852. The first recorded date of a rector is 1306, and the register dates from 1658. A war memorial stands in the churchyard to commemorate those who lost their lives in the two wars.

The Methodist church, on the Norwich/New Buckenham road, was rebuilt in 1904. On the site of Masters & Skevens Builders Merchants in Mill Lane once stood a windmill.

The village hall in Mill Lane plays a very active part in village life. Opposite the village hall is the playing field. The school was originally a voluntary controlled church school, but is now a county first school. There is a post office, but no village shop.

Bothway's farm house, in Ashwellthorpe Road, is a fine old building. In front is a pond which accommodates quite a few ducks, and one needs to drive carefully when the ducks decide to take a walk. The Bird in Hand public house has been extended to include a restaurant.

🍁 WROXHAM

Over 60 years ago Wroxham was already famous for the Broads and its boatyards. The season started at Whitsuntide and from that Saturday until September the train arriving from London at one o'clock at Wroxham station unloaded its passengers and their luggage to start their holidays. The train was met by the local boys with their wheelbarrows, who would carry holidaymakers' luggage from the station to the boatyards for the magnificent sum of twopence.

In those days Roy's really was the largest village store in the world. On its long mahogany counters complete with brass scales, tea, coffee and sugar were displayed in lovely decorated containers and weighed to the customer's requirements. Bacon was cut thick or thin by hand and all was personal service and no hurrying.

Monday afternoons were coach outing afternoons, when from Cromer, Sheringham and Yarmouth holidaymakers were taken out for a trip on the Broads.

Only the large houses had flush toilets then, and even they were connected to a septic tank in the garden. There was no tap water, only the wells serving five or six houses. You took your pail and pumped, hard work on bath night or family washday, although rain water was also collected.

Then came the Second World War and because of the airbase at Scottow water was laid on from Norwich. Real progress! There has been a lot of development since then. Colonel Charles' estate is now Charles Close, with well-designed houses and gardens. The avenue, once almost a country lane, now has its full complement of houses. Trafford Walk, named after the squire, is a grouped home, and Keys Hill, once a high class hotel, is now a council-run home for the elderly. There are also two private nursing homes.

In one of the gardens of a private house is a miniature steam engine which carries passengers and is open to the public from about April to October. The proceeds are given to local charities.

Roy's is no longer a village store. It is now a supermarket and gone are the days of personal service and delivery of groceries by horse and cart. There is a good shopping centre in the village, with hotels and restaurants. The village school is now a private school.

INDEX